Impacts of Cultural Capital on Student College Choice Process in China

Emerging Perspectives on Education in China

Series Editor: Gerard A. Postiglione

China's economic rise has been breathtaking and unprecedented, and this is no less true of its education system. Not only has China provided basic educational opportunities to more people in a relatively short period of time than elsewhere, but it has also helped spawn the largest higher education system in the world. Education in China is expected to reproduce a social order that can support a massive manufacturing economy, while producing innovative thinkers for a knowledge economy. As the work of new Chinese scholars becomes accessible in English to the larger global community, myths will be removed and replaced by more accurate and sophisticated analyses of China's fascinatingly complex educational transformation. This series, *Emerging Perspectives on Education in China*, presents the work of a unique breed of young Chinese scholars—those who undertook postgraduate study abroad or in postcolonial Hong Kong, where there is greater access to the international academic literature and more academic freedom than elsewhere in China. The studies in this series demonstrate a determination on the part of young scholars to explore emerging educational issues and grapple with the challenges of conducting research within mainland China. Their research is based on firsthand fieldwork data gathered by adapting research methodologies to diverse settings in different parts of mainland China. It is in this context that the series provides emerging perspectives about the transmission of culture through formal structures of education.

Impacts of Cultural Capital on Student College Choice Process in China, by Lan Gao

State Education and Ethnic Identity: The Politics of a Tibetan Neidi *Secondary School in China*, by Zhiyong Zhu

Muslim Uyghur Students in a Chinese Boarding School: Social Recapitalization as a Response to Ethnic Integration, by Yangbin Chen

Identity and Schooling among the Naxi: Becoming Chinese with Naxi Identity, by Yu Haibo

Becoming a Model Minority: Schooling Experiences of Ethnic Koreans in China, by Fang Gao

China's Mongols at University: Contesting Cultural Recognition, by Zhenzhou Zhao

Student Loans in China: Efficiency, Equity, and Social Justice, by Baoyan Cheng

Property Ownership and Private Higher Education in China: On What Grounds? by Spring Su

Impacts of Cultural Capital on Student College Choice Process in China

Lan Gao

LEXINGTON BOOKS

A division of
ROWMAN & LITTLEFIELD PUBLISHERS, INC.
Lanham • Boulder • New York • Toronto • Plymouth, UK

Published by Lexington Books
A division of Rowman & Littlefield Publishers, Inc.
A wholly owned subsidiary of The Rowman & Littlefield Publishing Group, Inc.
4501 Forbes Boulevard, Suite 200, Lanham, Maryland 20706
www.lexingtonbooks.com

Estover Road, Plymouth PL6 7PY, United Kingdom

British Library Cataloguing in Publication Information Available

Library of Congress Cataloging-in-Publication Data

Gao, Lan.
  Impacts of cultural capital on student college choice process in China / Lan Gao.
    p. cm. — (Emerging perspectives on education in China)
  Includes bibliographical references and index.
  ISBN 978-0-7391-3441-2 (hardcover : alk. paper) — ISBN 978-0-7391-3443-6
  (e-book)
  1. College choice. 2. Universities and colleges—Admission. 3. Educational
sociology—China. 4. Cultural relations—China. I. Title.
  LC191.G26 2011
  378.51—dc22   2011010330

∞™ The paper used in this publication meets the minimum requirements of
American National Standard for Information Sciences—Permanence of Paper
for Printed Library Materials, ANSI/NISO Z39.48-1992.

Printed in the United States of America

Contents

List of Figures and Tables   vii

1   Introduction   1

2   Literature Review and Empirical Research   7

3   Models of Student College Choice   29

4   Social Stratification and Higher Education Opportunities
in China   37

5   Research Design   59

6   Introduction of Wuhu and the Two High Schools   71

7   Fuzhong High School Students   83

8   Nancheng High School Students   123

9   Cross-Case Analysis   143

10   Findings, Limitations, and Implications   179

Appendix A   List of Universities in Project 985   195

Appendix B   Background Characteristics of the 14 Cases Excluded   197

Bibliography   201

Index   213

About the Author   215

Figures and Tables

FIGURES

3.1 Stages in College Decision Making and Elements of
Cultural Capital and Economic Capital Influenced by
Family's Socioeconomic Status   32

4.1 The Total Enrollment in Higher Education Institutions
in China from 1990 to 1995   47

4.2 The Net Enrollment and Gross Participation Rate in
Chinese HEIs from 1990 to 2004   48

4.3 The Percentage of Different Channels of Revenue to Public
Postsecondary Education in China from 1998 to 2001   50

6.1 Urban and Rural Populations in Wuhu from 2002 to 2004   72

6.2 Disposable Income per Urban Resident in Wuhu from 2002
to 2004   72

6.3 Annual Expenditure on Education and Cultural Goods
by Family Income in Wuhu from 2002 to 2004   73

6.4 Average Annual Family Income for Rural and Urban Residents
in Wuhu from 2000 to 2004   74

6.5 Enrollment Rates of Two-Year Colleges and Four-Year Universities
for Fuzhong and Nancheng High Schools from 2001 to 2005   80

TABLES

3.1 Variables Associated with Cultural Capital and
         Economic Capital   34

4.1 Different Channels of Revenue to Public Postsecondary
         Education in China from 1998 to 2001   50

5.1 Number of Interview Subjects by Family Type   63

5.2 Cases Presented in the Study   64

6.1 Central Government's Expenditure on Middle and
         High Schools (per student) and Number of Students
         in Schools (ten thousands)   75

1

Introduction

SIGNIFICANCE OF THE RESEARCH TOPIC

It is well known that the expansion of higher education in the post–World War II period in both developed and developing countries is unprecedented. For example, the participation rates to universities have increased fivefold between 1951 and 1979 in Australia (Lamb, 1989, p. 1). In China, the 1978–1994 period also witnessed a remarkable growth in the enrollment of public, regular higher education institutions—from 0.86 million in 1978 to 2.8 million in 1994 (World Bank, 1999, p. 3). However, despite the considerable expansion of higher education, worldwide there has been a constant gap between students in the lower social class and those in the higher social class students in terms of college attendance and persistence. According to the study of Fitzgerald and Delaney (2002), the gap in college enrollment rates was 32 percent (48 percent for low-income students versus 80 percent for high-income students) in the United States in 1970. Although the participation rate for low-income students has been increasing for the past few decades, the gap in participation between the students from low-income families and those from high-income families in 1997 was still 32 percent (p. 14). Fitzgerald and Delaney (2002) further point out that only 6 percent of the students from families in the lowest socioeconomic status earned a bachelor's degree in 1998, compared to 18 percent of students from families in the middle socioeconomic status and 40 percent of those from highest socioeconomic status (p. 15). Similarly in Australia, in spite of the substantial increase in college enrollment, the gaps in college participation rates among different social groups in the 1980s remained the same as those in the 1950s (Lamb, 1989, p. 1). As concluded by Premfors (1984), the social differences

1

in patterns of college attendance in most of the developed Western countries have remained remarkably stable in the post–World War II period.

The Task Force on Higher Education and Society (2000), convened by the World Bank and UNESCO, conducted research on 178 countries and concluded that expanding the enrollment to higher education and improving the quality of higher education are becoming increasingly critical to national development. It emphasized that knowledge has become the most important drive of economic growth and a key to a country's competition in the global economy. Since most technological innovations and the diffusion of knowledge are undertaken in universities, the role of higher education in knowledge accumulation and application is more influential than ever. At a time in which higher education has never been more meaningful to the economy, nor the economic returns to its citizens any greater, providing access to higher education regardless of race/ethnicity, social class, and financial ability should be a primary concern for policy making. This research is going to study the family-related factors that influence students' decision to enroll in college or to choose a particular college in China so as to shed light on the future policy making that is aimed at increasing college access and equalizing educational opportunities.

OVERVIEW OF THE STUDY

Socially structured differences—namely, social inequality—have been one of the primary theoretical issues addressed in sociology. Since the earliest years of sociology many different theories or paradigms have tried to explain the origins of social inequality, explore the process of social transmission, and uncover the necessity and possibility to eliminate human inequality. My study will draw on cultural capital theory, which views education as the main agent in transmitting social inequality from one generation to the next, to study the patterns of higher education participation among different social groups. Therefore, the second chapter will present and analyze the key concepts and major arguments of cultural capital theory, and then review and critique the prior empirical research. The discussion of related literature will indicate what is known and what is unknown on the research topic in order to identify the intellectual traditions that guide this study and to situate the research in the ongoing discourse of the topic about college access and choice for students from different family backgrounds. Extensive research reviewed in chapter 2 supports the basic argument of cultural capital theory by confirming that the likelihood of attending college is indeed associated with one's family socioeconomic status. Based on the theory and research outlined in chapter 2, the third chapter will present the conceptual framework for the study. The student college choice process is a complex developmental process influenced by many variables; a lot of conceptual models have thus been developed to study the dynamics of the process. This study uses Hossler and Gallagher's three-phase model (1987) to understand the complex process that determines college attendance and choice. Besides presenting the conceptual model that guides this study, chapter 3 also discusses the numerous social and economic variables that are used to present and analyze students' college planning in the study.

Considering the unique political and economic conditions of China, the fourth chapter is devoted to a discussion of the profound social changes that are taking place in the post-1978 reform era. The deterioration of the old planning economy, the bourgeoning new middle class, and the extensive reforms of higher education together brought about new income inequalities and educational stratification in China. Therefore, the overarching research question of this study is, how do class-based differences in a family's cultural capital and economic capital influence the students' decisions about applying for college and his or her choice of college. After identifying the major research questions, I will proceed with discussions about my research design in chapter 5. In this chapter, the site selection, sampling approaches, major data collection techniques, and preliminary data analysis methods will be presented. As discussed in this chapter, 25 students from two high schools in a middle-sized city in China were chosen as the cases for this study. Chapter 6 therefore provides a general introduction about the city and its educational system, a brief discussion of income inequalities in the city and its countryside, and unequal educational resources and opportunities for students from different family backgrounds.

Chapters 7 and 8 provide a detailed description of how 11 high school students from different family backgrounds and academic preparation made their decisions about whether or not to continue their education beyond high school and how they chose their colleges. Certainly, there exist differentials based on social class in participation in higher education. Therefore, chapter 9 explores the patterns of the college planning process for students with different socioeconomic status and examines influences of different variables, such as cultural capital and economic capital, on students' decision-making process of choosing colleges.

The last chapter is a concluding chapter that summarizes major findings of this study, indicates limitations of the research, and discusses implications for future research and policy making in China.

SIGNIFICANCE AND POTENTIAL CONTRIBUTIONS

The fact that students from families with lower socioeconomic status are less likely to attend college and, if they do attend, are less likely to graduate is well established from prior research. Educational researchers have long been concerned about the factors that influence the patterns of attendance in higher education and the extent to which higher education has been accessible to all students regardless of their socioeconomic status. Extensive research has indicated that a variety of class-related factors, such as cultural capital, social capital, and economic capital, exert remarkable impacts on the amount and type of education that one receives. However, how these different forms of capital influence one's chance to participate in higher education to a great extent remains unexplored. This limitation largely stems from the research method adopted by most of the prior research. Studies elevating the concept of cultural capital to a prominent position have exhibited a restricted methodological scope, primarily using quantitative techniques. Specifically concerning college access and choice, extensive quantitative research has been conducted. Although the regression models employed in prior quantitative research are varied, the research questions have been the type of "what" questions—what variables are powerful for predicting educational attainment and what factors are important in influencing college choices. Therefore, I argue that a qualitative study can make an important contribution by providing insights into the underlying actions that produce or make use of cultural capital, thereby complementing quantitative research and enriching our understanding.

Moreover, most of the prior research has been carried out in capitalist societies. Given the uniqueness of political and economic conditions in China, whether or not the relationship of family social origins and educational attainment resembles that found in the capitalist market economy is still debatable. This study will enrich cultural capital theory by applying it to the transitional period of China in which the transformation of classes is complex and distinctive.

Finally, little solid research has been done in China that looks exclusively at the state of access to higher education institutions for students from families with lower socioeconomic status. The rigid three-tiered examination system in China has for long been regarded as impartial in selecting people for advanced educational opportunities.[1] There was a common belief that "before the system of grades, everyone is equal." Not surprisingly, the unequal opportunity for college education was not a primary concern for either educational research or public policies until 1997 when tuition charges were universally introduced in Chinese colleges and universities. The introduction of tuition and the subsequent dramatic increase of college prices have created fears that college education will soon be out of the reach of all except those from wealthy families. The old faith that every member in Chinese society stands to have the same opportunity for education, and that those people who are intelligent and work hard get ahead, began to be challenged. However, the research interest of Chinese scholars is still limited to the financial barriers that low-income students are facing. Undoubtedly, an adequate financial aid system can significantly increase the likelihood of college enrollment for economically disadvantaged students. Nevertheless, financial constraints are not the only factors that exclude students with lower socioeconomic status from equal participation in higher education. Drawing on cultural capital theory, this study therefore endeavors to fill such a gap in the college access research in China by exploring the impacts of class-based cultural capital on students' chances to enroll in college, while recognizing the importance of the financial dimensions of access.

NOTE

1. The three-tiered examination system in China refers to the unified entrance examinations to middle school, high school, and college.

2

Literature Review and Empirical Research

According to Grabb (1990), "Social inequality can refer to any of the differences between people (or the socially defined positions they occupy) that are *consequential* for the lives they lead, most particularly for the rights or opportunities they exercise and the rewards or privileges they enjoy. Of greatest importance here are those consequential differences that become structured . . . that are built into the ways that people interact with one another on a recurring basis" (p. 4). Although inequality is one of the most pervasive and familiar facts of human life, there is no easy answer to the nature and causes of social inequality. The problem of social inequality has been the subject of lively debates for decades, and there have been competing theories and paradigms that attempt to answer the most basic question of how social order is possible. As previously noted, my study will draw on cultural capital theory, a branch of conflict theories, to explore the considerable impacts of family social origin on the educational inequality.

CULTURAL CAPITAL THEORY

Cultural capital theory stresses the extent to which individuals, groups, and classes within society are in competition with one another for whatever people in society consider to be important or worthwhile. In basic terms, some people will have more than their fair share of a society's valued resources and others will consequently have less than their fair share. Cultural capital theorists (Bernstein, 1982; Bourdieu & Passeron, 1977; Wexler, 1982) argue that the educational forms and practices in capitalist societies are grounded in the economic relationship in the productive sphere, and

So we can say they are influenced to go but outhomes?

thus it is aimed at legitimating rather than reducing social inequality. The reason behind the differences in academic achievement is what type of knowledge is actually taught in schools. Cultural capital theorists suggest that school knowledge is not neutral and is not a "shared" set of normative rules. Instead, it is closely linked to the ideological dominance of powerful groups in society. In the following, I will introduce the basic concepts and major arguments of cultural capital theory.

Cultural Capital

The cultural capital theoretical framework of Pierre Bourdieu has been applied to the study of education, language, science, and art, and has been most important in the sociological studies that focus on how and why social status influences educational achievement and occupational levels, which is also known as the literature on social reproduction. The underlying concern of all these studies is the relationships among class, power, and culture. Bourdieu identifies these relationships as fundamental to social stratification and intergenerational inequality:

> Different classes and class fractions are engaged in a specifically symbolic struggle to impose the definition of the social world most in conformity with their interests. The field of ideological positions reproduces in transfigured form the field of social positions. They may carry on this struggle either directly in the symbolic conflicts of everyday life or indirectly through the struggle waged by the specialists in symbolic production (full-time producers), in which the object at stake is the monopoly of legitimate symbolic violence—that is to say, the power to impose (and even indeed to inculcate) instruments of knowledge and expression of social reality (taxonomies), which are arbitrary (but unrecognized as such). The field of symbolic production is a microcosm of the struggle between the classes. It is by serving their own interests in the struggle internal to the field of production (and to this extent alone) that these producers serve the interests of groups external to their field of production. (1977c, p. 115)

From this paragraph we can see that, in Bourdieu's view of class relations and power, the meaning systems taken for granted by members of a society are the key to maintaining any system of domination and to transmitting class advantages from generation to generation. Cultural capital, therefore, is defined as competence in a society's dominant cultural codes and practices through which social background inequalities are translated into differential educational certificates and which in turn lead to unequal social and economic returns. Cultural capital is not a simple by-product or reflection of class position but a mechanism through which the social reproduction process is maintained and legitimized (Bourdieu, 1977a; Bourdieu & Passeron, 1977).

In Bourdieu's essay titled "Forms of Cultural Capital" (1997, pp. 46–58), he identifies three forms of cultural capital. The first is the embodied state of cultural capital, which is the disposition to appreciate and understand cultural goods through deliberate inculcation. Bourdieu argues that the embodied cultural capital cannot be transmitted instantaneously from one generation to the next generation, or from one person to another person. Instead, an individual can attain the certain tastes and attitudes only through inculcation and assimilation. The process of acquiring the ability to appropriate cultural goods depends on the cultural capital embodied in one's family—the offspring of families endowed with strong cultural capital obtain it in a faster and an easier way. In addition, the transmission of embodied cultural capital is better hidden compared to the heritage of other forms of capital, such as economic capital. Therefore, the role it plays in the reproduction of intergenerational inequality is less visible. The second state of cultural capital is the objectified cultural capital. As the name implies, objectified cultural capital refers to cultural goods and media, such as works of art, writing, and instruments. There is a strong relationship between objectified cultural capital and embodied cultural capital since a cultural object can become effective capital only when the owner of the object possesses the cultural ability to appreciate and appropriate it in order to wield power and gain profits from it. The third state is institutionalized cultural capital, which refers to educational credentials and the credentialing system. The academic qualification brings its holders both economic and symbolic profits, such as high salary and high occupational prestige. In this way, an individual converts his/her cultural capital into economic capital and symbolic capital.

In Bourdieu's formulation, children from higher social strata are born into a home environment in which societally valued knowledge of highbrow culture and cultural cues are more likely to be manifested (Bourdieu, 1977a; Bourdieu & Passeron, 1977). Therefore, children from families of higher socioeconomic status already possess more embodied and objectified cultural capital by the time they enter school than do children from families of lower socioeconomic status. More important, the initial differences in cultural capital are not reduced or eliminated but reinforced by an educational system that prefers certain types of cultural dispositions. Students with more valuable cultural capital thus do better than their otherwise comparable peers with less valuable cultural capital. Social inequalities that are perpetuated as initial differences in embodied and objectified cultural capital become systematically encoded in institutionalized cultural capital, such as educational credentials, which in turn channel individuals into different class positions. The exclusionary character of cultural capital is at the heart of Bourdieu's framework, according to Lamont and Lareau (1988). They therefore proposed to define cultural capital as institutional-ized—that is, it consists of widely shared high-status cultural signals (such as behaviors, tastes, and attitudes) that are used for social and cultural ex-clusion. Social exclusion refers to "exclusion from job and resources," while cultural exclusion to "exclusion from high status groups" (p. 156).

Together, these arguments indicate that differences in cultural capital ex-plain at least part of the association between the socioeconomic positions of parents and their children. Members of the dominant class possess the most valuable cultural capital and have the best opportunity to succeed in school, leaving most members of the lower classes with little hope of achieving social mobility. According to Perna (2000), there are three typi-cal ways in which those people with less valuable cultural endowment act to their disadvantaged positions. First, they receive fewer economic and symbolic returns for their educational investment compared to their coun-terparts with higher social status. Second, those who begin school with less cultural capital also acquire it at a slower rate. Therefore, to catch up with those who begin their schooling already possessing valuable cultural capital, they have to overperform to overcome the obstacles that are typi-cal for those in their class position. Third, students from families that lack the cultural skills and preferences rewarded in the schools are aware that people from their class are unlikely to succeed educationally, and thus self-select out of certain situations. For example, lower-class students tend to self-select out of the college-going track based on their view that college is not for people from their class.

Habitus and Field

Although cultural capital is an important part of Bourdieu's theory of social reproduction, it is not the only component of his theoretical frame-work. Bourdieu noted that capital, habitus, and field all work together to generate practices, or social action (1971, 1977b).

Habitus is the mechanism behind the effect of cultural capital. Bourdieu conceived of habitus as "a system of lasting, transposable dispositions which, integrating past experiences, functions at every moment as a matrix of perceptions, appreciations, and actions and makes possible the achieve-ment of infinitely diversified tasks, thanks to analogical transfers of schemes permitting the solution of similarly shaped problems" (Bourdieu, 1971, p. 83). That is to say, in a certain social group an individual's activity is greatly influenced by a set of subjective perceptions held by all the mem-bers of this group. Given that members from different social classes are dif-ferent in the nature of their primary socialization, each class has its unique habitus that can shape its members' attitudes, expectations, and aspirations. By observing other people's lives in their communities, an individual makes an assessment about what is possible and what is not possible for his/her own life and makes sensible or reasonable choices for his/her own aspirations accordingly. Dumais (2002) conceived of habitus as "one's view of the world and one's place in it" (p. 45). By internalizing one's beliefs about the social world and about one's life chances, an individual develops his/her own attitudes and expectations. This internalization takes places in early childhood, and the habitus resulting from this unconscious process is continually modified by the individual's encounter with the world (DiMaggio, 1979; Dumais, 2002).

According to Bourdieu, the consequences of the development of habitus are very important and play a key role in maintaining the existing social structure (1977a). On the basis of the class positions they were born into, people develop ideas about their individual potential. For example, working-class children usually believe that they will remain in the working class and thus have lower educational aspirations, and these beliefs are then externalized into their actions. Therefore, Bourdieu thinks that the low educational achievement of students from families with a lower socioeconomic status is "the product, not the cause, of the low statistical probability of their academic success." (DiMaggio, 1982, p. 1,465).

In summary, high expectations lead to high grades. A student's expectations are developed from what he/she has experienced in the past and believes is likely to happen for people from his/her particular background.

Field is another important concept in Bourdieu's social reproduction model. It refers to both the actors and organizations and the rules of interaction between them within a cultural or social domain. For example:

> The intellectual field, which cannot be reduced to a simple aggregate of isolated agents or to the sum of elements merely juxtaposed, is, like a magnetic field, made up of a system of power lines. In other words, the constituting agents or system of agents may be described as so many forces which, by their existence, opposition or combination, determine its specific structure at a given moment in time. In return, each of these is defined by its particular position within this field from which it derives positional properties which cannot be assimilated to intrinsic properties. (Bourdieu, 1971, p. 161)

From this example we can see that one of the most important characteristics of the concept of field is that field is an arena of conflict. In a certain field, dominant and subdominant groups struggle for control over resources. The objective of social life is to accumulate and monopolize different types of resources or capital. Therefore, each field is related to one or more types of capital. Capital, as defined by DiMaggio, is "attributes, possessions, or qualities of a person or a position exchangeable for goods, services, or esteem" (1982, p. 1,463). Capital can take many forms, such as cultural capital, economic capital, and social capital (Coleman, 1988). In a certain field, the interaction of actors is shaped by multiple forces, including different forms of capital the actors possess, positions of the actors, and the rules governing the field. In one word, a field is a cultural or social domain in which participants have a stake and compete with one another for the accumulation of some sort of capital.

EDUCATION AND SOCIAL INEQUALITY

Having elaborated on the key concepts and major arguments developed by cultural capital theory, I will proceed in the following section with discussion about how education acts as the main agent in maintaining the status quo from the perspective of cultural capital theory.

Educational System

According to Bourdieu (1977a), in a capitalist society, where demands for democracy and equal opportunities of success have been increasing, social reproduction through direct mechanisms such as intergenerational inheritance and class-based promotion loses its legitimacy. Instead, indirect mechanisms of reproduction, like cultural capital, become important in transmitting social inequality from one generation to the next. Without doubt, educational institutions are among the most important places where power struggles between dominant and subordinate groups take place (Spring, 1998). In the following, I will examine how people from different classes interact with one another in the educational field.

The central tenet of cultural capital theory is that educational institution is the main agent where a class-based society is reproduced through the use of economic, cultural, and hegemonic capital of the dominant social class (DeMarrais & LeCompte, 1999; Coleman, 1988; Lin, 1999; Spring, 1998). Schools are not socially neutral, and the apparently neutral academic standards actually function as a biased screening mechanism that favors those students who come from dominant social classes and derive from their families the specific cultural resources that are most rewarded in schools. This suggests that social class position and class culture become a form of capital—cultural capital—in the school setting.

The school system is a mechanism of distributing certain ideas and values. School knowledge is not neutral and is not a shared set of normative rules (DeMarrais & LeCompte, 1999; Grabb, 1990; Spring, 1998). Instead, it is closely linked to the ideological dominance of powerful groups in society. Students from high-status origins bring with them cultural preferences, attitudes, and behaviors to school, where their cultural capital is most highly valued (Bourdieu, 1977a; Bourdieu & Passeron, 1977). Although the educational system presupposes the possession of this kind of cultural capital by all, only a small section of students in fact possess it. Since the lower- and working-class students do not benefit from their background and do not derive the prerequisites from their family, they are left behind by students from better-off families at the very beginning of their educational journey.

Of course, one might expect the school to impart to all the students the set of skills and bodies of knowledge that it demands and assesses. However, to acquire the social, linguistic, and cultural competencies, students need to have the ability to receive, decode, and internalize it, while schools are not very efficient in cultivating in all students the highly valued habits of thinking, the tastes, and the interest (Bourdieu, 1977a; Bourdieu & Passeron, 1977; Lamont & Lareau, 1988). Rather, the initial inequalities in terms of possession of cultural capital among different social classes are not recognized in teaching practices, and the content and methods of teaching tend to favor students who are already familiar with them. Students from lower classes are penalized for lack of social and cultural cues. Therefore, schools widen rather than diminish the initial academic differences associated with social status through its selection and socialization. As Bourdieu put it,

> By doing away with giving explicitly to everyone what it implicitly demands of everyone, the educational system demands of everyone alike that they have what it does not give. This consists mainly of linguistic and cultural competence and that relationship of familiarity with culture which can only be produced by family upbringing when it transmits the dominant culture. (1977a, p. 494)

Cultural capital certainly plays an important role in determining academic achievement. Nevertheless, despite the fact that students from lower and working classes are seriously handicapped by the academic standards adopted in schools, the differences in academic achievement are normally explained by differences in abilities rather than by cultural capital (de Graff, 1988; Jonsson, 1987; Katsillis & Rubinson, 1990). Schools reward students who have cultural capital, and the ultimate reward is in the form of educational credentials. As Parkin (1971) pointed out, educational certificates help their holders monopolize advantageous positions in the social and economic system. Bachelor's degrees or more advanced diplomas in all fields make for the formation of privileged strata.

Bourdieu's argument makes it clear that cultural capital is critical for us to understand the relationship between knowledge and power because through control of the knowledge-preserving and -producing institutions

of a particular society, the ideological dominance of certain classes are en-
hanced. As Apple (1990) put it, "The 'reality' that schools and other cultural
institutions select, preserve and distribute . . . may not serve the interests of
every individual and group in society" (p. 27).

In his book, Spring (1998) discussed how the issues of knowledge and
power are related to struggles over economic advantages, culture, language,
and religion. One aspect of using schooling as an instrument of power is
to control access to the labor market by academic sorting. Students from
families with low socioeconomic status are less likely to graduate from high
schools and less likely to go to college. As a result, students with lower social status are channeled into lower rungs of the labor market, and students
from families of high status to the top positions. That is to say, well-placed
families are able to confer their economic and cultural advantages to their
younger members through the educational system, and thus encourage
social self-reproduction from generation to generation. As Parkin (1971)
indicated, because of the ability of elite status groups to transmit cultural
capital to their offspring, "there often develops a pattern of social and cultural differentiation which, in turn, reinforces the system of occupational
recruitment and so crystallizes the class structure through time" (p.14). In
other words, family position is indeed associated with education, and education in turn makes a sizable difference in early and subsequent economic
achievement and social status.

Family Factors

According to cultural capital theory, family background is crucial to the
patterning of students' achievement (Bourdieu, 1977a; Bourdieu & Passeron, 1977; Katsillis & Rubinson, 1990). First of all, family is a primary
source of cultural capital for children. Parents from higher social classes
have more cultural capital than do parents from lower social classes. This
is the so-called background effect. Second, students with more endowments of cultural capital are more able to adapt and further develop the
cultural preferences and skills rewarded in schools. This is the cultural
capital effect. Third, family background indirectly influences the academic
rewards through cultural capital. Besides emphasizing the direct effects
of early cultural socialization, cultural capital theory also points out that
those moving through the educational ladder who begin with more initial cultural capital accumulate their cultural capital at a faster rate than
those from lower classes. This is called the transformation relationship.
In conclusion, social differences in levels of cultural capital influence
opportunities of achievement through the culturally selective academic
standards adopted in schools. In the following, we are going to see how

the different dimensions of family environment contribute to the maintenance of educational inequality.

A particularly important aspect of family background is the educational resources parents can provide to their children (Bourdieu & Passeron, 1977; Coleman, 1988; DiMaggio, 1982;). Valuable educational resources, such as books, newspapers, and computers, can cultivate and foster children's motivation to learn and shape orientations to school. Family lifestyles and cultural consumption patterns are another critical source of children's cultural formation. Bourdieu (1977a) considers art, classical music, and literature as "beau arts" and contends that they play an important role in formal education. Art museum visits, concert attendance, and literature reading are all concentrated in the upper- and middle-classes families, which represent distinctively different cultural traits, tastes, and styles from those of lower- and working-class families. Through these beau arts activities, parents' cultural capital establishes the intellectual atmosphere in which children feel more comfortable and motivated to learn. The participation in cultural activities at home make children become acquainted with the cultural cues in the formal school education and also leads to the development of knowledge or skills, which both in turn enable students to succeed in school. For example, parents who regularly read books and newspapers at home have better linguistic skills and can pass these educational skills on to their children. They also contribute to a stimulating learning environment at home and act as role models for their children (DiMaggio, 1982, 1985). For those children who have grown up in a home climate in which reading is emphasized, it is much easier for them to adapt to classroom learning once they enter school. In contrast, for those children who have not learned to deal with certain cultural practices, such as reading, school experiences could be shocking and frightening (de Graaf, 1988; Lamont & Lareau, 1988).

Although lower- or working-class parents share a desire with upper- and middle-class parents for their children's educational success, parents with different social statuses engage in different types of involvement for their children's education (Horvat, Weininger, & Lareau, 2003; Lareau, 1987). Lareau (1987) has suggested that a variety of factors influence parental involvement in children's education. She points out that "parents' educational capabilities, their view of the appropriate division of labor between teachers and parents, the information they had about their children's schooling, and the time, money, and other material resources available in the home all mediated parents' involvement in schooling" (p. 79). For example, as previously noted, parents with high social status are more likely to socialize their children into highbrow cultural activities, which make their later educational practices more familiar and friendly to them.

Besides the different cultural capital parents can pass on to their children, parental expectation is another important factor influencing children's academic performance (de Graaf, 1988; Horvat, Weininger, & Lareau, 2003; Lareau, 1987; McDonough, 1997). Although most parents encourage their children to do well academically, parents with lower social status are less likely to establish specific rules with regard to homework and grades. In addition, because of their own educational experiences, they tend not to hold high expectations for their children. This family habitus also influences the way children view their own potential. Students from working-class families tend to believe that they will remain in the working class, and these beliefs are then externalized into their motivation and behavior at schools, which usually leads to lower academic achievement.

Another important family factor playing in children's educational development is parents' social capital. Bourdieu defines social capital as "the aggregate of the actual or potential resources which are linked to possession of a durable network of more or less institutionalized relationships of mutual acquaintance or recognition"(Bourdieu 1997, p. 249). In his discussions of the social context of education, Coleman (1994) also points out that social capital is the norms and networks that allow collective actions. Unlike other forms of capital, social capital inheres in the structure of social relations. Coleman (1988) has discussed the role of a family's social capital in the younger generation's development.[1] According to Coleman, social capital can be defined as investment in social relations and use of the resources flowing through those relationship. He argues that social capital can be found "in the community consisting of the social relationships that exist among parents, in the closure exhibited by this structure of relations, and in the parents' relations with the institutions of the community" (p. 113). One of the important class-based factors influencing students' educational achievement is the social network of parents. According to Horvat, Weininger, and Lareau (2003), there are significant class-specific differences in the structures of parents' social network. They argue that middle-class parents have a more comprehensive and strong network with parents of their children's peers at school, while the social network outside of working-class families is predominantly organized along kinship lines. The social capital that is made available to middle-class families through their social network of school peers has positive effects on a variety of aspects of their children's school life. For example, middle-class parents can obtain information about their children's performance at school through other parents, which also enables the reciprocal monitoring of children in schooling and in the organized activities outside of school. In contrast, the kinship network of working-class families has little to do with their children's school performance. Rather, the ties with relatives usually help them with some economic problems, such as childcare, transportation, or

clothing. Another significant difference is that middle-class families' social network involves more professionals. As a result, middle-class parents have considerably greater resources at their disposal when some problems come up in the course of their children's schooling. For working-class parents, when dealing with problems about their children's education, they are highly dependent on the school.

The different architectures of social network, parents' educational level, and their views of the appropriate division of labor between teachers and parents all determine the various family-school relationships associated with class positions. Lareau (1987) argues that schools have a standardized view of what kind of parental involvement is proper; however, the cultural resources possessed by different classes are not equally valuable in terms of complying with schools' requests for parental participation. For example, schools usually emphasize positive, affirmative, and supportive family-school relationships. The middle-class parents are privileged in the sense that they feel more comfortable dealing with schools (Horvat, Weininger, & Lareau, 2003; Lareau, 1987). On one hand, they have more trust in teachers and school administrators. On the other hand, if there were any problems, they feel more confident to intervene. In contrast, working-class parents begin to construct their relationships with schools with less ease and more suspicion. However, when presented with problems regarding their children's education, they usually depend on educators to solve the problems and feel much less comfortable speaking their own opinions. Their relatively poor educational skills and lower occupational prestige compared to teachers make them feel less confident and less comfortable in monitoring and supplementing their children's schooling.

Social Status and Higher Education Opportunity

Clearly, higher education is a component of the whole mechanism of social reproduction. Educational certificates, such as a bachelor's degree, admit individuals to the dominant and respectable status group. According to cultural capital theory, students from middle- and upper-class families are more likely to get a college education (Aschaffenburg & Maas, 1997; McDonough, 1997; Steelman & Powell, 1991).

As previously discussed, in the early phase of educational careers, family factors have a major impact on the development of those cognitive skills, tastes, and attitudes. Children from families with high status have already possessed the certain kinds of cultural capital that are recognized and highly rewarded in schools, which gives them precedence over their lower-class counterparts.

As children move through the educational system, those well-educated parents can provide their children with instrumental assistance, information about college application, the importance of college education, and future opportunities. They also establish and reinforce norms of expected behavior and achievement and offer support whenever their children are experiencing success or failure. All of these parental behavior foster better academic performance and therefore better chances of their children getting into a college.

In addition, social capital is also important for educational achievement. Social capital, posited by Coleman (1988), consists of the relationship between (1) parents and children and (2) parents and other individuals and institutions that affect children's development and is important for educational achievement. Parental networks may provide information about colleges and college application. As previously noted, the middle-class parents' network involves more professionals, who may provide connections to colleges and may facilitate the complicated process of college application, while working-class parents are often ill-informed.

Some researchers argue that with the educational expansion in capitalist countries after World War II, there appears to be increasing equality of educational opportunity. However, although the expansion of schooling has been successful in reducing socioeconomic influences at lower levels of educational transitions, familial influences remain stable and strong at the college level (Katsillis & Rubinson, 1990; Marks & McMillan, 2003). Besides cultural capital and social capital, financial capital is another factor influencing students' chances of obtaining a college education.

Clearly, sufficient material support is important for family well-being. On the primary and secondary educational levels, the lack of financial resources put low-income students at a disadvantage in terms of their access to diverse types of material resources, such as books, clothing, and stable housing. On the tertiary level, good academic preparation is certainly one of the prerequisites for admission to college, while students from higher-income families are more likely to obtain higher achievement (Cabrera & La Nasa, 2001; Perna, 2000; Perna, 2002). Higher family income is significantly associated with children completing higher levels of education because higher-income families are likely to have the economic capital to move to a good neighborhood, send their children to good schools, afford the cost of private preparation for standardized examinations, and provide the necessary time and attention to children's schooling (Behrman, Pollak, & Taubman, 1989; Stafford, Lundstedt, & Lynn, 1984). In other words, economic factors are also associated with school success.

Some researchers (Steelman & Powell, 1989) argue that different types of capital have different impacts on children's schooling at various points of an educational career. The researchers suggest that social and cultural capital provided by the family have profound influences on students' academic development in childhood and adolescence, while the impact of financial capital is more significant on their opportunities to obtain a college education. Compared to elementary and secondary education, equality of opportunity for higher education is more problematic because in most countries higher education is only partially subsidized by the government and paying for a college education is largely the responsibility of students themselves and their parents (Fitzgerald & Delaney, 2002; Gladieux, 2002; McDonough, 1997). Students from low-income families have great difficulty paying the tuition and cannot afford to forgo the earnings associated with pursuing college education. Clearly, sufficient financial support from their families is important for students to be able to continue their education on the tertiary level. It is argued that since access is contingent on unequally distributed parental income and wealth, the well-off families are able to secure a college education for their offspring, and therefore maintain their advantageous positions in the occupational attainment contest.

The extent to which parents are willing to sponsor their children's college education is highly associated with their family income (Steelman & Powell, 1991). By definition, low-income parents possess less economic resources to pay for college education. The lack of security in terms of financial capital also makes them less willing to get loans. Being ill-informed about the opportunities of financial aid makes them unaware of the net cost of college education and therefore less willing to invest on it.

CULTURAL CAPITAL RESEARCH

Cultural capital theory has inspired many scholars who are interested in how education replicates existing social inequalities. Most of the social reproduction research found the concept of cultural capital to be useful, especially as articulated in the work of Bourdieu and his associates (Bourdieu, 1977a, 1977b, 1984, 1990; Bourdieu & Passeron, 1977). In the following, I will review research that has employed cultural capital theory to study the patterns of educational attainment across social groups.

Drawing on Weber's notion of status groups and status cultures and Bourdieu's cultural capital theory, DiMaggio (1982) examines the impact of status culture participation on high school students' educational performance in the United States. Following Bourdieu's idea about prestigious cultural activities, DiMaggio measured high school students' cultural capital by their involvement in highbrow cultural activities, such as art, music, and literature class attendance. He concluded from his study that a composite measure of cultural capital has a significant impact on high school grades even when family background and measured students ability are taken into account. In a subsequent study, DiMaggio and Mohr (1985) found that cultural capital has a positive net effect on higher education attendance and completion in

the United States and that the effect is stronger than the effect of the fathers' education and that of the students' former high school grades.

One drawback of DiMaggio's studies (DiMaggio, 1982; DiMaggio & Mohr, 1985) is that he and his colleagues only included students' own cultural capital in their models but didn't consider parents' cultural capital. Aschaffenburg and Maas (1997) is one of the first studies that tries to examine how the cultural capital possessed by parents and the cultural classes taken by students influence students' educational careers in the United States.[2] By examining the impact of cultural capital in different stages of educational process, they point out that there is a strong interaction between parental cultural capital and children's cultural participation for beginning college. For those students whose parents have a college education, their own participation in cultural activities has larger positive effects on the likelihood of going to college compared to those students whose parents do not have a college education. They further argued that since higher education is key to later life chances, the fact that children from families with high social status benefit more from the cultural participation in the transition from high school to college lends support to Bourdieu's cultural capital theory and social reproduction model.

Some American studies extend cultural capital theory to include ethnic minority groups in their research. For example, Roscigno and Ainsworth-Darnell's study (1999) examines the link between racial inequality in educational attainment and family background. The findings they obtained from both general and race-specific models suggest that a family's social status largely determines the cultural capital and household educational resources available to the children, which is consistent with sociological explanations for the association between cultural capital and class differences. They further point out that family socioeconomic status, which is a particularly important factor of family background, varies significantly by ethnic groups, and that the racial gap in educational achievement is largely a function of the differences in cultural capital and household educational resources.

Research conducted in European countries has also found similar patterns. A study carried out by Paul de Graaf (1986) in the Netherlands found that parental cultural capital has significant effects on children's educational attainment. Cultural capital accounted for 9–14 percent of different age cohorts of the effects of parental socioeconomic status on educational attainment of the younger generation, after controlling for parents' education and fathers' occupational prestige. In his other study, Paul de Graaf (1988) examines the relationship between parents' cultural resources and children's grades and transition to secondary education by using data from a West German survey. The findings suggested that not only do parents' educational and occupational levels have substantial impacts on grades in arithmetic and language, the reading climate at home also directly affects the grades. Using representative data for the Netherlands, Nan Dirk de Graaf and his colleagues (2000) also demonstrate that parents' reading behavior has a significant impact on children's educational attainment. They argue that parents who read frequently not only have more linguistic and cognitive skills at their disposal and pass them on to their children, but they also provide a stimulating learning environment at home that resembles the school climate. In contrast, those children, whose parents do not read often usually experience school as a hostile environment. They also lack the educational skills and attitudes that are rewarded in school.

Using the data from her own survey of senior high school students in England, Sullivan (2001) examines the distribution of cultural capital among different social classes and its impact on children's educational attainment. Sullivan found that parents' social classes and education are strongly associated with the cultural knowledge they possess. Moreover, there is a positive correlation between parents' cultural capital and children's cultural activities. These two findings back Bourdieu's view that cultural capital is unevenly distributed according to social class and educational level and that it is passed down from parents to children. However, Sullivan also points out that parents' social class remains a significant influential variable on students' educational achievement even when cultural capital is controlled. She therefore indicated that cultural capital is not the only mechanism through which high-class families transmit their educational advantages to their offspring. There must be other mechanisms, such as family financial resources, that can explain the remaining differential in educational attainment for students from different social backgrounds. Similarly, Wong (1998) was also concerned about the roles that different forms of family capital play in the educational attainment of children. Using national representative data in Czechoslovakia, Wong examines four components of family resources, which are human capital measured by father's education, financial capital measured by family income and assets, cultural capital measured by eight highbrow cultural activities, and social capital measured by the political membership status. His research indicates that each form of family capital is positively associated with children's educational attainment. An increase in either form of family capital leads to higher educational attainment, especially at the tertiary level. The cultural capital possessed by parents exerts a particularly strong impact on children's college attendance. His findings point to the dependence of educational destination on social origins and therefore support Coleman and Bourdieu's theory about the family's active role in an intergenerational conversion process.

Most of the research presented above measures their respondents' cultural capital by highbrow cultural activities they participated in or cultural classes they took in and out of school. Habitus, an important concept in Bourdieu's cultural capital theory, was not identified as a single variable in the research previously reviewed. Dumais's study (2002) filled this gap by joining cultural capital and habitus in her model for studying the relationship between social background and educational success in the United States. She used students' occupational aspirations for the measure of habitus and found that for both female and male students habitus has a considerable effect on their schooling success. For those students who aspire to have occupations with high social prestige, they have higher grades on average than those who do not have high expectations for their future careers.

As previously noted, cultural capital theory argues that social classes are highly associated with the patterning of family-school relationships. The standard parental roles required by schools are not neutral. Instead, the school's request for parental involvement may be laden with the social and cultural experiences of intellectual and economic elites. Therefore, parents with different class positions approach family-school relationships with different cultural capital and thus construct different forms of parental participation in their children's schooling. Lareau (1987) conducted a qualitative study in two schools concerning the association between social classes and family-school relationships. Her analysis points to the importance of class and class cultures in facilitating or impeding parents' negotiation of the process of schooling. First, she found that although all parents think highly of educational success and all want their children to succeed in school, working-class parents have lower expectations for their children's educational attainment compared to middle-class parents. Second, working-class families have fewer economic resources, which makes it more difficult for working-class parents to respond to requests for attendance at school events. Third, middle-class parents develop a more extensive and strong network with other parents and educational professionals, which provides them with more information about their children's schooling and promotes the social ties between home and school. Generally, the difference observed in the patterning of parental involvement for different classes in this study "suggests that the concept of cultural capital can be used fruitfully to understand social class differences in children's school experiences" (p. 73). Horvat, Weininger, and Lareau's more recent study (2003) focuses on social class differences in parental networks and the roles the network plays in children's schooling. Consistent with the earlier study, their findings demonstrate that parental networks vary across class categories. Their findings also suggest that because of the resources they can obtain from parents of their childrens' school peers, educators, and other professionals in their social networks, middle-class parents are more likely to be able to "customize their children's educational careers in important ways—for example, by contesting a placement decision or obtaining additional resources for a learning-disabled child" (p. 332). In contrast, working-class and poor parents lacking these resources were less likely to obtain a desired outcome for their children when dealing with such situations.

COLLEGE ACCESS RESEARCH

I have discussed the prior research that has examined the impacts of cultural capital in different stages of the educational process, now I will turn to its implication in higher education. Broad-range studies have been conducted in the United States to examine different factors that influence students' chances to go to and graduate from college. In this section, I will present and analyze the prior research concerning college access and choice.

Family Background

Research in education usually uses socioeconomic status (SES), which is a combination of parental education, occupation, and family income, to predict educational outcomes. Prior research (Cabrera & La Nasa, 2001; Coleman, 1988; McDonough, 1997; Perna, 2000) has consistently shown that the socioeconomic status of a student's family is the most powerful predictor for college enrollment. Students from families of low SES are less likely to go to college and less likely to persist in college and graduate. Peng's (1977) study suggested that independent of academic ability, the college enrollment rate for students from the bottom socioeconomic quartile is still about half of that for those from the top socioeconomic quartile. Moreover, social class is also highly correlated with institutional choice (Gladieux, 2002; Peng, 1977). According to Gladieux (2002), the most recent longitudinal data from the U.S. Department of Education show that about 66 percent of students from families with high SES who attend college are enrolled in four-year institutions, 44 percent higher than their counterparts from the lowest socioeconomic quartile (p. 47).

Moreover, some studies in sociology that examined the social factors influencing students' decisions to enroll in college also indicate that family income and parental education and occupation are all pivotal predictors for college enrollment when examined separately (Blau and Duncan, 2000; Fitzgerald & Delaney, 2002; Hauser, 1993; Kane, 1999; Sewell, Hauser, & Wolf, 1980).

In their study of intergenerational inheritance of social inequality, Blau and Duncan (2000) point out that occupational and social status are to an important extent self-perpetuating. Occupational and social status are associated with many other factors, such as education, family structure, and social networks, which together confine individuals to certain status groups and make it hard to change. Blau and Duncan (2000) call such a situation "a vicious circle" in which "each factor acts on the other in such a way as to preserve the social structure in its present form, as well as the individual family's position in that structure. . . . The cumulation of disadvantages (or of advantages) affects the individual's entry into the labor market as well as his later opportunities for social mobility" (p. 42). In their study, Blau and Duncan (2000) found that fathers' education and occupations are the most powerful variables for predicting participants' educational attainment and occupational achievement. When comparing race differences in college attendance across gender and class positions, Thomas and his colleagues (1979) also found that the father's education is a strong predictive factor of college enrollment across race groups. Students whose fathers have college degrees are two-and-a-half times more likely to enroll in college than were those whose fathers did not have a high school diploma.

Other studies (Fitzgerald & Delaney, 2002; Kane, 1999) point out that family income is central to family decisions about college application. Kane (1999) indicates in his study that the college entry rate for low-income students is much lower than that of students from better-off families even when students from both groups have similar high school performance and similar test scores. Gallagher (1950) also points out that a lot of previous research, either with large quantitative data from statewide samples or qualitative data from case studies, all suggested that family income is a much more important factor than students' ability and academic performance in deciding who has access to college.

Previous studies have suggested a hierarchy of effects that students' background characteristics have on college enrollment. The order of effects, from strongest to weakest, is SES, race, and gender. In his study about college entry among African Americans, Hauser (1993) indicates that the odds of African Americans being enrolled in college within one year after high school graduation were less than half of the odds for whites in 1984. Despite the increasing rate of college participation among minority groups in recent years, Breneman and Merisotis (2002) point out in their study that the college enrollment gap between whites and those of other races has been persistent in the last 25 years. Perna (2002) also indicates in her research that African Americans, Hispanics, and American Indians continue to be underrepresented among college participants and degree recipients.

Although whites are more likely to attend college than blacks, this difference can be largely attributed to class background and family income. Other research (*Journal of Blacks in Higher Education*, 1994, 2001) suggests that there is a strong correlation between black family income and college participation and graduation rates. The studies point out that the average wealth of black families is only one-seventh of that of white families, and black families are three times more likely to be poor than white families

(*Journal of Blacks in Higher Education*, 2001, p. 8). The financial reason is believed to contribute considerably to the college enrollment gap between blacks and whites. The findings suggest that as blacks move up the income ladder, their college enrollment rates increase significantly. For those blacks from families with an annual income of $40,000 or more, the college participation rate of the age cohort 18 to 24 is double the rate of black youths from families with income under $10,000 (*Journal of Blacks in Higher Education*, 2001, p. 9). Moreover, this group of blacks from families with income more than $40,000 is also more likely than their white counterparts to attend college. The research further points out that low family income is the primary deterrent for keeping low-income blacks from completing their college degrees. Because of the lack of adequate financial support from home, low-income students have to take part-time or full-time jobs in order to pay tuition and fees while enrolled in college, which makes it more difficult for those students to keep up with their studies and, hence, they receive poor grades. Many of them have to drop out of school due to poor academic performance. The research emphasizes that this situation is more common for black students given that low-income students tend to be disproportionately black.

Parental Involvement

The existing research has also shown that parental encouragement and involvement is the important force in students' college participation (Cabrera & La Nasa, 2001; Coleman, 1988; McDonough, 1997; Perna, 2000; Swail and Perna, 2002). Students from the higher social class are more likely to have academic support from their parents and a home environment in which they can acquire the intellectual skills they need to do well in school (Jencks et al., 2000). Parents in the lower social class are less likely to be involved in their children's academic activities and less able to provide necessary information about college access and choice (Hagedorn & Fogel, 2002).

High School Climate

In her study, McDonough (1997) investigates a variety of organizational contexts and cultures in high school as they have an influence on students' decision-making about college enrollment and choice. Her research shows that students in prestigious high schools are highly encouraged to attend college, not only by counselors, but also by almost everyone in the school. Teacher-student interactions, course content, and college counseling are all directed to support college planning. In contrast, schools serving working-class students are less likely to be involved in students' college enrollment

decisions. Jencks and his colleagues (2000) also found that there is a relationship between high school status and its students' educational attainment. Their study suggests that "attending a high school in the top fifth
boosts the average student's eventual attainment about half a year above
the expected level, while attending a high school in the bottom fifth lowers
high probable attainment about half a year" (p. 172).

Self-Expectation and Academic Preparation

Prior research also shows that students' self-efficacy and academic preparation are important predictors of college enrollment decisions (Cabrera &
La Nasa, 2001; Kuo & Hauser, 1995; Perna, 2000; Perna, 2002). In their
study, Cabrera and La Nasa (2001) show that academic qualification is one
of the defining characteristics of college participants. Perna (2000, 2002)
also points out that academic ability, as a combined measure of test scores
and academic track, is powerful at predicting college enrollment regardless
of race. Peng and his colleagues (1977) found that students from academic
high school programs are far more likely to attend college than their counterparts from the nonacademic track when socioeconomic background is
controlled. Not surprisingly, the findings of Thomas and his colleagues'
study (1979) suggest that students from lower-class families are less likely
to be placed in college preparatory programs compared to their middle-
class counterparts when academic ability is controlled. Kuo and Hauser
(1995) indicated that students' self-efficacy and aspirations provide useful
and valid clues for their college enrollment plans. Students' aspirations for
schooling and careers exert impacts on their school performance and thus
influence their postsecondary education opportunities.

Financial Aid

Financial aid is money provided to needy students to help pay for higher
education costs. It can be used toward tuition fees, room and board, books
and supplies, transportation, living expenses, and other costs associated
with going to college. As suggested by numerous American researchers, an
adequate financial package is a necessity to making higher education affordable to all. The package should include need-based grant assistance for
the most promising students from low-income families, student loan programs available to all eligible students, and a work-study program (Cronin
& Simmons, 1987; Fesco, 1993; Hauptman & Koff, 1991; Lee, 1999). The
grants and loans should be sufficient in amount to make possible the enrollment of financially disadvantaged but academically qualified students.

Previous research (Cabrera & La Nasa, 2001; Coleman, 1988; Perna,
2000) consistently demonstrates that there is a powerful correlation be-

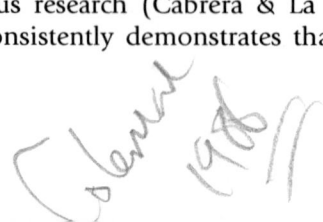

tween good academic performance and high family socioeconomic status. Students from families of lower socioeconomic status are less likely than others to get high achievements that are good enough to qualify for an award. That is to say, when aid is based on personal achievement such as academic performance, the students who are most in need of financial assistance to make a college education even possible are the least likely to get a scholarship. Moreover, research (Jackson, 1978) also reveals that low-income students are more responsive to financial aid than other students. Therefore, targeted, need-based financial aid is the most effective strategy to expand college access for students from families with low socioeconomic status.

Research in American higher education (Gladieux, 2002; Heller, 2002; Lee, 2002; McPherson & Schapiro, 2002) reveals that grant dollars are more effectively targeted at low-income students and do encourage enrollment, whereas loan funds do not appear to affect many decisions to go to college. Instead, the prospect of debt likely discourages economically disadvantaged students from considering applying to college. Moreover, if these low-income students drop out of college, the situation for them would get even worse. As indicated by Gladieux (2002), they will have to leave college "with no degree, few skills, and student loan debt to repay" (p. 48). Jenson's research (1984) also suggests that financial aid is positively correlated to college persistence. The larger the amount of assistance students receive, the more the likelihood for them to complete their degrees.

CONCLUSION

Bourdieu's cultural capital theory analyzes how culture and education interact and thereby contribute to the social reproduction of inequality. Expansive college access research inspired by Bourdieu's theory has shown that student's college access is a complex product of family backgrounds, high school climate, parental involvement, and students' self-efficacy and academic preparation. Since students' process of college choice is a complex procedure that involves many variables that play different roles at different stages, numerous conceptual models have been developed to examine the process. In the next chapter I will review different economic, sociological, and combined models for understanding students' college planning process and then discuss the conceptual framework for the study.

NOTES

1. The concepts social capital and cultural capital are sometimes used interchangeably in discussions of the social context of education, such as in McDonough,

Korn, and Yamasaki's research on college counseling (1997) and Perna's discussions of underrepresented minority students' college decisions (2000). However, social capital can be broadly defined as the norms and networks that enable people to act collectively and has been used in research other than educational studies (Woolcock & Narapan, 2000).

2. Cultural classes are used as a measure of cultural capital in some research. According to Aschaffenburg and Maas (1997), cultural classes usually include lessons or classes in the following cultural domains: "(1) music (voice or instrument); (2) visual arts (sculpture, painting, print-making, photography, or film-making); (3) performance (acting or ballet); (4) art appreciation or art history; and (5) music appreciation and music history" (p. 578).

3

Models of Student College Choice

The previous chapter presented and discussed the theory and literature on status attainment and college access and choice. Cultural capital theory argues that social stratification is closely linked to the system of education and, specifically, to higher education. Whether a person continues his/her education at the postsecondary level and in which kind of postsecondary institution he/she chooses to enroll have a major impact on life chances, occupational status, and wealth. Research reviewed in chapter 2 supports the premise of cultural capital theory by proving that family socioeconomic status, parental expectation and involvement, and student achievement all play a large role in the likelihood of attending college. Based on the theory and research outlined in chapter 2, this chapter will present the conceptual framework for the study.

PERSPECTIVES ON STUDENT COLLEGE CHOICE

According to Hossler, Braxton, and Coopersmith (1989), college choice process can be defined as "a complex, multistage process during which an individual develops aspirations to continue formal education beyond high school, followed later by a decision to attend a specific college, university or institution of advanced vocational training" (p. 234). Although the previous research has identified a variety of factors that influence students' decisions to enroll in college and their interrelationships, the student college choice process is still difficult to study because it is a longitudinal and developmental process during which the different factors play different roles. Many conceptual frameworks and models have thus been developed to explain the complexities and dynamics of the choice process. Hossler, Schmit, and Vesper (1999) identify three types of college choice models: economic models, status-attainment models, and combined models. Each type of model postulates an important variable set in order to understand a student's choice of whether or not to attend a college and of which college to attend.

Economic models assume that individual students strive to maximize their utility and minimize risk (Hossler, Braxton, & Coopersmith, 1989; Hossler, Schmit, & Vesper, 1999; Hossler & Stage, 1992). Therefore, an individual will choose to attend college if the perceived benefits of college attendance are greater than noncollege alternatives. Following the same logic of cost-benefit analysis, economic models suggest that students will select a particular postsecondary education institution (PEI) if the perceived benefits of attendance at this institution outweigh those of other PEIs. Economic models are rooted in the assumption that individuals are rational and obtain all needed information to make decisions that are in their best interest. Economic models take into account college costs, financial aid, student background characteristics, and high school and college characteristics.

Status-attainment models of college choice focus on the identification of factors, such as family background, cultural capital, social networks, and schooling conditions, that influence aspirations for a college education. As pointed out by Hossler, Schmit, and Vesper (1999), status-attainment models are largely concerned with the role of family socioeconomic status in education and career decisions, which in turn lead to the development of social stratification. Different from economic models, status-attainment models reject the assumption of students and parents as rational decision makers who have ready access to all the necessary information. Instead, status-attainment models emphasize that an individual is guided by his/her position within structures of access and constraint when making choices and that the consequences of the choices are also shaped by these structures. For example, family socioeconomic status has a direct impact on student college choice and also influences a series of other attitudes and behaviors that are related to college choice.

COMBINED MODELS OF STUDENT COLLEGE CHOICE

Although both economic models and status-attainment models have indicated important sets of variables that influence student decision making with regard to college attendance and college selection, neither of these conceptual frameworks successfully explains the student college choice as a longitudinal and cumulative process. A group of combined models, by drawing on the strengths of both economic and sociological models, has been developed in order to provide a better conceptual approach to explain student college choice. Litten (1982) outlines a three-phase model, which depicts three distinctive steps in the college choice process. The first phase refers to a period during which a student first develops his/her aspiration to attend a college and then makes the decision to pursue a college education. The second phase involves collecting information and identifying postsecondary options. The final phase includes application for submission and enrollment in a particular institution. Jackson's college choice model (1982) shares some similarities with Litten's model. His model also includes three stages: preference, exclusion, and evaluation. In the first stage, students develop their preferences for certain options. In the second stage, students form a choice set. Some students might exclude colleges as unfeasible, and others might not consider anything other than a college education. The final stage is that of evaluation. Students evaluate the available alternatives and choose one institution to attend.

Based on Litten's (1982) and Jackson's (1982) models of student college choice and Chapman's work (1981) on the important variables and their interrelations on students' decision making about college choice, Hossler and Gallagher (1987) develop a comprehensive and accessible three-phase model for the college-going process. Since the introduction of this model, researchers have heavily relied on it and widely used it as a conceptual framework for understanding the complex processes that determine college attendance and choice. The three phases of the model are labeled as (1) predisposition, (2) search, and (3) choice. In their 1987 article, predisposition is defined as "a developmental phase in which students determine whether or not they would like to continue their education beyond high school" (Hossler & Gallagher, 1987, p. 209). For those students who decide to pursue a college education, the second phase is the time when they begin to seek information about colleges and universities that they might be interested in attending and develop a list of these colleges and universities, which is known as the "choice set." As Hossler and Gallagher (1987) describe it, "The choice set is the group of institutions to which students will actually apply" (p. 209). The final stage is the choice stage. At this stage, students evaluate their choice set developed in the second stage and make a decision to attend one of those colleges or universities based on the institutional characteristics that are most important to them and their own background characteristics. Hossler and Gallagher distinguish themselves by forming a comprehensive three-dimensional model of college choice that includes both individual and organizational influences at each dimension. That is to say, in their model each phase is understood as containing a set of individual and organizational variables that interact with one another and work together to culminate in specific outcomes.

Combining status attainment and econometric theories, Hossler and Gallagher's model has provided a conceptual framework in which both traditions can assess each other and allow researchers to more holistically examine the phenomena of college access and choice. A number of scholars have relied on this model to explore influential factors that affect different stages of the college choice process. By combining traditional econometric measures and measures of social and cultural capital, Hossler and Gallagher (1987) provide a framework that views college choice as more than an economic investment, but as a cultural and social decision as well.

CONCEPTUAL FRAMEWORK OF THE STUDY

The conceptual framework proposed for this study (Figure 3.1) is based on the model of Hossler and Gallagher (1987), but expands the three stages of college choice (predisposition, search, and choice) to four. Previous research on college access and choice has indicated that the process of student college choice starts approximately in middle school (Hossler, Braxton, & Coopersmith, 1989; Hossler & Gallagher, 1987; Nora & Cabrera, 1992). However, Hossler and Gallagher (1987) also note that one of the most important background characteristics, students' SES, has a "cumulative effect on college enrollment plans that begins in pre-school and continues throughout the formal years of schooling" (p. 210).

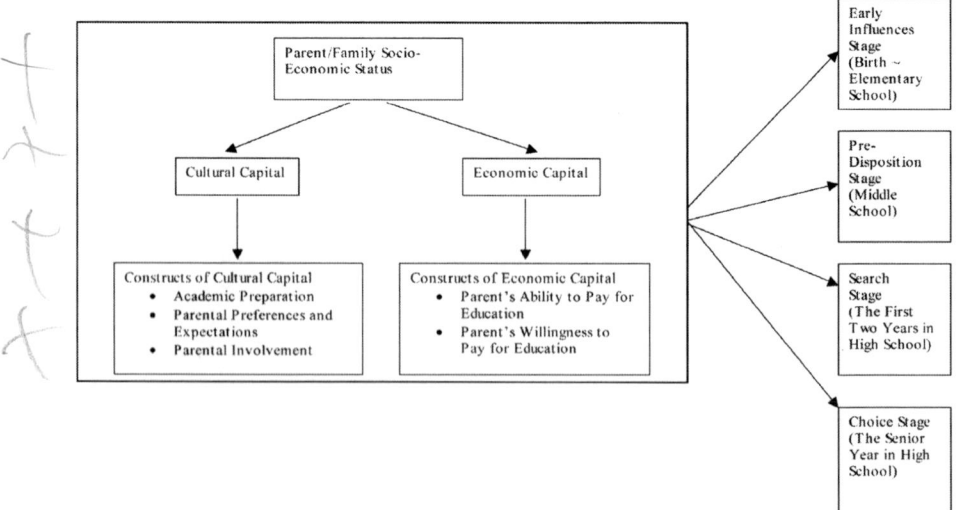

Figure 3.1. Stages in College Decision Making and Elements of Cultural Capital and Economic Capital Influenced by Family's Socioeconomic Status

Focusing on the factors that contribute to success in school, Bempechat's study (1998) also indicates the importance of early childhood effects on cognitive development and academic achievement. Her findings demonstrate that high-achieving children have experienced similar early family education and have similar perceptions about their parents' educational beliefs and practices. The prior research presented in the literature chapter also reveals the importance of early family education and of the role of academic performance in demand for education. A number of studies point to the role that stimulating academic performance could play in the breaking of cycles of disadvantages based on socioeconomic status. Therefore, considering these two points: (1) early childhood family education has a strong impact on academic achievement, and (2) academic performance is one of the most powerful variables influencing student college choice, the conceptual framework for this study expands the three stages of college choice to four by adding an earlier stage, "early influences," to the three stages proposed in Hossler and Gallagher's model—predisposition, search, and choice. The early influences stage covers the period from birth to the end of elementary education.

In the conceptual framework, the two important elements that affect the whole process of the student college choice are cultural capital and economic capital. The cultural capital element includes three constructs: academic preparation, parental preferences and expectations, and parental involvement. The constructs that represent the economic capital are parents' ability to pay for education and their willingness to pay. Table 3.1 presents these constructs and the individual variables that make up the constructs. These variables are taken from the literature on cultural capital in chapter 2.

The construct "academic preparation" includes early family education, education planning, reading and learning environment at home, and school choices. A number of studies (Cabrera & La Nasa, 2001; Kuo & Hauser, 1995; Perna, 2000; Perna, 2002) indicate that as students' academic achievement increases, so does the likelihood of college attendance. As previously discussed, according to cultural capital theory, family factors have a major impact on the development of cognitive skills, acquaintance with cultural cues, and cultivation of certain attitudes with studying that are recognized and highly rewarded in formal school education. A stimulating reading and learning environment at home can also contribute to the development of linguistic and educational skills, which increases students' academic abilities. Finally, there is a relationship between family's socioeconomic status and school status (Jencks, et. al, 2000), which in turn has an influence on students' decision making about college enrollment and choice (McDonough, 1997).

Five variables identified in the literature of cultural capital and college access make up the construct "parental preferences and expectations." The

Table 3.1. Variables Associated with Cultural Capital and Economic Capital

Elements	Constructs		
	Academic	*Parental Preferences*	
Cultural Capital	*Preparation*	*and Expectations*	*Parental Involvement*
Variables	Early Family Education	Parents' Expectation about School	Parental Participation in College Visits
	Education Planning	Parents' Encouragement for Schoolwork	Helping with College Set
	Reading and Learning Environment at Home	Communication Styles	Final Decision about College Choice
	School Choices	Discipline at Home Rules about Schoolwork and Grades	
		Parents' Ability to	*Parents' Willingness to*
Economic Capital		*Pay for Education*	*Pay for Education*
Variables	Spending on Books and Other Educational Objects Spending on Extracurricular Activities and Other Afterschool Classes Choosing a Middle School Choosing a High School Criteria for College Choice (such as institutional cost and financial aid)		

five indicators include parents' expectation about school (as communicated to the student), parents' encouragement for schoolwork, communication styles, discipline at home, and rules about schoolwork and grades. The extant research has also shown that parental preferences and expectations are an important force in students' college participation (Cabrera & La Nasa, 2001; Coleman, 1988; McDonough, 1997; Perna, 2000; Swail and Perna, 2002). There is a strong relationship between the amount of parental encouragement students receive to attend college and their subsequent college plans. As cultural capital theory indicates, parents play an important role in shaping students' attitude toward schooling in general and higher education in specific. Students with parents who had college experiences and strongly encourage the student to attend college are more likely to be planning to go to college. Of course, parental knowledge and expectations can be effective only if the student can take advantage of this cultural capital. To make the sources of cultural capital available to the student also depends on how often and how well parents and the student communicate with each other. Therefore, the conceptual framework of this study will take into account the importance of early and sustained discussion about educational topics and the importance of a high level of discussion between parents and the student relevant to college decisions.

Three indicators make up the construct "parental involvement." While there may be some overlap between "expectation" and "participation," this construct assumes more concrete resources and actions that are related to college planning. It includes parental participation in visiting college campuses, helping select a set of institutions for application, and making the final decision to enroll in a particular college. Prior research indicates that parental involvement is a strong predictor of the student's postsecondary plan. Having a parent with a high level of education affects not only the student's academic achievement and aspirations but, more important, the actual process of college choice. The parents' knowledge of and comfort with navigating particular aspects of the college search can facilitate a student's successful matriculation. The parents' experiences with college application and actions like going on college visits can benefit the student and promote college access.

The two constructs that represent economic capital are parents' ability and willingness to pay for education. Family income, an important aspect of a family's socioeconomic status, directly affects college decisions. As prior research indicates, students from high-income families are more likely to go to college and choose four-year institutions. In the choice stage, family income can limit what students believe are their realistic options. Furthermore, family income interacts with other factors, such as cost of educational materials, and thus impact student's academic performance, which, in turn, is related to college planning.

On the primary and secondary school levels, low-income students can be put in a disadvantaged position because of the lack of financial capital, limiting their access to educational resources, such as books and afterschool classes. On the tertiary level, sufficient financial support from their families is even more important for students to consider pursuing a college degree and to persist in college. Researchers point out that parents' willingness to pay for education is highly associated with family income (Steelman & Powell, 1991). By definition, low-income parents possess fewer economic resources. Because of the lack of security in terms of financial capital, low-income parents are less willing to invest in their children's education. Since there is an overlap between parents' ability and willingness to pay for education, these two constructs share four indicators: spending on books and other educational objects, spending on extracurricular activities and other afterschool classes, choosing a middle school and a high school, and assessing criteria for college choice (such as institutional cost and financial aid).

CONCLUSION

Figure 3.1 presents the conceptual framework of this study that identifies how the various social and economic factors affect the different stages of students' decision-making process about college planning. As discussed earlier, the conceptual framework is a derivative from Hossler and Gallagher's model of the student college choice, with its key phases of predisposition, search, and choice. The first stage, early influences, is added to Hossler and Gallagher's model in order to capture the importance of early family education and the unique characteristics of habitus for different social classes. The treatment of the predisposition phase also requires some comments. According to Hossler and Gallagher (1987), the predisposition stage refers to the phase in which students determine whether or not they want to pursue a college education, which usually happens in the third year of middle school or the first year of high school. However, later on, Hossler and his colleagues (Hossler, Braxton, & Coopersmith, 1989) define the predisposition stage as the time when "students arrive at a tentative conclusion to continue, or not continue, their formal education after high school graduation" (p. 249). The inclusion of the word "tentative" is important because it gives the model more flexibility. Elsewhere, Hossler also points out that students with parents having a high level of education might make their college plans earlier (Hossler, Schmit, & Vesper, 1999). Therefore, the conceptual framework of this study expands the predisposition stage to cover the time from the beginning of middle school to the beginning of high school. It aims at revealing the early college planning of some students while capturing the tentative decisions about college attendance from other students.

This study is aimed at contributing to our understanding of students' college choice process in China. To better understand this complex process, the following chapter will provide some background information about the profound social changes that have been undertaken in China and the resulting inequalities of participation in higher education. In chapter 4, I will discuss the unique Chinese political and economic conditions, the social stratification in China, and the unequal opportunities for higher education.

4

Social Stratification and Higher Education Opportunities in China

The political and economic situation in China has been changing dramatically in the wake of post-1978 market-oriented reforms. The political reform is mainly embodied in the emphasis shifting from class struggles to economic development. Instead of mobilizing the masses for continual political campaigns with class struggles to strengthen the proletarian dictatorship, the emphasis of government policies switched to extensive economic revitalization. The new leadership after Mao wanted to make its national power strong by realizing "four modernizations."[1] The economic reform aimed at transferring the former planning economy to a market-oriented economy. With the establishment and development of a market-oriented economic system, the previous highly centralized planning and control began to be replaced by more local enterprise initiatives and a certain degree of market regulation. These changes in the political and economic fields inevitably brought about a process of class transformation, creating new mechanisms of social stratification and causing new income inequalities and unequal educational opportunities.

CHANGING MECHANISMS OF SOCIAL STRATIFICATION

It is well established that different political and economic institutions produce different patterns of social stratification and inequality (Szelenyi, 1978). Therefore, in order to understand the changing mechanisms of stratification in China, one needs to recognize the differences in the government-controlled redistributive economy and the market economy regarding the redistribution of resources and the allocation of welfare among social groups and intergenerational mobility.

The Redistributive Economy

The economic structure in state socialist China before the 1978 reform can be described as a redistributive economy (Nee, 1989). Redistributive economy refers to the institutional basis that the state owns economic resources, collects the returns to these resources, and distributes the earnings and welfare to individuals according to their political power and their positions in the state's bureaucratic system. Given the fact that the state systematically redistributes resources and opportunities, the state undoubtedly plays a central role in the stratifying mechanism. As argued by Zhou, Tuma, and Moen (1996), the state policies and political processes exerted significant impacts on individuals' life chances in state socialist China. Only when one's family social origin was supported by state policies could an individual get ahead in terms of educational attainment and work opportunities. According to Szelenyi (1978), in the redistributive economy, the members of the elite class actually control the resources under the disguise of the state. These elites are "redistributors," including high-ranking officials and professionals, who are in a conflict of interest with "immediate producers," such as workers and peasants.

However, it should be noted that in state socialist China under Mao's leadership, the working class was politically favored and regarded as the leading class. Urban working class and peasants were regarded as the most trustworthy and supportive class of the newly founded communist China under the leadership of the working class. Therefore, although the working class and peasants were still in disadvantageous and powerless positions compared to cadres and high-ranking party members, some of the state polices were carried out in favor of workers and peasants. In a later discussion, we will see how the college admission policies in Mao's era benefited children from working-class or peasant families.

The Market Economy

The status hierarchy mainly based on political criteria, which was anchored in the redistributive economy in state socialist China, has eroded since the 1978 reforms. The emerging market-oriented economy introduced new mechanisms of resource allocation and also created conditions for new patterns of social stratification. As put by Zhou and his colleagues (Zhou, Tuma, & Moen, 1996),

> In the market economy, political and economic transactions are based on the principle of exchange. In this institutional structure, initial endowments

of resources have a lasting effect on social position because private property rights prevail and stabilize the relative opportunities of various groups based on their preexisting social and economic resources. Not surprisingly, then, until very recently social mobility and stratification in industrialized market societies have been characterized by persistent advantages of initial resource endowments. (p. 762)

As we have seen in the literature review chapter, extensive research conducted in capitalist societies has consistently found that children from high socioeconomic backgrounds are more often exposed to highbrow cultural activities at home and that those who enter the school with more cultural endowments are more likely to do well in school and subsequently have better chances of achieving high levels of schooling. Cultural capital is a principal vehicle through which background inequalities are translated into differential academic rewards and which in turn lead to unequal social and economic rewards, thereby maintaining and legitimizing the reproduction process. In the industrialized market societies, economic capital, human capital, and social capital all operate in the same way as cultural capital. These different forms of family based resources can be invested to enhance profitability and facilitate upward mobility. Therefore, different from the redistributive economy in which individuals' socioeconomic status is largely determined by the state polices and political conditions, individual life chances in industrialized market societies reflect "a high degree of stability of the relative social status of social groups" (Zhou et al., 1996, p. 763).

China has now undergone more than two decades of reform. During this period of time, the Chinese government gradually whittled away the institutional basis for the redistributive economy and introduced market-based economic transactions. Meanwhile, the old system remained and played important roles in shaping the transition from one system to the other. The creation of a mixed "socialist-market" economy has drawn attention from both Chinese and Western scholars. Victor Nee's market transition theory is one of the earliest attempts to examine the social changes brought by the economic reforms in China. His thesis emphasizes the role of markets in societal transformation and predicts that markets would ultimately diminish the power of the state and alter stratification. According to Nee (1989), "The transition from redistributive to market coordination shifts sources of power and privilege to favor direct producers (i.e., entrepreneurs) relative to redistributors (i.e., cadres)" (p. 663). Besides Nee's market transition theory, some other scholars have proposed alternative explanations that emphasize the persistence of political power (Bian & Logan, 1996) or the co-evolution of politics and markets (Zhou, 2000), which also considerably contributed to the study of large-scale social changes in the transitioning

Chinese society. The interaction between politics and emerging markets has brought about substantial changes to the stratification order.

The Changing Social Stratification

During the 30 years of Mao's reign, China's pattern of stratification and mobility has been determined by politically ascriptive standards. People were divided into two opposing classes: "people's classes" and "class enemies" (Lin, 1991). People's classes included Communist Party members, revolutionary cadres, and soldiers, workers, and peasants, while class enemies consisted of the former landlords, entrepreneurs, and intellectuals. As previously noted, although workers and peasants were politically favored, the resources were controlled and redistributed by party members and cadres in the name of the state. In this cadre-dominated social hierarchy, class enemies were abused, tortured, and even persecuted to death, especially during the period of the nationwide political turmoil—the Cultural Revolution (1966–1976) (Lin, 1991).

Class structure and income stratification have experienced fundamental changes in China for three decades. The previous social order based on political positions and loyalty to the Communist Party has eroded while China transitions from the redistributive economy to the market economy. Nevertheless, cadres are still in an advantageous position in market transactions compared to other social groups, argue many scholars (Zhou, 2000). Those who once held or still hold political positions can influence the state policy making in order to advance their group interests. Moreover, these cadres in powerful positions can use their social networks and their political power to capitalize on opportunities and economic benefits. As put by Zhou (2000), "Those with positional power have advantages in access to both resources and the market-induced opportunities, relative to other social groups: previous 'redistributors' may now profit from economic arena in the role of 'regulators' in market transactions or as parties of economic transactions."

The state policy of discriminating against certain classes, such as entrepreneurs and intellectuals, was officially discontinued after the 1978 reform. Researchers argue that a "dual-elite model" exists in the transitioning Chinese society (Bian, Breiger, Davis, & Galaskiewicz, 2005). Besides those cadres who use their political positions and social ties to actualize economic interests, intellectuals gain high-paying jobs in the market sectors and new entrepreneurs also receive high earnings to their investments. Some scholars (Bian, Breiger, Davis, & Galaskiewicz, 2005; Lin, 2006) argue that these skilled professionals (such as professors, lawyers, doctors, and engineers) and new entrepreneurs form the emerging "middle class" in China. Nevertheless, defining Chinese middle class with accuracy remains challenging.

Reputable sources disagree considerably about the size and criteria of the middle class in China. Recent definitions of what constitutes the middle class in China range from approximately 10 percent to more than half of the population. In 2007, Goldman Sachs put the figure at 100 million people (Wagner, 2010). In contrast, the Asian Development Bank (August 2010) defines Asian middle class as those consuming between $2 and $20 per day, which means 800 million Chinese are qualified as middle-class members, about 60 percent of the country's population. More confusing, there is no one agreed-upon definition of Chinese middle class.

How much income qualifies one for being middle class in China? The Chinese Academy of Social Sciences released a report in 2004 defining the Chinese middle class as families with assets valued from $18,100 to $36,200 (150,000 to 300,000 yuan) (Lin & Sun, 2010). In 2005, after surveying more than a quarter of a million people and taking into consideration the exchange rate and purchasing power, China's National Bureau of Statistics categorized the Chinese middle class as households with an annual income ranging from $7,250 to $62,500 (60,000 to 500,000 yuan) (Lin & Sun, 2010).

This study adopted the most common definition of middle class used in Western sociology, which takes into account education, profession, and wealth. Here a middle-class member is defined as someone who works as salaried professional and has received at least college education. Because of the varying income standards used by different organizations when defining the Chinese middle class, this study uses educational attainment—a college degree—as the main distinguishing feature of middle class.

In contrast to the continuing privileged positions of cadres and the rising social status of intellectuals and entrepreneurs, the high status recognition of manual workers and peasants has substantially declined while the role of market institutions is increasing. Manual workers, who were provided with lifetime employment and an impressive array of collective benefits, including state-owned housing and health insurance, are now exposed to intense economic competition in the newly reconstructed urban labor markets. And, millions of manual workers who used to work in the state-owned industries were laid off (Lin, 2006). The effect of unemployment has been devastating for laid-off workers, especially middle-aged female workers who were least likely to find a job in the labor market. Peasants, who have been always among the poorest, are now still living at low economic levels. Some peasants therefore choose to leave the countryside and come to the urban area in search of job opportunities. Most of them end up in heavy manual labor, but it is low-paying work with poor conditions and benefits (Bian, Breiger, Davis, & Galaskiewicz, 2005; Lin, 2006). The unemployed workers, the ever-increasing migrant "peasant workers," and retired workers have formed the new urban poverty stratum. As indicated in Lee and

Selden's article (2007, p. 10), a new class of urban poor emerged in China, which was estimated to be about 15 to 31 million and comprised 4 to 8 percent of the urban population.

HIGHER EDUCATION REFORMS IN MAO'S ERA

Educational reforms in China often, if not always, respond to some political campaign or economic readjustment. Therefore, the development of higher education in the People's Republic of China has followed an uneven road since 1949 when the republic was founded. Educational policy and practice have shifted and adjusted in response to numerous political campaigns and state policies. In the following, I will briefly introduce the higher education reforms in the 1950s and then discuss the several changes made to college admission policies under Mao's leadership and the associated different forms of social inequalities in terms of educational opportunities.

The Formation of the "Soviet Model"

Before discussing current reforms in Chinese higher educational system, we must be aware of the first wave of reforms coming in 1952, which was an extensive restructuring of the existing institutions of higher learning at that time. The period from 1949 to 1957 is the early period of socialist construction. The most important and urgent task for the Chinese Communist Party at that time was to revitalize the national economy after the eight-year Sino-Japanese War and the four-year Civil War.[2] Thus, the main task for future higher education development set forth at the first National Education Work Conference held in June 1952 was to serve economic construction, which is the foundation for all other construction (Hayhoe, 1996).

The reforms carried out under Soviet guidance as a part of the efforts associated with the First Five-Year Plan (1953–1957) have been summarized under the phrase "the reordering of colleges and departments" (Hayhoe, 1984). In this round of reforms, Chinese universities that had fairly comprehensive departments and programs, including liberal arts, sciences, engineering, agriculture, and medicine, were dismembered. Former colleges of engineering, agriculture, law, and medicine within comprehensive universities split off and became independent colleges or were combined with other similar departments or colleges and then transformed into independent institutions (Du, 1992; Hayhoe, 1984). By the end of 1953 when the restructuring had been basically completed, comprehensive universities in China were reduced to 14, while the specialized colleges markedly increased (Chinese Ministry of Education, 1985). Thus, a new higher educational system patterned on a "Soviet model" has been built up in China.

The Evolution of College Admission Policies

The primary concern in this reform was to restructure the whole higher education system in ways that would gear it to the needs of economic and social development and to produce a large number of specialized personnel for the nation's rehabilitation and economic revitalization (Du, 1992). To achieve this goal, the college admission policy placed an emphasis on academic qualifications by recruiting students who had high test scores in the national unified college entrance examination. It was biased in favor of the bourgeois intellectuals because children from these families had better parental coaching and thus performed better in the examinations.

The 1958–1965 phase witnessed an economic contraction following the economic disaster of the early 1960s. The state policies gradually shifted from economic revitalization to political campaigns. In higher education, the college admission policy also increasingly emphasized family background and downplayed academic qualifications (Zhou, Moen, & Tuma, 1998). The rationale behind this change was that class conflicts and struggles still existed in the Chinese society and that the former exploiting classes would try to overthrow the Communist Party governance. In order to prevent this from happening, the college admission policy in this period was biased in favor of students from working-class and peasant families because they were of the people's classes, which the Chinese Communist Party had to rely on to fight against those class enemies (Niu, 1992).

The next period, 1966–1976, encompasses the years of the Cultural Revolution. Education, especially higher education, was seen as the most important institution for cultivating successors for the proletariat cause (Lin, 1991). As a result, labor and political loyalty were valued over academic achievement. In this phase, the national unified college entrance examination was eliminated, and social origin became the one and only criterion for deciding who was eligible for higher education. Children from intellectual families or former landowning families were totally shut out of higher education institutions. In contrast, all colleges and universities were mandated to open their doors to students whose parents were labor workers and peasants (Du, 1992; Niu, 1992).

The changes in educational priorities reflected the shifts of state policy concerns. The different college admission policies decide which social groups have better access to higher education and have carried direct implications for the social inequalities in a particular period. In general, the emphasis on academic achievement has resulted in a high proportion of children from intelligentsia families being admitted, while the consideration of class background or political stance has favored children from working-class or peasant families as well as the children of political cadres.

HIGHER EDUCATION IN THE REFORM ERA

Using class background and political loyalty as the only criteria for college admission was discontinued in 1977. With the new leadership coming into power, the state policy priorities once again shifted to economic development. The three-tiered national examination system was restored in order to select and train the most talented for the revitalization and development of the national economy.

During the ten years of the Cultural Revolution, educational processes and institutions were severely disrupted. It was only after the 1978 reforms that relatively systematic and balanced efforts began to be made to develop higher education. A series of policy readjustments have been made in Chinese higher education with regard to management, finance, structure, and curriculum during the nearly two decades of reform. In the following, I will review the development of higher education in the reform era, with a focus on two important national policies that were implemented in the 1990s regarding enrollment in and the financing of higher education.

The Institutional Amalgamation Policy

In the 1980s, the Chinese economic and political reforms had been carried out for several years, the Chinese government decided to start a series of reforms in the higher education system that attempted to overthrow the Soviet model built up in the 1950s.

One of the primary features of the Soviet model is the government's strong control over colleges and universities (Hayoe, 1996). The higher education administrative system in the early 1980s was still the one that was developed in the state-planning economy and concordant with the rigid political control at that time. With the state government controlling higher education planning and policy making and with excessive uniformity and a rigid system of management, colleges and universities had no autonomy in their own development. Institutions that were responsible for the same field of study had the same course outlines and unified textbooks fixed by the central government. The enrollment quotas set by the government had to be filled every year. Moreover, the government set the national unified placement for college graduates, and this kind of placement had to be fulfilled by each institution (Du, 1992). Under such a strong control by the state, colleges and universities were unable to take the initiative to make adjustments to their programs and course offerings to meet the needs of economic and social development. When nationwide political and economic reforms brought about local initiatives, enterprise autonomies, market regulations, and a certain degree of political democratization, the problems of the Soviet model became prominent. With the high tide of economic and political reforms sweeping over the country, both the state government and academia called for reforms in higher education

The central government carried out a series of policies with regard to the higher education administrative system in the reform era. I will only focus on the institutional amalgamation policy and higher education expansion.

As noted before, changes in the political and economic fields in China brought the crucial role of education into sharp focus and, at the same time, gave impetus to educational reform. At the National Educational Work Conference in April 1978, President Deng Xiaoping emphasized the importance of education by saying, "To realize the four modernizations, science and technology are the keys . . . and education is the foundation" (Niu, 1992, p. 43). To build the relatively poor and backward China into a modern and powerful nation "before the end of the century" (Chinese Communist Party Central Committee, 1978), a great challenge was presented to Chinese higher education, which was charged with the important task of producing sufficient human capital for national development. Therefore, higher education in China had to undergo corresponding changes to provide and foster the personnel and knowledge required for the development of the national economy and the accomplishment of the four modernizations.

Among several policies initiated by the Chinese government in the higher education field, the institutional amalgamation policy was carried out to increase the capacity of higher education institutions and nurture talents with multiple intelligences. The institutional amalgamation policy was enacted and implemented by the central government in 1992 (Zhao, 1998). "Amalgamation" means encouraging institutions of higher learning to merge with one another in order to build up more comprehensive universities (Jian, 1998; Zhu, 1995). Because colleges and universities were relatively small and extremely specialized in the Soviet model, there was a lack of economies of scale. As a result, the ability of institutions to recruit students was quite low (Zhao, 1998). The aim of the amalgamation policy was to increase enrollment by increasing economic scale and encouraging universities to share educational resources. In terms of physical resources, students and faculty can share laboratories, libraries, lecture halls, classrooms, and other places that were not open to students and faculty of other institutions before the merger. In terms of human resources, the merged institutions had free access to exchanging faculty and staff (Hayhoe, 1996; Jian, 1998).

The main stimulus for expanding enrollment in higher education institutions was the rapid economic development in China and the urgent demand for highly educated personnel. In the 1980s and early 1990s, the higher education participation rate in China (just over 4 percent) was incompatible with China's rapid economic growth, which had an annual average gross domestic product growth rate of 9.89 percent between 1978 and 1994 (World Bank, July 2001). The World Bank advisors and Chinese scholars all point out that without a corresponding substantial increase in the higher education participation rate, China could not sustain its rapid economic growth. The college enrollment expansion was to be aimed at producing more human resources for China's long-term development. Moreover, China was being urged by advisors from the World Bank to consider a rapid expansion of the higher educational system toward the threshold of mass higher education, which has been identified as 15 percent of the age cohort of young people between 18 and 22 years old who are enrolled in higher education (World Bank, 1986).

The amalgamation policy was carried out under these concerns about efficiency and equity and reached its apex of implementation in late 1994 and early 1995. Between 1992 and 1995, more than 70 institutions merged into 28 institutions and more than 100 institutions set up cross-institution consortia (Zhu, 1995). Admittedly, the institutional amalgamation policy did increase enrollment to higher education. According to a project document of the World Bank about China (World Bank, 1999), the 1978–94 period witnessed remarkable growth in the enrollment of public, regular higher education institutions—from 0.86 million in 1978 to 2.8 million in 1994. Full-time students in undergraduate and short-cycle courses grew at an annual growth rate of 7.7 percent (p. 3). Especially during the 1992–95 phase, the annual growth rate of enrollment to higher educational institutions was as high as 11.6 percent (see Figure 4.1).

Higher Education Expansion

Although the consolidation of institutions certainly increased enrollment to higher education, China's level of human resource development in the late 1990s still lagged behind the world average of 1970 (Zha, 2007). On the other hand, China continued to enjoy magnificent economic growth and became a major player in the world economy. Responding to the fast economic development, Chinese higher education was charged with the tasks of creating more human resources and generating knowledge for China's long-term development. Moreover, with the rapid development of China's economy and resulting improvement of people's life, the social demand for higher education has become significantly greater. As a report

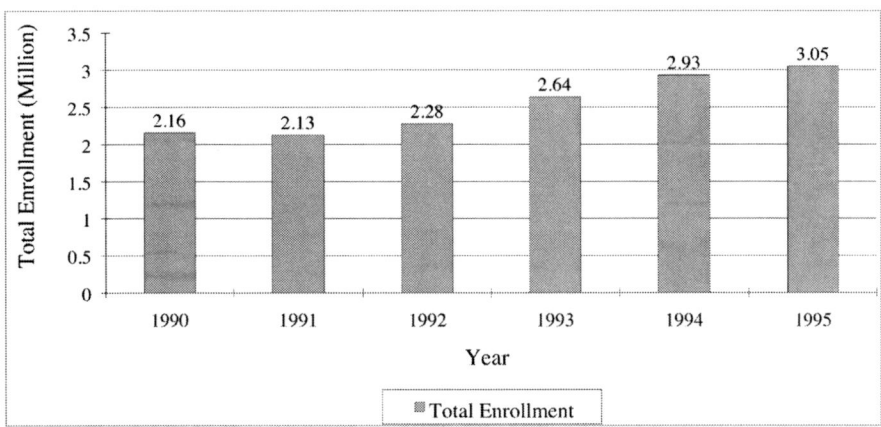

Figure 4.1. The Total Enrollment in Higher Education Institutions in China from 1990 to 1995 (in Millions)
Source: Zhao, F. (1998).

points out (China Education and Human Resource Task Force, 2003, p. 43), education has become the second largest consumption item in China in the late 1990s, next only to food. To meet the economic demand for more human resources and the social demand for greater access to higher education, higher education massification was put on the Chinese government's policy agenda. The East Asia Financial Crisis in 1997 also triggered higher education expansion in China. Influenced by the serious financial crisis that happened in most Asian countries in 1997, China also faced a rising unemployment rate and economic stagnancy. Prime Minister Zhu Rongji, being advised by two economists in the Asian Development Bank, decided to propel the consolidation of higher educational institutions (Wei, 1999). The intention was to encourage the investment in higher education, stimulate college students' consumption on campus, such as expenditures on food and board, and reduce the demands for employment by keeping a large number of students in school. Because of the belief that households' expected large-scale consumption and investment in higher education would stimulate domestic economic development, the expansion of higher education thus received much importance.

The further expansion of higher education in the late 1990s brought about significant increase in enrollment to Chinese heigher education institutions. As indicated by Zha's report on higher education massification (2007, p. 1), less than 4 percent of people in the 18–22 age-group enrolled in higher education institutions in 1990 compared to 19 percent in 2004. The total number of college students in 2004 exceeded 11 million, while the number in 1990 was only about 2 million. Figure 4.2 shows this great increase in access to higher education.

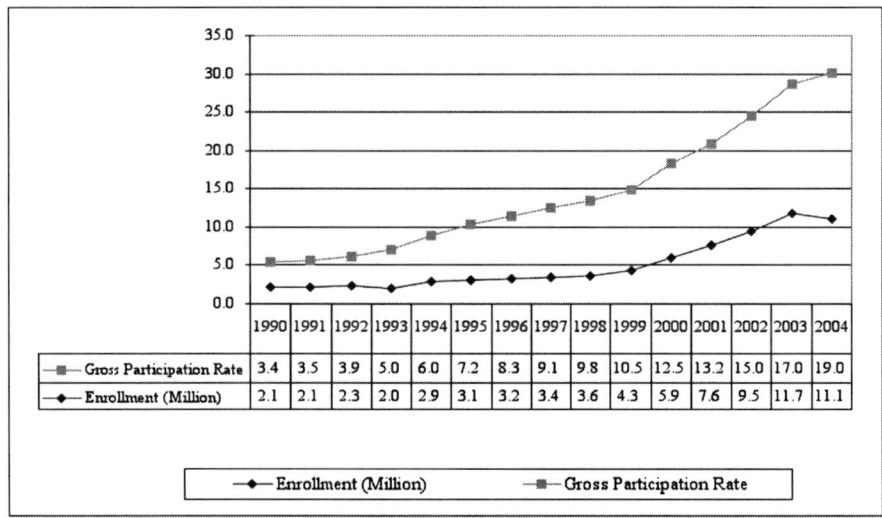

	1990	1991	1992	1993	1994	1995	1996	1997	1998	1999	2000	2001	2002	2003	2004
—■— Gross Participation Rate	3.4	3.5	3.9	5.0	6.0	7.2	8.3	9.1	9.8	10.5	12.5	13.2	15.0	17.0	19.0
—◆— Enrollment (Million)	2.1	2.1	2.3	2.0	2.9	3.1	3.2	3.4	3.6	4.3	5.9	7.6	9.5	11.7	11.1

——◆—— Enrollment (Million)   ——■—— Gross Participation Rate

Figure 4.2.   The Net Enrollment and Gross Participation Rate in Chinese Higher Education Institutions from 1990 to 2004

Source: Zha, Qiang (2007, p. 1).

However, with the rapid increase in enrollment, the Chinese government was no longer able to provide sufficient funds to colleges and universities. The higher education system, which was exclusively reliant on government funding, had to quest for alternative revenues. In the face of cost pressures accelerated by increased enrollment, the central government enacted the Pay-to-Learn policy in the mid-1990s (Tang, 1998a).

Pay-to-Learn Policy

When the government finances could no longer satisfy the development of higher education institutions, tuition and fees were introduced for the survival of Chinese higher education. The "Pay-to-Learn" policy set out to make parents and students responsible for shouldering part of the costs of college education. The rationale behind this policy was that "those who benefit from it should pay for it" (International Comparative Higher Education Center, 2000, p. 2). At the National Conference on Higher Education in 1992, Zhu Kaixuan, the deputy commissioner of the State Education Commission, stated, "The whole society's concept of higher education should be changed. It should be made clear that higher education does not fall into the category of compulsory education and, in principle, all university students should pay for their way" (Wang, 2001, p. 208). The proponents of cost-sharing argue that college students tend to be drawn from wealthier families that have the capacity to help their children study and place more importance on their learning performance. Therefore, providing college students with free higher education, which is actually paid by regressive taxes, is to use government funding to support elites from the socially and economically advantaged families and thus is not equitable. Moreover, higher education is a good personal investment because it raises its beneficiaries' incomes later in life. Thus, college students should pay for their education by themselves (*The Economist*, 1997).

In 1994 the state commission mandated 46 pilot colleges and universities implement the Pay-to-Learn policy. For the first time in the history of the People's Republic of China, institutions of higher learning charged students for tuition and fees. Since 1997 this policy has spread out over the whole higher education system (Tang, 1998b).

Tuition varies considerably for different institutions, different majors, and different grades (Central Education Research Institute, 2001; International Comparative Higher Education Center, 2000). First, prestigious universities charge more than other universities and colleges. Second, within the same university, popular and marketable majors, such as computer science, foreign languages, and economics and business, charge higher tuition than others, such as agriculture, forestry, and geology. Some other majors without high market values also charge relatively higher tuition because of their higher instructional costs, such as performance arts and music. Third, because amounts of tuition are fixed for the whole four-year or two-year undergraduate period and tuition increases every year, students in lower grades are generally charged higher tuition than those in higher grades within the same institution.

As noted before, the huge enrollment expansion to higher education led to more demands for revenue. To meet higher education's daunting financial requirement, government revenue has been growing in China since 1997. The central government appropriation to higher education was increased from RMB (renminbi, Chinese dollar[3]) 342.6 billion in 1998 to RMB 613.3 billion in 2001—an increase of 80 percent (Shanghai Academy of Education and Technology, 2002). Meanwhile, the central government authorized institutions more autonomy to develop new ways of raising revenue. Running institutional enterprises, offering executive training programs, providing various other services such as contractual research and consultancy, and seeking donations from alumni and corporate entities all provided valuable income to institutions (Wang, 2001). Therefore, the institutional revenue has grown at an annual rate of 58.8 percent, from RMB 202.2 billion in 1998 to RMB 553.3 billion in 2001 (Shanghai Academy of Education and Technology, 2002). However, the most astounding fact is that the tuition and fees have grown fourfold in this period (1998–2001). The revenue from tuition and fees was RMB 73.1 billion in 1998 and increased to RMB 298.7 billion in 2001 (See Table 4.1).

Table 4.1. Different Channels of Revenue to Public Postsecondary Education in China from 1998 to 2001 (in Billions)

Year	1998	1999	2000	2001
Total Revenue	544.8	704.2	904.4	1166.6
Government Appropriation	342.6	429.5	512.7	613.3
Institutional Revenue	129.1	153.9	199.1	254.6
Tuition and Fees	73.1	120.8	192.6	298.7

Source: Shanghai Academy of Education and Technology (2002).

Obviously, government appropriation accounted for a smaller percentage of the total revenue to higher education in 2001 (52.6 percent) than that in 1998 (62.9 percent). The share of the total revenue from institution-generated funds also decreased, though at a lower rate. In contrast, students and their families were asked to pay for a larger portion of their college education in the form of tuition and fees, which accounted for 25.6 percent of the total revenue in 2001 compared to 13.2 percent in 1998 (see Figure 4.3).

FINANCIAL ASSISTANCE POLICIES IN HIGHER EDUCATION

Given the dramatically increasing tuition and fees, today's students, particularly students from low-income families, are facing enormous financial challenges in achieving access to higher education. To help these low-income students overcome the financial barriers, China began to establish a financial aid system in the late 1990s that included scholarships, grants, and subsidized and unsubsidized loans (Han, 2002).

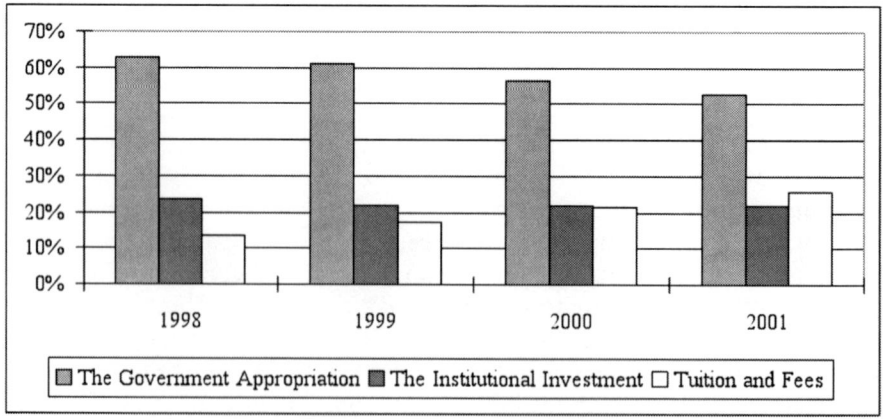

Figure 4.3. The Percentage of Different Channels of Revenue to Public Postsecondary Education in China from 1998 to 2001
Source: Shanghai Academy of Education and Technology (2002).

Financial aid is money provided to needy students to help pay for higher education costs. It can be used toward tuition fees, room and board, books and supplies, transportation, living expenses, and other costs associated with going to college (Lee, 1999). The overriding goal of the financial aid system is to ensure college access and choice to low-income students (Kane, 1999; Lee, 1999). Ensuring college access means that lack of money should not be the primary obstacle preventing needy students from continuing their education at the postsecondary level, while ensuring college choice means that needy students should have the right to choose the academic field according to their professional aspirations and interests.

Financially Needy Students

Before discussing the financial aid system in Chinese higher education, it is necessary to make clear the standard for identifying so-called "needy students" and who they are. The economic development in China is substantially unbalanced throughout the country. Some areas fall away behind the more progressive areas. In general, the central and western regions are behind the eastern part of China in progress, and the rural area is less developed in comparison to the urban area. Because of such uneven development, the standards for distinguishing needy students and the ratios of needy students in the whole student population vary largely in different areas and different institutions. In Beijing, the capital of China, students from low-income families made up 15 percent of the total enrollment in universities and colleges at all levels in 2001 (Gui, 2002). Among them, students whose family income is under the poverty level account for 5 percent of the total. In the same year, Shanghai, the biggest and wealthiest city in China, had 230,000 students enrolled in colleges and universities. Among them, there are 36,800 students whose monthly family income is below RMB 280 (the local basic living level), which is 16 percent of the total enrollment. The number of students whose monthly family income is below RMB 195 (the local poverty level) is 18,700, accounting for 8 percent of the total (Liu & Liu, 2002). The average ratio of financially needy students in the total college student population across the nation is 20 percent. In some backward regions and some least marketable and competitive majors, the percentage of low-income students reaches 30 percent of the total enrollment (Zhang, 2001).

In a survey conducted in Shaan'xi province, the data show that 70 percent of the needy students come from the rural area (Central Education Research Institute, 2001). Actually, given that the annual per capita net income of rural residents is less than a half of the per capita disposal income of urban residents (Chinese National Statistics Bureau, 2000), most needy students coming from the countryside are to be expected throughout the nation.

Before the cost-sharing policy was implemented in China, higher education had acted as a powerful mechanism for upward mobility, allowing the talented to thrive despite their social origins. Especially for those students who were born in farming families, going to college and then finding a job in the urban area is the only way they can expect to lead better lives. How to help those academically qualified but financially needy students go to college is becoming a substantial problem that the Chinese government and institutions must deal with. Means-tested grants and student loan programs are possible approaches to addressing this problem, which will be discussed in the following section.

Scholarships and Grants

Recognizing that financial barriers are severely restricting accessibility to higher education, the Chinese government created a series of programs designed to help students pay for college education. There are two basic types of financial aid offered by the government: merit-based and need-based grants. Merit-based scholarships are awarded to students based on their individual achievements, such as test scores, activities, special talents, community service, and so forth. Need-based grants are awarded to students and families based on their eligibility and demonstrated need.

All public institutions of higher learning in China have established the Outstanding Student Scholarship (OSS), supported by the central government. Generally, this scholarship is awarded to students based on their academic performance and extracurricular activities (Liu, 2002), and the precise standards for selection are decided by individual institutions. However, the central government set specific requirements for the amount of this scholarship and the number of students awarded. There are three levels of OSS. Five percent of students of the total can be awarded the first level of OSS, which is RMB 350 for an academic year. Ten percent of students are able to gain the second level of OSS, of which the annual amount is RMB 250. Another 10 percent of students are qualified for the third level of OSS and can gain RMB 150 for an academic year. Institutions are allowed to reduce the ratio of the first level of OSS winners and increase the third level of OSS gainers according to their specific institutional circumstances. However, the OSS students at all levels should account for no more than 35 percent of the whole student population (China Education News, 2001).

The second form of scholarship is the National Specialty Scholarship (NSS) (China Education News, 2001; Liu, 2002). Similar to the OSS, the amount of NSS and the quota of students being awarded are prescribed by the central government, and the specific requirements are regulated by individual institutions. Students who are currently enrolled in education, agriculture, forestry, geology, and marine sciences are all eligible for the

NSS. The NSS is also classified into three levels. Five percent of students in these majors are awarded the first level of NSS, which is about RMB 500 for an academic year. Ten percent of students are granted the second level of NSS, of which the annual amount is RMB 400. The rest of students are eligible for the third level of NSS, which is RMB 300 per year.

The third form of scholarship is the form of National Career-Based Grants (NCBGs) (China Education News, 2001; Liu, 2002). Students who pledge to go to work in the remote and backward area or in mining, forestry, and geology fields for a minimum of five years after graduation enjoy this grant. The service obligation is required. Students who fail to fulfill the promise would be obligated to repay the subsidies in one lump sum to the institution. There are also three levels of NCBGs, with the maximum award of RMB 500, RMB 450, RMB 400 per student per year, respectively. Different from OSS and NSS, for which students need to compete for different levels of awards every academic year, career-based grants are automatically renewed for the whole four-year or two-year undergraduate period.

National Scholarship for Outstanding Needy Students (NSONS) is based on both merit and need (Liu & Lan, 2002). China established this national scholarship on September 1, 2001, to help outstanding students from low-income families pay for their college education. The central government spends RMB 2 billion a year on the NSONS program. This national scholarship has two levels of grants. The first level is awarded to 10,000 students nationwide. The amount is RMB 6,000 per student per year. The second level is awarded to 35,000 students nationwide and is RMB 4,000 per student per year. For those who are awarded the NSONS, institutions must exempt their tuition and fees for that year.

Tuition reduction or tuition remission is an institutional-level grant that is aimed at helping needy students pay for their college education (Liu, 2002). In theory, students who are disabled, orphaned, from minority ethnic groups, or from a family in which parents are revolutionary martyrs are eligible for the reduction or remission of tuition. However, in practice, since these awards represent a loss of tuition revenue, many institutions try to shirk the responsibility by simply not publicizing this policy. Therefore, few eligible students actually pay reduced tuition or get exempted from paying tuition.

Student Loans

China started the National College Student Loan Program in the fall of 1999, "marking the country's first partnership with the private sector in higher education" (McMurtrie, 1999). Under this program, the state-owned Chinese Industrial and Commercial Bank provides funds to students who are currently enrolled in public colleges and universities. An experimental loan program was first established in eight cities, including Beijing, Shanghai, Chongqing, Wuhan, Shenyang, Xi'an, Nanjing, on September 1, 1999, and eventually reached to all colleges and universities throughout the country in the fall of 2000 (China Education News, 2001). There are two basic types of student loans. One is the subsidized student loan, and the other is the unsubsidized student loan.

The subsidized student loan is also called the Student Credit Loan (SCL) (China Education News, 2001). Students whose family income is below the national poverty level are eligible for this loan program. The amount of the loan equals tuition and fees plus living expenses minus family contributions minus other forms of scholarships and grants. The subsidized loan can be further classified into two types, loan for tuition and fees and loan for living expenses. The maximum loan for tuition and fees is the actual tuition and fees charged by specific institutions. The loan is distributed annually and deposited to the institution directly from the bank. The amount of loan for living expenses is no more than the minimum living expenses in the city in which the institution is located. The loan is distributed monthly and deposited to the student bank account (Chinese Ministry of Education, 2001).

The Student Credit Loan program does not require any kind of financial guarantee. However, applicants need to have one introducer (usually the officer in student financial office) and two eyewitnesses (could be teachers or classmates) who can prove that the information provided by the applicant is accurate. Applicants must be 18 years or older and currently enrolled in a two-year or four-year public college or university as a full-time degree-seeking undergraduate student. Applicants must provide information about annual family income and demonstrate financial needs (China Education News, 2001; Chinese Ministry of Education, 2001).

For the subsidized student loan, the interest rate is the same as the prevailing commercial rate (10.8 percent in the spring of 2000) (Johnstone, 2002, p. 9). Students need to pay 50 percent of the interest charge when they are still enrolled in college, and the central government pays the other half. The length of repayment is up to eight years for four-year university students and six years for two-year college students. In other words, students only have four years to repay the loan after graduation. If they continue their study in master's or doctoral programs, the repayment period can be extended to four years after they graduate from their master's or doctoral programs. If students cannot repay the loan within the time limit, their parents are legally responsible for paying the loans (China Education News, 2001; Chinese Ministry of Education, 2001).

The student financial office in individual institutions is responsible for reviewing application materials for the Student Credit Loan program. The number of needy students should be no more than 20 percent of the total enrollment (China Education News, 2001). The institutional student financial office then reports to the Student Loan Center periodically. The Student Loan Center was established in the fall of 1999 and is a nonprofit agency backed by the central government (McMurtrie, 1999). Its headquarters are in Beijing, the capital of China. For every province, a division in the provincial capital runs the Student Credit Loan program.

The Student Loan Center makes the final decision about the amount of individual student loans and sends its decision directly to the bank that is associated with the institution in which the student is registered. The bank does a final review of application materials and then informs the institution of the names of eligible students and the amount of loans after ensuring the authenticity of their information. Institutions are responsible for helping students fill out application forms (Liu, 2002).

The Student Credit Loan is the largest loan program in China. Besides this national subsidized loan program, there is a Neediest Student Loan program in each individual institution designed to help low-income students cover the expenses associated with university participation (China Education News, 2001; Liu, 2002). The institutional Neediest Student Loan is awarded only to students with financial need. Students borrow directly from the institutions where they are currently enrolled. Under this loan program, students are charged no interest. The length of repayment is up to six years after graduation. The loan amount equals the tuition and fees plus the living expenses minus other forms of financial assistance. Higher education institutions select the recipients and are responsible for collecting the repayments.

Students from middle-class families may be too wealthy to receive the subsidized loan but lack the resources to pay the sticker price out of their own pockets. For those students, the unsubsidized loan is helpful. The state-owned Chinese Industrial and Commercial Bank provides unsubsidized loans to any student who is attending a postsecondary institution as a full-time undergraduate. The interest rate is the prevailing commercial rate. Students and banks can negotiate the specific repayment period.

INEQUALITIES IN CHINESE HIGHER EDUCATION

Prior research has indicated that the stratification order in Chinese society has substantially changed in the reform era and that the reforms have brought about profound inequalities in terms of income and educational opportunities. With the socialist market economy emerging, the educational stratification in China came to resemble that of a capitalist society (Zhou, Moen, & Tuma, 1998). Using the representative data from 20 cities in China, Zhou and his colleagues analyzed that in the post-Mao era

(1978–94), a clear pattern of high school and college participation across social groups has been emerging. Their analysis supported the cultural capital argument that fathers' educational level, fathers' occupational status, and family's socioeconomic status all have significantly positive effects on children's educational attainment. Drawing on her extensive field work conducted in a number of schools and universities, Lin (2006) also points out that the burgeoning new middle class in China could send their children to expensive private schools or key public schools by paying astoundingly high tuitions, making private donations, or using social networks. Receiving a better basic education in these privileged schools, in turn, promotes the children's chance to enroll in college. This era of economic transformation clearly favors the children of cadres and professionals, while those from working-class and peasant families are facing declining access to college education.

Besides being ostracized for their low academic standing, the children of workers and peasants are also facing enormous financial challenges to achieving access to higher education. As previously noted, the tuition charges have skyrocketed in the recent years. Some low-income students are being forced to terminate their higher education, and others are discouraged from applying for university admission. As Seeberg and Zhang (2001) point out, the problem that concerns many Chinese people is that "the imposition of private tuition has reinforced the basic critique of the post-Mao reforms as reinstating or exacerbating invidious social inequalities and education, once again reproducing class privilege" (pp. 3–4). Although efforts have been made to establish a financial aid system that is aimed at mitigating the adverse effects of tuition and fees on financially disadvantaged students through grants and loans, the extremely low capacity of financial aid cannot truly relieve the financial pressures of needy students. For example, in 2001, 534,000 students applied for what the government promised would be RMB 400 million in student loans. Only 170,000 students received loans, and they received an average of 37 percent of what they asked for, reaching a total of RMB 145 million (Jiang, 2001).

Last but not least, the stratification of colleges and universities in China became more manifest in the reform era. As part of the administrative reforms in higher education, the central government carried out Project 211 in 1993. This policy expressed intentions of the state to identify a hundred top universities and give them special financial support (Wang & Wu, 1993). Interestingly, this policy encouraged the implementation of the amalgamation policy since the size of campus, the diversity of programs, the number of faculties and students are all under consideration. Presidents of colleges and universities and faculty and staff all became more active in merging with other universities in order to position their institutions in such a way as to qualify for selection into Project 211. The amalgamation policy and Project 211 therefore joined hands with each other to classify the universities. Those universities in this elite group are now receiving considerably more government appropriations, have better faculty and more advanced facilities, and recruit students with higher scores in the college entrance examinations (Hayoe, 1996). In 1998 another policy, Project 985, was conducted by the Chinese government and aimed at developing world-class universities in the twenty-first century by providing those universities with substantial state government funding (Zhu, 2007).[4] Undoubtedly, graduates from these elite institutions have a better chance of achieving high-ranking positions in the labor market.

The prior research conducted in capitalist societies indicate that social class is highly correlated with institutional choice (Gladieux, 2002; Peng, 1977). According to Gladieux (2002), the most recent longitudinal data from the U.S. Department of Education show that about 66 percent of students from families with high socioeconomic status who attend college are enrolled in four-year institutions, 44 percent more than their counterparts from lowest socioeconomic quartile (p. 47). In his study about educational stratification in Japan, Ishida also shows that students who are from economically and socially advantaged families disproportionately attend elite institutions. Whether or not such a pattern of college enrollment and choice exists in China is part of my research. In the next chapter, I will first elaborate on my research and then discuss the methodology employed. In addition, the next chapter outlines fieldwork and discusses data collection and analysis.

NOTES

1. At the National Educational Work Conference in April 1978, President Deng Xiaoping brought up for the first time the phrase "four modernizations." Four modernizations refer to the modernization of national defense, industry, agriculture, and science and technology.

2. The second Sino-Japanese War, 1937–45. The Civil War, 1946–49.

3. Renminbi (RMB), also called Chinese Yuan (CNY) or yuan, is Chinese currency. One U.S. dollar (USD) equals 7.5 CNY. The exchange rate was last updated on January 3, 2008.

4. Project 985 comprises 39 universities (see appendix A).

5

Research Design

As Shulman (1988) suggests in his book about disciplines of inquiry in education, research method is the quality ascribed to research activity and thus distinguishes a disciplined inquiry from mere observation and speculation. He further argues that since research findings are unlikely to be commensurable if researchers disagree on the research method, debates have been going on for a long period of time about the strengths and weaknesses of different research methods. The dominant research paradigm guiding educational studies has been the quantitative research method. The philosophical assumption underlying quantitative research is that educators can investigate the social world in the same way as the scientists study the natural world, and that a researcher's job is to discover the one objective reality (Mertens, 1997). In contrast, qualitative research is based on the philosophy that reality is socially constructed. That is to say, no research on social phenomena can be value-free. The social construction of reality in research can only be conducted through the interaction between investigators and participants (Marshall & Rossman, 1999).

I reviewed prior cultural capital research and college access research in the second chapter. Most of the studies employed quantitative techniques to examine the impacts of cultural capital on educational attainment. When concerning higher education opportunities, although prior research has consistently demonstrated a strong relationship between students' college access and choice and their family background, students' decision-making process is to a large extent still unexplored. I argue that a qualitative study can make an important contribution by providing insights into the underlying actions that produce or expend cultural capital, thereby complementing quantitative research.

RESEARCH QUESTIONS

According to Yin (2002), what distinguishes research methods from one another is the nature of research questions. Case study, in particular, deals with "how" and "why" questions because these kinds of questions are more explanatory, for which case study is suitable. Other researchers (Merriam, 1998; Stake, 1995) also agree that it would be fruitless to start research without identifying research questions, and that the nature of research questions decides the research method.

As previously noted, there has been a strong tradition of quantitative research on the topic of college access and choice. Although the studies are different in the design of the regression models, with different focuses on parental cultural capital (Graaf, Graaf, & Kraaykamp, 2000), students' cultural participation (DiMaggio, 1982), and structures of the parental social network (Horvat, Weininger, & Lareau, 2003), the main research questions have been the type of "what" questions—what variables are powerful for predicting educational attainment, and what factors are important in influencing college choices. The multivariate analysis has indicated that social class, cultural capital, and social capital all have statistically significant impacts on college plans. Nevertheless, how those variables shape students' opportunities for a college education largely remains unknown. Therefore, this study endeavors to fill such a gap in research by exploring how class-based differences in family cultural capital and economic capital influence students' decision about college application and their choice of college. This study addresses two major questions:

1. How does a high school senior in today's college admissions environment in China make decisions about whether or not to go to college? And, if the student has decided to apply to college, how does he/she make decisions about where to go to college?
2. How does this decision-making process vary by the student's social class?

DEFINITIONS OF A CASE

As defined by Creswell (1997), "A case study is an exploration of a 'bounded system' or a case (or multiple cases) over time through detailed, in-depth data collection involving multiple sources of information rich in context" (p. 61). The question is, however, how to define this "bounded system," or a case. There is a divergence in understandings about what consists of a case. Stake (1995) regards a case as an integrated and clearly bounded system. Therefore, a person or a program is very likely to become a case in the view of Stake, while a relationship, an event, or a process is less likely to fit the definition of a case and thus is less likely to become an object of case study research. Yin (2002) also thinks that an individual or an organization might be a well-defined case, but decisions, programs, implementation process, and organizational reforms also can be regarded as the case. He defines case study research as "an empirical inquiry that investigates a contemporary phenomenon within its real-life context, especially when the boundaries between phenomenon and context are not clearly evident" (p. 13). From his definition about case study research, we can clearly see two points about a case from Yin's perspective. First, a case study is to study "a contemporary phenomenon." Therefore, a case should be bounded by time. If there is no practical or theoretical end to a program, event, or process, this specific program, event, or process is not bounded enough to qualify as a case for case study research. Second, it is important for case study research to explore the relationship between a case and its context. As Yin points out, an experiment purposefully separates a phenomenon from its context in order to explore several variables of the specific phenomenon. In contrast, case study research is to study a case in its physical setting and investigate it in its historical, cultural, and economic contexts.

In this study, the cases are bounded by place and time. Two high schools were chosen—one is a provincial key high school, and the other is an ordinary high school. Both of the schools are located in the city of Wuhu. Wuhu is a middle-sized city in eastern China. The city has a total area of 3,317 square kilometers.[1] As of the 2004 census, it had a total population of more than two million. Compared to Beijing, the nation's capital, or Shanghai, the largest industrial center in China, both of which enjoy better opportunities than other urban areas in China, the political, economic, and educational situations and the social structure in Wuhu are more representative. A general description of the city's demographic characteristics, economic conditions, and educational system will be presented in the next chapter in order to provide a context for the investigation of the two high schools. At each high school, ten students were chosen as the cases for the study. The period of time for observations and interviews was April 2006, which is one month before high school senior students took the national unified college entrance examinations in China. Generally speaking, by the end of April, high school seniors are supposed to make their mind about their college application and college choice.

SAMPLING AND UNITS OF ANALYSIS

After identifying initial research questions, the researcher needs to concern himself/herself with the issue of sampling. As Patton (1990) points out,

"Perhaps nothing better captures the difference between quantitative and qualitative methods than the different logics that undergird sampling approaches" (p. 169). Because of the aim of striving for generalization, quantitative research is typically based on large and randomly selected samples, which is usually called "probability sampling" (Patton, 1990, p. 169). In contrast, qualitative research usually opts for "purposeful sampling" (Patton, 1990, p. 169). Purposeful sampling is to choose information-rich cases from which investigators can gain broader and deeper understandings about the phenomenon under the study, and thus the samples are usually small. There are different strategies for purposeful sampling recommended by several authors (Merriam, 1998; Patton, 1990; Yin, 2002). First, a single case is selected for study when the case is critical in testing a preexistent theory. Second, a case can be selected because of its uniqueness. Third, a case is likely to be chosen if it's typical and helpful for understanding other cases. Fourth, maximum variation sampling is to try to include cases of a great diversity, from which researchers can discover some patterns. Fifth, convenience sampling is to choose cases based on concerns about money, time, and location. Finally, snowball, chain, and network sampling is to ask participants or interviewees to refer the researcher to other informants. Each sampling approach serves a particular research purpose.

As mentioned earlier, 25 students from two high schools in a middle-sized city in China were chosen as the cases for the study. One of the two high schools is a key high school, and the other is an ordinary high school. Key schools in China enjoy privileged governmental appropriation, better school facilities, and recruit more highly qualified teachers than ordinary schools. Therefore, one of each kind was chosen for the study to better present the diverse educational contexts. The key high school selected for the study is my alma mater. I contacted two of my old teachers, one of them is now the principal of the school and the other is the director of the student affairs office. I had formal interviews with both of them in order to better understand the school's historical, cultural, and economic contexts. From the student affairs office, I obtained some descriptive data about its student population, including age, gender, origin of residence, and family background. Based on the data acquired from the office, I selected ten students for interviews that represent different combinations of gender, origin of residence, and family socioeconomic status. Their homeroom teachers and some of their parents were also interviewed whenever it was possible (see Table 5.1). The director of the student affairs office put me in contact with the principal of one ordinary school. Basically, the same research procedure was carried out in the ordinary school. However, to my surprise, no student in the class picked for the study at the ordinary school was as qualified as a middle-class student.[2] Because this situation was unexpected, I had to go back to the key high school to oversample its middle-class students. I

Table 5.1. Number of Interview Subjects by Family Type

Family Type	School Type	Students Interviewed	Parents Interviewed	Homeroom Teacher	Principal
Middle Class	Provincial Key High School	7	10	3	2
	Ordinary School	0	0		
Working Class	Provincial Key High School	5	7		
	Ordinary School	8	4		
Farming Family	Provincial Key High School	2	2		
	Ordinary School	3	1		

ended up interviewing 14 students at the key high school, including seven middle-class students, five working-class students, and two students from farming families, and 11 students from the ordinary high school, including eight working-class students and three students from farming families. In total, 25 students were interviewed. Their family and school backgrounds are presented in Table 5.1.

However, after having done the transcriptions, I compared the narratives of the students from the same kind of family background and found that their stories often had some similarities. For example, the two students from farming families who were studying at the key high school had a very similar experience: they both came from a low-income family, both went to a key university, and both made some compromises when choosing the college major because of financial concerns. Considering the limited time and funding, I decided to choose only one of the two students for more thorough examination. The one chosen for more complete description and detailed analysis had more information available—his parents were both interviewed. For the same reason, only three out of seven middle-class students and five out of 13 working-class students were described and examined in detail. When reducing the sample size, I followed two rules. First, I picked those cases that I regarded as unique and representative. Second, I selected those cases with more information available. Altogether, 11 cases were studied in detail. Table 5.2 summarizes their socioeconomic status, school type and ranking in class, and final college choice. The background characteristics of the 14 cases that were excluded from in-depth analysis are presented in appendix B.

Table 5.2. Cases Presented in the Study

School Name	Student's Name	Family Type	Gender	Class Ranking (Out of 45 Students)	University Attended
Fuzhong High School	Cai Shuang	Middle Class	Female	2	Beijing University
	Ruan Wei	Middle Class	Male	32	Greenwich University
	Wang Yicheng	Middle Class	Female	14	Fudan University
	Shi Juan	Working Class	Female	28	Anhui Normal University
	Zhang Peng	Working Class	Male	19	University of Science and Technology in China
	Li Qunhuan	Farming Family	Male	22	Shanghai Transportation University

School Name	Student's Name	Family Type	Gender	Class Ranking (Out of 63 Students)	University Attended
Nancheng High School	Gao Manyue	Working Class	Female	57	Not Admitted
	Huang Xiaomin	Working Class	Male	3	Anhui Normal University
	Zhang Huifeng	Working Class	Male	5	Anhui University
	Xie Erping	Working Class	Male	43	Not Applied
	Lin Congbo	Farming Family	Male	26	Not Applied

DATA COLLECTION

Internal Validity

According to Merriam (1998), "Internal validity deals with the question of how research findings match reality" (p. 201). To qualitative researchers, there is no one objective reality. The concept of objectivity is replaced by confirmability (Guba & Lincoln, 1989). Researchers construct "reality" on the basis of accurate interpretations of the data with the help of participants who are the providers of the data. Data, interpretations, and outcomes are all rooted in contexts and can be traced to their sources. Moreover, the logic used to assemble interpretations should be clear and explicit (Merriam, 1998; Mertens, 1997).

Researchers have suggested several strategies to improve the internal validity for case study. One of them is to use multiple sources of information—a process of triangulation (Merriam, 1998; Stake, 1995; Yin, 2002). Yin (2002) identifies six major sources of evidence for conducting case study research, which are "documentation, archival records, interviews, direct observations, participant-observation, and physical artifacts" (p. 85). Each source of evidence has its strengths. Documentation and archival records usually provide the researcher with extensive information about the issue under study. Interviews directly focus on the research question, while direct observations and participant-observation can provide additional information about the phenomenon in its naturalistic context. Both Merriam (1998) and Stake (1995) agree with Yin to a great extent in data collection and suggest that data gathering in case study research at least involves observations, interviews, and documents analysis. It is suggested that the systematic use of different sources of evidence can corroborate the fact or phenomenon being studied and thus make research findings more valid and compelling.

Understanding that an important strength of case study research is to make use of different sources of information, I relied on three different categories of data sources when conducting my research. First of all, I read through documentation and archived records released by the Department of Education in this middle-sized city in order to provide a general description of the local educational system in which I could situate the selected high schools for my study. During my school visits, I reviewed local official documents in regard to the school's organizational and cultural contexts. As previously noted, I also collected descriptive data about the school's student population. Second, I conducted both structured and informal face-to-face interviews with people working in the student affairs office, 25 students with different family backgrounds, and some parents and teachers. Students were interviewed individually. Parents were sometimes interviewed separately from the student and sometimes with the student. Each interview ranged from one to three hours. The initial interviews were followed up by phone conversations and emails to get to know the student's final college choice after I had left the site. Third, besides documents and interviews, I also collected observational data from family visits, bulletin boards, meetings, and sometimes when walking around on the campus to obtain a better understanding of the family environment and the school culture.

Besides triangulation, member checks and peer review are the other two important criteria in establishing internal validity for qualitative research (Merriam, 1998; Mertens, 1997). "Member checks" is to take the data and tentative findings to the people interviewed or studied and ask them if the results are plausible in order to rule out any inaccuracy or incompleteness of the data. In my study, I summarized what had been discussed in the interview and asked the participants if the notes reflected their positions by the end of the interview. When analyzing the data, I tried not to impose my own framework on the perspectives of the participants and tried to understand the meanings they attached to their words and actions. Moreover, I also asked colleagues to comment on the findings emerging from my data analysis in order to avoid being influenced by my personal biases concerning certain issues and thus present a holistic interpretation of what is happening.

External Validity

According to Campbell and Stanley (cited in Schofield, 1990, p. 201), "External validity asks the question of generalizability: To what populations, settings, treatment variables, and measurement variables can the effect be generalized?" Campbell and Stanley's definition of external validity represents the classical conception of external validity for quantitative research. It is impractical to make precise replication of such a criterion of generalizability for qualitative work. In his article about generalizability for qualitative research, Schofield discusses several ways to reconceptualize generalizability for qualitative work suggested by different researchers (1990, pp. 206–209). For example, Goetz and LeCompte (1984) replace "generalizability" with the concepts of "comparability" and "translatability." These two terms can be used to judge how well components of a qualitative study, such as concepts, sampling, and settings, are defined and described and to which degree the findings of the study can be used as a basis for comparison. However, no matter what we call it, external validity concerns the issue of whether one study in one situation can be used to speak to or help form a judgment about other situations. Yin (2002) admits that the strength of a case study sometimes is on its particularizing analysis. However, it doesn't mean that a case study can't provide little basis for scientific generalization. Because of the limited number of samples and the entangled situation between phenomenon and context, it might be difficult for a case study to be generalizable to populations or universes, but it doesn't reduce its ability to generalize theoretical propositions.

Given the number of the student samples, the findings of this research might not be applicable to different situations or generalizable to wider populations. However, the design of this study is easily replicated and applied to other populations. Similar studies can also be conducted in private schools, schools in rural area, or urban schools in other cities to test the validity of the findings that might be derived from this study. Furthermore, the constructs and the variables consisting of the constructs examined in this study can also be tested in other educational contexts.

Yin (2002) suggests that multiple-case studies sometimes are more compelling and robust compared to single-case studies. Because of the limited time and research funding, I was only able to discuss 11 cases in depth. However, I believe that the design of my case study can be easily translated into a multiple-case study on a big scale, which will allow other researchers to track my reasoning from evidence to conclusions and thus be able to test the reliability of my study. In this sense, the model constructed in my research has external validity.

DATA ANALYSIS

Merriam (1998) strongly recommends researchers carry out data collection and data analysis simultaneously. In her view, without the ongoing analysis, it is easy for researchers to get confused by the overwhelming data. It is true that case study research usually relies on a high volume of materials and thick descriptions about phenomena. The fact that data analysis in case study research does not have any formulas to follow as in quantitative research makes it even more difficult to interpret the data. Yin (2002) thus provides us with three strategies for performing data analysis for case study (pp. 111–114). The first and most important one is to let the theoretical propositions guide the data analysis. Yin argues that the original research design should be based on theoretical propositions that also reflect the research question and guild the data gathering. Therefore, by following the theoretical propositions, researchers also will be able to pick out the useful information and define alternative explanations. The second strategy is to test the rival explanations in order to place more confidence in the original theoretical propositions you hold or the findings you conclude with. The third one is to provide a theoretical framework.

Although case study research usually is not designed to test hypotheses or previous theories, it does not mean that qualitative research can be conducted without any theoretical framework. To build a theoretical framework, I first attended to the literature on the topic of my interest. From a review of a body of theories and related empirical studies, I was able to identify important concepts, terms, and theories. The findings of the prior research that differential resources (both economic and cultural) contribute to the persistence and reproduction of a social-class-based, stratified system of college education opportunity clearly guide my study. However, I did not select and analyze the data in a way that I could make my findings fit the existing theory or my preconceptions. I also paid attention to discrepant data and considered alternative explanations or understandings of the phenomena whenever possible.

Like Merriam, Maxwell (1996) also points out that one of the most common problems in qualitative studies is letting unanalyzed field notes and transcriptions pile up, making the task of final analysis much more difficult and discouraging. Therefore, I began my data analysis immediately after finishing the first interview. I recorded and organized field notes the same day as the interview took place. After I did the first round of interviews with my student subjects, I created a separate file for each of the students and put each set of field notes and transcriptions under their names, and thus built up a journal for every student I had interviewed. This strategy helped me keep the data physically well organized and made it easy for more thorough data analysis later on. Furthermore, from the first day when I entered into the field, I set up a field diary for myself in order to record important insights, comments, reflections, and hunches that came to me during the data collection. I read through all of the field notes, transcriptions, and reflections every week and wrote up a preliminary narrative for what I had learned from all the interviews and observations. I did this practice by way of memo writing and summarization regularly, which helped me form initial codes when I had finished all of my field work. In summary, my data analysis in the filed involved working with the data, organizing them, breaking them into manageable units, and synthesizing them. The work of developing categories, searching for patterns, and discovering the preliminary findings were left until the data collection had been completed.

CONCLUSION

I have indicated the specific research methodology that my study will adopt, defined my research questions, and also discussed the way that I carried out my data collection and analysis. In this concluding part, I will give a brief discussion of ethical considerations.

There are certain associated risks in any study that require some form of interaction with live subjects (Merriam, 1998). My data collection inevitably involved asking sensitive questions. Students may be reluctant to share their experiences because of potential embarrassment about reporting struggles with financial issues or academic life in school. Parents may be hesitant to share their feelings about teachers and school administrators. Therefore, this study assured the participants of privacy and confidentiality by using pseudonyms. Personal information was secured and concealed. However, the use of fake names did not corrupt the data. Internal validity of the study ensures that the substantive information and its interpretation are reliable and trustworthy.

NOTES

1. One kilometer equals 0.62 mile.
2. I used parents' education and profession to define middle-class students. If at least one of the student's parents has received higher education and was working as a professional, the student was regarded as a middle-class student.

6

Introduction of Wuhu and the Two High Schools

Wuhu is a middle-sized city in eastern China. It is the second largest city in the Anhui province. Anhui's economic development level remained low to medium compared to other provinces in China during 1990s. For example, the gross national product per capita was 6,048 yuan nationally in 1997 and, yet, it was only 4,378 yuan in Anhui. Wuhu has a total area of 3,317 square kilometers. As of the 2005 census, its population totaled more than two million, 41 percent of which were urban residents and 59 percent resided in the countryside (*Wuhu Statistical Yearbook*, 2005, p. 55).

Wuhu is a port and industrial center on the lower Yangtze River. Major manufacturers only began to be developed in Wuhu after 1949, and they include the textile industry, paper mills, motor vehicles, and machinery. However, despite the large development of industries, Wuhu remains primarily a commercial and collecting center for trade in rice, silk, cotton, tea, and wheat, which determines that the majority of its population are agricultural workers (see Figure 6.1).

As Lee and Selden (2007) indicate in their article, "Measured by income distribution, China has evolved from being one of the world's most egalitarian societies on the eve of reform to becoming, by 1995, one of the most unequal in Asian, and then, by the early 2000s, in the world" (p. 10). Research on China's class structure points out that the relatively homogeneous urbanite in Mao's era has spited into different classes in the reform era (Bian, Breiger, Davis, & Galaskiewicz, 2005; Lin, 2006; So, 2003). The rich class, newly formed middle-class, urban workers in the private and collective enterprises, and workers in the state sector have differentiated income. The

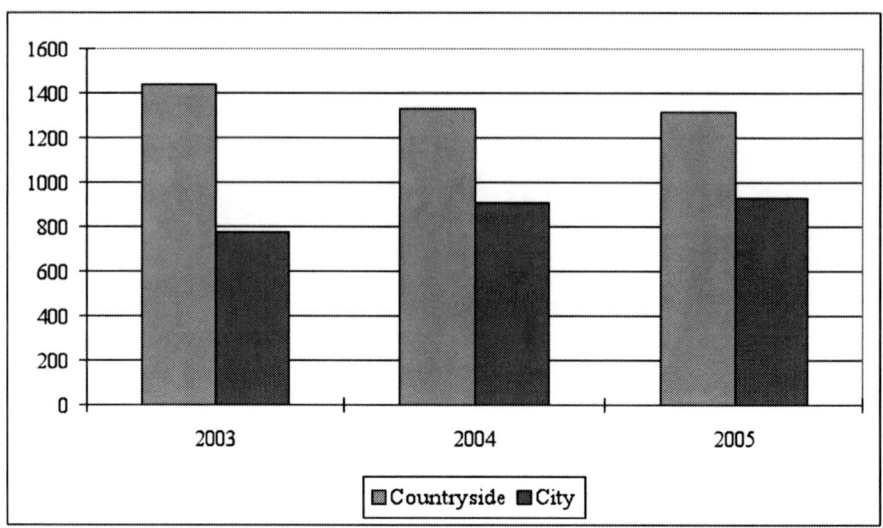

Figure 6.1.　Urban and Rural Populations in Wuhu from 2002 to 2004 (in Thousands)
Source: Wuhu Statistical Yearbook, 2003, 2004, and 2005.

inequalities of income distribution can also be observed in Wuhu. Figure 6.2 presents the annual disposable income per person for different income families in the urban area of Wuhu for the years 2002, 2003, and 2004.

Not surprising, families with various income levels have different consumption patterns. As pointed out by Bourdieu (1977a), certain cultural

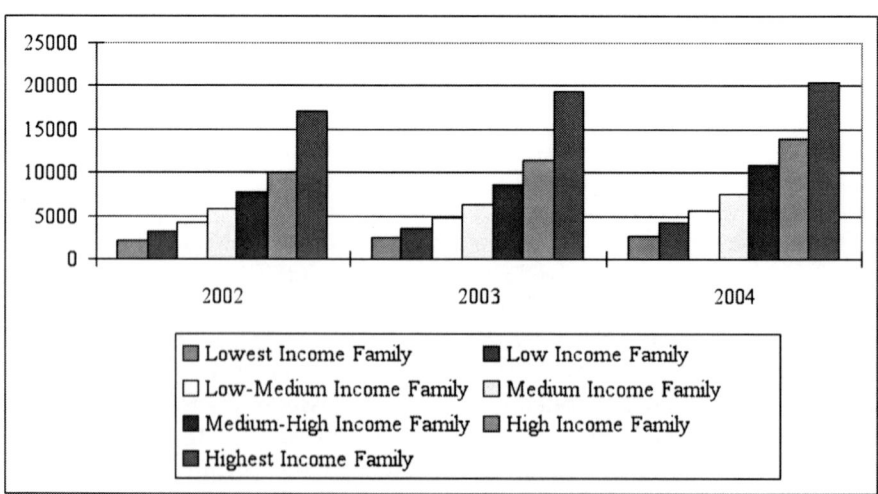

Figure 6.2.　Disposable Income per Urban Resident in Wuhu from 2002 to 2004 (in Chinese Dollars)
Source: Wuhu Statistical Yearbook, 2003, 2004, and 2005.

consumption and activities concentrate in the upper- and middle-class families, which represents distinctive cultural traits and lifestyles. The following figure shows the amount of money spent on cultural goods and educational objects by urban residents from different income families in Wuhu. Figure 6.3 illustrates that high-income families tend to spend more on cultural consumption. For example, in 2004 the lowest income family spent about 7 percent of their annual income on education and cultural goods, which was about 294 yuan for the year. In contrast, the highest income family spent about 2,704 yuan, or 13 percent of their annual income, on education and cultural items.

Nevertheless, the main locus of income inequality is between urban and rural areas. Analysis of Chinese income surveys in 1988, 1995, and 1998 by Riskin and his colleagues (2001) shows that in terms of income, the gap between urban and rural areas is the major source of overall income inequality in China. This urban-rural cleavage is also manifest in Wuhu. As Figure 6.4 shows, the average income of urban residents has been more than twice as high as that of rural residents from 2000 to 2004 in Wuhu.

Research has revealed that the gap between rural and urban residents in China—not only in terms of income but also in consumption patterns, access to public goods and opportunities, and lifetyles—has remained significantly large in the last century. In terms of cultural consumption, rural residents in Wuhu spent 5 to 8 percent of their annual income on education and cultural goods from 2000 to 2004, which was about same as the

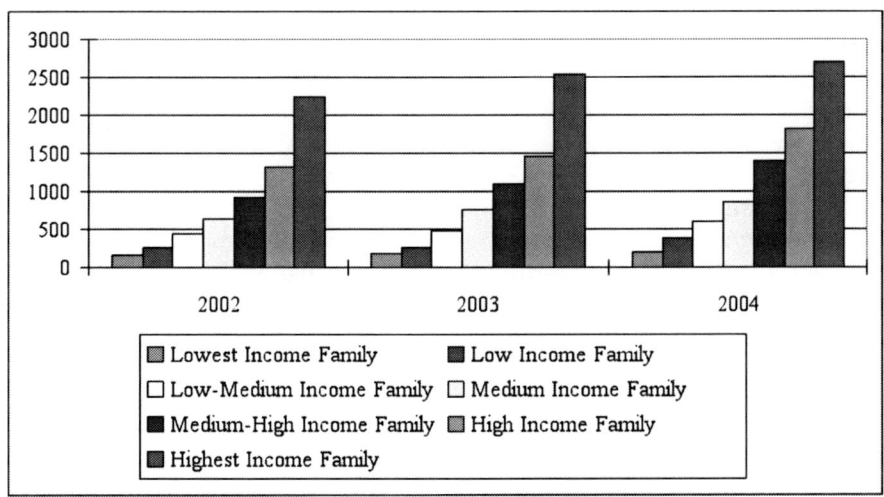

Figure 6.3. Annual Expenditure on Education and Cultural Goods by Family Income in Wuhu from 2002 to 2004 (in Chinese Dollars)

Source: Wuhu Statistical Yearbook, 2001, 2002, 2003, 2004, and 2005.

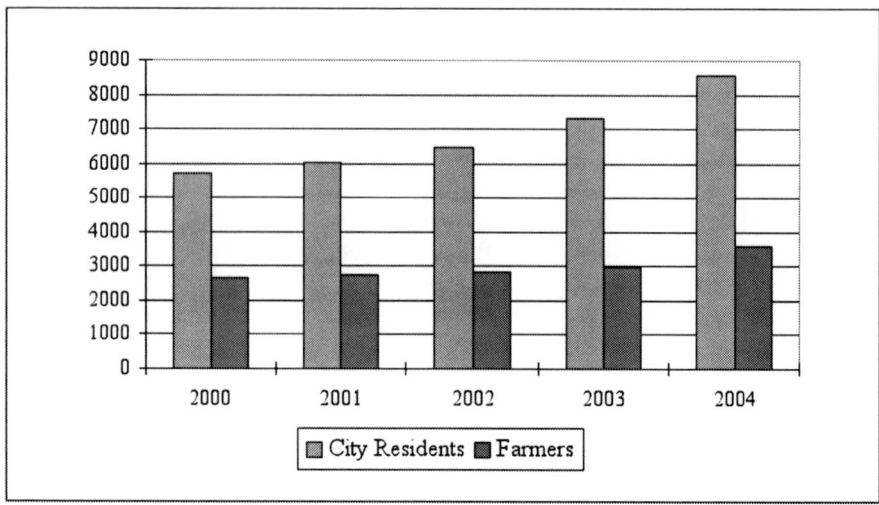

Figure 6.4.   Average Annual Family Income for Rural and Urban Residents in Wuhu from 2000 to 2004 (in Dollars)
Source: Wuhu Statistical Yearbook, 2001, 2002, 2003, 2004, and 2005.

lowest and low income urban families in Wuhu (*Wuhu Statistical Yearbook,* 2001–2005).

More crucially, children from the rural area do not enjoy equal opportunities to obtain education as their urban counterparts. Scholars have long been aware of the uneven distribution of educational resources between rural and urban areas in China (Hannum, 1999; Lin, 2006; Wu, 2002). Generally speaking, rural schools are less widely available and are generally of inferior quality. Government policies and educational appropriation are in favor of urban schools. The following table presents the central government's educational expenditure on junior and senior high schools and the enrollment numbers across the country from 1997 to 2005 (Chen, Zhang, &Yang, 2010). Table 6.1 shows that in 1997, the total educational appropriation from central government for rural middle and high schools were about a third of that for urban middle and high schools. Although the government's educational expenditure on rural schools have been steadily increasing over the past decade, the gap between the educational investment in cities and in rural area has been widening instead of shrinking. In 2004, the government expenditure per student in urban middle and high schools was 2.5 times of that in rural areas. Although there is no statistics available for the average educational expenditure on urban and rural schools in Wuhu, we do not expect the situation radically different from the average in the nation.

Table 6.1. Central Government's Expenditure on Middle and High Schools (per student) and Number of Students in School (ten thousands)

	Year	1997	1998	1999	2000	2001	2002	2003	2004
Expenditure per Student	Urban	1679	1814	1839	2123	2137	2386	2758	3067
	Rural	843	886	962	880	884	1014	1129	1220
Number of Students	Urban	597.83	579.92	589.26	626.13	720.98	727.2	688.68	631.35
	Rural	345.26	365.34	393.22	417.91	386.12	390.74	403.93	412.26

EDUCATIONAL SYSTEM IN WUHU

The Chinese educational system is highly differentiated, with schools being classified into national key schools, provincial key schools, municipal
key schools, and ordinary schools. The elaborate examination system helps
place students in schools with different rankings as early as middle school.

The "key school" system was first established in the 1950s when the
Chinese educational system was charged with providing professional talents required for the revival and development of the national economy
(*China Daily*, 2006). Given the very limited educational resources at the
time, some schools were designated by the government to be "key schools."
The philosophy was that allocating limited financial and human resources
to those selected schools could make training the needed manpower for
China's reconstruction more efficient. Key schools were shut down during
the Cultural Revolution because it was against the idea of equalism, which
was an essential value held by the Communist Party (Worden, Savada, &
Dolan, 1987). However, in the late 1970s and the early 1980s, when the
Chinese government needed to revive the lapsed education system and to
boost the poor national economy, the key school system was reinstalled
by the government. In cities and county seats, educational authorities designated those schools with records of past educational accomplishment to
be key schools and gave them priority in the assignment of teachers, equipment, and funds. They were also allowed to recruit the best students for
special training to compete for admission to top schools at the next level.
Naturally, key schools with better financial conditions, teaching staff, and
students become better compared to those ordinary schools. Key schools
constitute only a small percentage of all regular junior and senior high
schools and are disproportionately concentrated in cities, which favor urban areas and children from better-off families.

Wuhu has 288 public elementary schools, 85 middle schools, and 20
high schools (Wuhu Bureau of Education, 2006). Primary education in
China follows a six-year cycle. There is no diversification of curriculum or
differentiation of schools at this level. Junior secondary education is a uni-
form three-year cycle. Since it is part of compulsory education, there is usually no diversification of curriculum at this level either. However, middle
schools in Wuhu are classified into three categories according to their educational accomplishments—provincial key middle school, local key middle
school, and ordinary middle school. Fuzhong, one of the two high schools
studied in this research, is a provincial key high school and has its own
middle school section that funnels most of its graduates to Fuzhong high
school. Nancheng high school, the other high school chosen for the study,
is an ordinary high school and does not have a middle school.

Compulsory education in China includes only elementary schools and middle schools. Senior secondary education is not a part of the compulsory education. Like middle school, senior secondary education is also a three-year cycle. There are four types of senior secondary schools: general senior secondary, technical or specialized secondary, vocational secondary, and craftsmen schools. The general senior secondary school is also commonly known as the ordinary high school. It has an academic curriculum, with university entrance as its sole aim. Technical or specialized secondary schools are designed for the training of technicians. Vocational high schools mostly offer courses that prepare students for employment in the service sector. Craftsmen schools are mostly attached to factories or enterprises and they train craftsmen.

Due to the recent large expansion of higher education enrollment, more and more graduates from middle schools are opting to continue their education at general senior secondary school and hoping to eventually enroll in college, rather than going to secondary, specialized, vocational high school, or craftsmen schools. For example, in 2006, 61 percent of senior secondary students were enrolled in the general education track in Wuhu, while the other 39 percent were enrolled in specialized, vocational, or craftsmen schools (Wuhu Bureau of Education, 2006). The general senior secondary school is the most popular among students and parents as it is the only channel that may lead students to institutions of higher education. The general senior secondary school is highly differentiated, with the provincial key high school at the top, the local key high school following, and then the ordinary high school. Wuhu has two provincial key high schools, one local key high school, nine ordinary high schools in the city, and eight high schools in its four suburban districts. Different from the situation in America, the city high schools in China generally provide a better schooling environment than those in the suburbs and countryside. Especially the key high schools, which are most likely located in the inner city, usually have better school facilities, better qualified teachers, and higher annual revenue and spending per student. This study includes two high schools, both of which are city high schools. One is Fuzhong, a provincial key high school. The other is Nancheng, an ordinary high school.

Because of the hierarchy of the Chinese educational system, admission to the key middle and high schools is inevitably competitive. Before 1998, all elementary school graduates had to take the middle school entrance examinations to compete for the very limited seats in three key middle schools in Wuhu. Because admission was completely based on achievement scores on the entrance examinations, graduates from the elementary school experienced tremendous pressure when preparing for the entrance examinations and many scholars as well as parents were concerned about their physical and psychological conditions. Therefore, in the name of relieving elementary school graduates from serious pressure for academic achievement, the policy makers in Wuhu introduced a voucher system into the middle school enrollment process in 1998 (Tang, 2006). Every elementary graduate was assigned a series of numbers. Lottery was used to determine which students got the vouchers. Students with vouchers could go to the key middle school in their districts. However, each key middle school only enrolled one-third of their freshmen through the voucher system. The other two-thirds of freshmen had to pay additional tuition and fees to get into any of the key middle schools even though the public middle school education is supposed to be free. Policy makers in Wuhu did not introduce this reform into the high school enrollment process. That is to say, the admission to high schools was still determined by achievement scores on the entrance examinations administered by the city's bureau of education. The key high schools apparently had higher admission scores than the ordinary ones. However, each school had some quotas assigned by the bureau of education to recruit a few students who did not achieve their admission scores but were willing to pay extra tuition and fees.

FUZHONG HIGH SCHOOL

Fuzhong is a key high school at the provincial level, as well as one of the model high schools in the Anhui province. It was founded in 1903, and over the past hundred years it has educated a stunning number of students who have succeeded in a variety of fields. Fuzhong is located at foot of the phoenix hill, one of the most scenic areas in the city, covering a total area of 6.34 hectares, with 30,000 square meters used for teaching buildings. The campus also includes a fine arts center, a learning center, a student union, laboratories for biology, physics, and chemistry, and an impressive library. The athletic facilities include a soccer playfield, a ping-pong room, indoor basketball and volleyball courts, and a grassy playground.

Fuzhong has a total of 189 employees, 164 of which are faculty members. All the faculty members hold baccalaureate degrees from an impressive array of national universities, and 37 percent of them have graduate degrees. Moreover, 7 faculty members hold national special-class teacher licenses, and another 64 have national first-class teacher licenses.

There are 405 members of the senior classes in Fuzhong and 2,100 students in grades 10 through 12. The students are predominantly from Wuhu; however, since Fuzhong is one of the outstanding high schools in the Anhui province, it also has the permission to admit students from other cities in Anhui who have outstanding overall academic performance and are especially gifted in science. Fuzhong has a nice two-story dormitory building for its current 50 resident students who are admitted from other cities.

Fuzhong students from the senior class preceding the students of this study collected a stunning number of college acceptances and modeled attendance at some of the finest public postsecondary institutions. In the past five years, more than half of the senior students went to key universities across the country, and the enrollment rate to four-year universities has been staying around 80 percent. The remaining 20 percent of the students have gone to two-year or three-year colleges.

The admission to Fuzhong is largely based on the unified high school entrance examinations administered by the city's bureau of education. Those students who have achieved certain a level of scores in the examinations are admitted to Fuzhong. Their average tuition for one semester is 850 yuan. The school is also allowed to admit a number of students whose scores are no more than 30 points below the cut-off point. The number of this group of students cannot exceed 20 percent of the total student population. Their average tuition is 7,000 yuan per semester. In addition, the school recruits around 10 to 20 outstanding students across the whole province every year who do not have to take the local entrance examinations. Generally, they are champions of provincial or national-level competitions in science and admitted as gifted students. In my conversation with principal Ma, he shared that the school sent out a special recruiting group of teachers every year to track down those champion students in a variety of competitions in math, physics, and chemistry and persuade them to come to Fuzhong, sometimes attracting them with scholarships. There is no need-based aid offered at this school.

The annual revenue from the city's bureau of education is four million Chinese dollars, which is only about 22 percent of the school's total funding. According to principal Ma, the tuition from students totals more than seven million Chinese dollars and the school's own investments bring in around another five million every year. Moreover, if the school has additional campus construction plans, it usually can get donations from individuals or companies.

NANCHENG HIGH SCHOOL

Although administratively Nancheng is one of the nine city high schools, it is actually located in the suburbs of Wuhu. There is a big farmers' market right next to the school, which is a nearly burned-out neighborhood. Of the rows of shacks in the community, most were roughly built and need major repair. The school buildings actually stand out among other buildings in this neighborhood. Nancheng high school was founded in 1958 as an ordinary high school. In the 1980s, it was once converted into a vocational high school, but then it was changed back to an ordinary high school in the early 1990s. The campus covers a total area of 2.4 hectares, with 16,000 square meters devoted to teaching purposes.

Nancheng high school has 95 faculty members and 13 administrative employees. Two-thirds of faculty members hold baccalaureate degrees, and three of them have master's degrees. When this study was conducted, there were 1,300 students spread across grades 10 to 12, of which 230 students were in the graduating classes. Annually, 70 percent of graduates go directly to college. However, most of them attend two-year community colleges. In the past five years, the average rate of students admitted to four-year institutions is 8 percent (see Figure 6.5).

The average score in the city's unified high school entrance examinations is 480 out of 700. Those students who passed the cut-off point of 465 get admitted to Nancheng high school and need to pay 350 yuan for tuition per semester. The school is allowed to admit a certain number of students whose achievement scores in the examinations are slightly below the cut-off point, which cannot exceed 20 percent of the total freshman population. These students have to pay 2,000 yuan per semester for their tuition and additional fees.

The annual revenue from the city's bureau of education for Nancheng high school is also four million Chinese dollars. According to the principal Cao, government appropriation is their major avenue. The tuition from students is a little more than one million. The school also has its

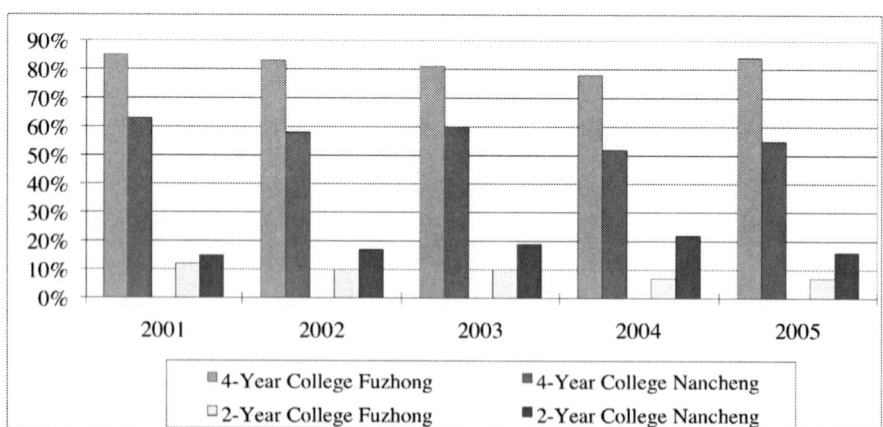

Figure 6.5. Enrollment Rates of Two-Year Colleges and Four-Year Universities for Fuzhong and Nancheng High Schools from 2001 to 2005

Source: School Documents from Fuzhong and Nancheng High School, 2006.

own investments, but the returns are very limited. The school receives no donations. Generally, the city's bureau of education supports its campus construction plans.

COLLEGE ADMISSION CRITERIA AND COLLEGE APPLICATION PROCESS

As indicated previously, college admission policy in China has undergone many changes responding to political campaigns and economic reforms since the foundation of the People's Republic of China in 1949. However, after the Cultural Revolution, the college admission policy has placed an emphasis on academic qualification. The National College Entrance Examination (NCEE) is an academic examination held annually to determine who is qualified for admission to college. Applicants have to hold a high school diploma or the equivalent to be eligible to participate. The NCEE is usually taken by students in their last year of high school, even though there has been no age restriction since 2001. It is arranged at the end of the spring semester and high school graduates across the country take the examination simultaneously. Three subjects are mandatory: Chinese, math, and a foreign language. In addition, science students need to take physics, chemistry, and biology, while students in arts and humanities need to take politics, history, and geography.

In most places, students have to complete their college application prior to the exam. That is to say, applicants do not know their achievement score in the examination when filling out their college application, although their achievement score is the single decisive factor in college admission. In China, the recruitment of college students is administered uniformly within each province or special municipality. In most places, the whole recruitment process is carried out in four stages. First is the so-called advanced stage. During this stage, military schools and a few schools with specialties recruit their students. It is relatively small-scale recruitment and does not affect most of the college applicants. The following stage is when national key universities carry out their recruitment, which is actually called the first stage of the college recruitment process in China. Regular universities recruit their students in the second stage. The last are the training-type colleges and community colleges. Accordingly, the college application form comprises four sections—military schools, national key universities, regular universities, and community colleges and others. Because these four types of universities carry out their recruitment at different times, they do not interfere with one another. However, within each category only the first-choice school has the highest chance for the applicant to enroll in, although theoretically the applicant can put in four to six schools and programs in order of preference. For example, most key universities claim that they would be willing to take those applicants who do not list the university as their first choice. However, key universities only do that under two conditions. The first is when they cannot fill their quota by recruiting those students who regard the university as their most preferred one. However, it rarely happens to those prestigious universities. Second, some universities do take students who have the university as their second choice but require a much higher achievement score in the entrance examinations, ranging from 30 points to 90 points (the total achivement score is 750), making it practically impossible (Shi, 2007). Therefore, for each category, only the first-choice college or university really matters. In the following chapter, we will see that most students only took their first-choice university seriously even though they still put four to six schools in their application in order of preference.

7

Fuzhong High School Students

There were seven classes in the twelfth grade in Fuzhong high school. Class size averaged 45 students. The class chosen for this study had 30 students from middle-class families, 11 from working-class families, and 4 from farming families. In this graduating class, 100 percent of the students went on to college, 78 percent specifically to national key four-year institutions, and 22 percent to ordinary four-year universities. The ten students interviewed for the study were A/B students in this class and attended Beijing University, University of Science and Technology in China, Fudan University, Shanghai Transportation University, Zhejiang University, Anhui University (2), and Anhui Normal University (3) in fall 2006.

CAI SHUANG

Family Background

Cai Shuang is from a small city in the Anhui province. Her father holds a baccalaureate degree in economics and a master's degree in business management and is the president of Ninguo Transportation Company. Her parents were college classmates. Her mother also has a B.A. in economics but specialized in taxation for her master's degree. She now works as a senior accountant for a private accounting firm. Their family income is about 250,000 yuan a year.

Early Influence Stage

Cai Shuang is the only child, so her parents have given her their undivided attention since the day they had her. Her parents admitted that they had always had high expectations for Cai Shuang's education even when she was still in her mother's uterus. Shuang's mother said,

> When we had her, we both just got out of graduate school and started working. We talked about her education plan when we just learned that I was pregnant. We worked out this specific schedule for me to listen to classical music and for him [Shuang's father] to read poems to my belly.

Shuang's father added that they studied a book about fetus education in the early stage of pregnancy and decided to follow its guidance to promote the development of infantile intelligence and behavior by exposing the mother to sweet music and rhythmic poems.

Shuang learned to speak at age one. Her parents began to teach her poems when she turned three. Her mother shared the experience:

> We picked those very simple poems from Tang Dynasty to begin with. You know, those poemss with five words per sentence and four sentences per poem. They are very rhythmic and the musical sound attracted her. So, we didn't have to force her to learn. We taught her a sentence here and a sentence there and assembled them together once she learned all of them separately. . . . We sometimes made her recite poems in front of other people, such as her grandparents and our friends. Everyone was impressed with her performance. And, she liked the attention and the admiration and became more motivated to learn. We then moved to more complicated ones, like those with seven words per sentence and eight sentences per poem. . . . She did really well. By the time she went to elementary school, she could recite at least 50 poems.

Shuang's parents began to teach her Chinese characters when she was five. Every night they sat her down and taught her a few Chinese characters. They taught her how to remember the different parts of one character by linking them to plants, animals, and other little things in real life that she was already familiar with. "We'd say something like, 'See, this is like a hat,' or, 'Here is a little dot, just like your doll's eye,'" her mother said with pride. "Shuang was a very good child and always cooperated with us, even when she was that little. . . . She learned quickly and could recognize around 100 [Chinese] characters before she went to elementary school and could write at least half of them." Around the time when they began to teach Shuang Chinese characters, Shuang's parents also made her start practicing Chinese calligraphy. Shuang's mother has a cousin who is a member of the Anhui Association of Calligraphy. Therefore, her parents took advantage of this and sent her to their relative's home to learn calligraphy once per week.

Shuang has been practicing calligraphy for ten years since then. She stopped taking private lessons with her relative in the last year of senior high school because her teacher thought she was good enough as an amateur while she had no intention to develop it as her career. According to Shuang's father, sending her to learn calligraphy was to cultivate her serious attitude to do things. Calligraphy practice is very detail oriented and requires patience and hard work. Therefore, they sent her to practice calligraphy before she went to elementary school, which they believe helped her form a good attitude toward study.

Not surprising, Shuang performed very well in elementary school. She was not only a straight-A student but also very active in extracurricular activities, such as participating in the school play and the literature club. "School work was very easy in elementary school," Shuang said. "I only needed to spend a little bit time on homework after school, and my parents would check for mistakes. For the rest of the night, I'd practice calligraphy or read all kinds of books they bought for me." Shuang's parents also confirmed that Shuang absolutely loved school and did not have any problem with schoolwork. Their job was just to double-check her homework and make sure that she understood everything taught in class. They often brought her to visit bookstores during the weekend and encouraged her to read. At the beginning, Shuang's mother read to her a lot. Since third grade, Shuang has learned enough Chinese characters to be able to read herself. Her mother recalled Shuang cuddling up often with books and enjoying reading a book for a whole afternoon. "We had to drag her to the dinner table," her mother added.

After elementary school, Shuang passed the middle school entrance examinations with flying colors and admitted to Ninguo No. 1 middle school, which was the best school in the city.

Predisposition Stage

Shuang continued to perform well in middle school. During the three years in middle school, Shuang developed special interest in history and biology. Because of her strong interest in these areas of knowledge, her family subscribed to a few magazines that were relevant, such as the *Journal of Biology for Middle School Students*, *Exploration of History*, and *Youth in Science*. Both of her parents liked to read for fun. Often all of them liked to crowd in her father's study room to read together and sometimes share what they had been reading.

Shuang's parents indicated that through these kind of reading activities, they not only wanted to help Shuang develop good reading habits but also intended to cultivate her ability to express her opinions and ideas. Shuang's father recalled that at the beginning Shuang used to read her favorite paragraphs aloud and give them a short comment, such as, "This is interesting." Gradually, with encouragement from her parents, Shuang started to articulate why she thought certain propositions were interesting. "Sometimes we'd provide her with alternative perspectives on a certain historical event. She often appreciated that. Sometimes she'd argue with us, and I think that was beneficial to her, too," Shuang's father said. "Or, if she was reading an interesting biology article, we'd ask some questions and she'd be happy to explain them to us."

Because of her outstanding performance in chemistry and biology, Shuang was often taken out of her class and given special training for competitions. She has participated in many chemistry and biology competitions within the school district, in the city, and at the provincial level. She has won quite a few awards from all the competitions, which include two championships in provincial biology competitions. Therefore, when graduating from middle school, she was recruited as a gifted student in science by Fuzhong high school, one of the best high schools in the Anhui province.

In addition to excellent academic performance in school, Shuang continued to be active in extracurricular activities. As previously noted, Shuang stopped taking private lessons for calligraphy in the last year of middle school. Instead, she began to take a piano class during the weekend. Although she started rather late, she made significant progress within one year, and thus she was able to give a performance at the graduation party in school, which, according to her parents, was well received. Shuang said that all the extracurricular activities she has been involved in were all very important to her:

> Practicing calligraphy cultivated my patience. You have to practice a hundred times just to make one character look perfect. . . . I learned to be patient. . . . I've also become more confident in myself because I know that it just takes time and practice to make one character look perfect, and I can do it if I wish to. Everything is like practicing calligraphy. If I really want to and invest enough time and effort, I can make it happen.

Shuang's parents indicated that their initial intention to send Shuang to dance class and piano class was to prevent her from becoming a "bookworm." As her mother pointed out, Shuang spent so much time reading in elementary school that sometimes it was hard to pull her out of her books. So, Shuang's parents signed her up for a dance class from the first year of middle school. Shuang immediately fell in love with dancing and told her parents she would like to learn to play piano when she stopped taking calligraphy class. Her parents were very supportive of all the extracurricular activities Shuang has participated in, and also believe that it cultivated her self-confidence.

While she continued to excel in academic performance and shine in a variety of extracurricular activities, Shuang also developed her aspiration to attend a college in middle school. Shuang always knew she would go to college even before she understood what a college really was. "When I was very little . . . before I went to elementary school, my parents began to talk to me about college," Shuang recalled. "They asked me, 'Where does Shuangshuang [Cai Shuang's nickname] want to go to college?' and then they'd answer for me, 'Our Shuangshuang wants to go to Beijing University!'" However, not until late in middle school did Shuang start to seriously consider going to college. Once she developed her preference for a college education, Beijing University, the top university in the country, became the top option on her list.

Search Stage

Beijing University is the first Western-style university founded in China. No other institution in the country is as synonymous with quality as Beijing University. The very name conjures up images of smartly dressed students, fearsome professors, and glamorous campus buildings with traditional Chinese architectural and artistic style. Its campus, known as Yan Garden, is located close to the Royal Garden of Qing Dynasty and the Summer Palace.

Shuang had set her college goal on Beijing University as far back as in middle school. As noted earlier, Shuang's father is the president of Ninguo Transportation Company. Taking advantage of his job, Shuang's father scheduled at least one family trip every summer. When Shuang was in fifth grade, she and her parents went to visit Beijing. Among all of the temples, palaces, monuments, and parks and gardens, Shuang's father made sure that they spent one day in the college district in the western suburbs of Beijing, where ten national key universities were located. Beijing University was surely the most attractive one. Shuang fell in love with the lake, the tower, and the arch bridge immediately:

> It was like a beautiful picture. . . . I was intimidated by those students who were walking past us and holding heavy-looking books and folders in their arms. They looked smart and awesome, and I wanted to be one of them. From then on, going to Beijing University has become one of my dreams, a dream that I can make come true by working hard.

During her middle school years, Shuang continued to be exposed to many different colleges and discussions about them. She learned about quite a few national key universities and their programs in chemistry and biology. However, none of them impressed her like Beijing University. As noted previously, Shuang was recruited as a gifted student to the science class at Fuzhong high school because she had won two championships in biology competitions on the provincial level. She decided to accept the admission and come to Wuhu, a city that was a two-hour drive from home, because she believed that a better high school would give her a better chance to get into Beijing University. Her mother was hesitant about the idea of sending her to Fuzhong as a boarding student, while her father was very supportive of her decision. "So, we voted," Shuang said. "Two versus one, so I came here."

Choice Stage

Although the science class at Fuzhong high school was full of gifted students in science, Shuang still managed to stay among the top ten in her class. She also continued to participate in all kinds of chemistry and biology competitions in high school and won one championship in a provincial chemistry contest and fourth place in a national biology competition.

Because of her outstanding academic performance in chemistry and biology, the University of Science and Technology in China offered her admission to its biological chemistry department at the end of the fall semester in her senior year. She had one month to decide whether she would accept the offer or not. There were a lot of struggles, discussions, and arguments with parents. For the first few moments, Shuang got all excited about the offer and wanted to take it. The University of Science and Technology in China is among the top three science universities in China, so the offer was very tempting. Moreover, if she accepted the offer, she would not have to go through the last semester of high school, which is always full of stress and pressure. Also, she would not have to take the national unified college entrance examinations, which single-handedly decide millions of students' destiny within two days. She was worried that she would fail the examinations because of overwhelming anxieties. Her mother was very supportive of her decision to go to the University of Science and Technology in China:

> Undoubtedly, it is a very good university. A friend's son went to that university four years ago, and now he is going to the United States to pursue his graduate education. I learned from my friend that two-thirds of her son's classmates were going abroad for advanced study. I thought it was good enough for my daughter, and I couldn't see why we should risk it for Beijing University.

Unlike her mother, Shuang's father did not express any opinions about this offer. He simply asked Shuang to think more about the offer and not to accept it immediately. In the week after she received the offer from the University of Science and Technology in China, she and her father talked about this issue over the phone every night. Her father constantly made comparisons between these two universities in terms of their environment, reputations, ranks of chemistry- or biology-related disciplines, and chances to study abroad after the undergraduate program. Shuang was still very hesitant about her choice. Her father came to visit her in Wuhu that weekend and took her to Hefei, where the University of Science and Technology in China is located, to visit its campus. It has a large and beautiful campus, too, but not as impressive as Beijing University. As Shuang said,

> It is a nice university. It is just that I have emotionally committed myself to Beijing University since I was a little girl. And, it would be foolish for me to just give up my dream like that. My father was right that we do not have many precious dreams during our lifetime and I should fight for and even take some risks for my dream college.

After her visit to the University of Science and Technology in China, Shuang gave herself a couple of more days to think about her decision. Then, one night she called her parents and told them that she decided to deny the offer. Her parents drove to Wuhu overnight in order to accompany her the next day to sign certain files to make her decision official. They went to see her homeroom teacher right after that in order to request a special permission for Shuang to participate in the early admission examinations for Beijing University. Permission for early admission examinations are only given to provincial-level champions in math, physics, chemistry, and biology. Technically, Shuang was qualified for the early admission examinations. However, if she had accepted the offer from University of Science and Technology in China, she would be automatically denied permission to take the early admission examinations for any other school. Therefore, the first thing Shuang's family did after they turned down the offer was to request permission to participate in the early admission examinations for Beijing University. A couple of months later, her father accompanied Shuang to Beijing University to take the early admission examinations. Unfortunately, she did not do well in the exams and therefore did not get early admission. However, Shuang's father had a lot of confidence in her and encouraged her to go ahead and apply to Beijing University through the normal admission program:

> It was a disappointment, of course. However, I believe that failure can also be a good education. She failed, she learned, and she would do better in the future. . . . I do not think that she should have settled for the University of Science and Technology in China. She has been dreaming about going to Beijing University ever since her first visit when she was only 11 years old. I believe that she deserves the best education, and as her father, I will do my best to support her dream.

Shuang took the national unified college entrance examinations in June 2006 and scored 625 out of 750 in the exams. In July when the word came that she was offered a place in the biology department at Beijing University, she jumped at the chance to attend her dream school.

Money was not an issue in Shuang's college decision making. She and her parents never talked about tuition and fees or anything related to finances. Her understanding was that her choices were only limited by her academic ability. Her parents confirmed that finances were never a concern. As her father commented,

> She tried her best to shine academically and got into the best university in China. We are so proud of her, and paying for her college education is the happiest thing we've ever experienced.

WANG YICHENG

Family Background

Wang Yicheng's parents are both college educated. Her mother holds a baccalaureate degree in physics and is currently teaching physics in high school. Her father has a master's degree in computer science and used to teach in a community college as an associate professor. When Yicheng was in high school, her father quit his faculty job and went back to school to work on his Ph.D. full time. He studied in Shanghai, which is about 400 kilometers southeast of Wuhu, and came back home every other weekend. The year Yicheng graduated from high school, her father also obtained his doctoral degree and got an offer from an international computer company in Shanghai.

Early Influence Stage

Yicheng's parents began to teach her to recite poems from Tang Dynasty when she was four years old. Tang Dynasty poetry is the most popular volume of Chinese classics. Yicheng's parents thought that reciting poems from Tang Dynasty would cultivate Yicheng's interest in learning the Chinese language. Yicheng's mother recalled,

> We began to ask her to recite certain pieces of poems when she was four. Every time she learned a new sentence, we'd give her a little something as a reward, such as a piece of candy or chocolate. Although she didn't really enjoy the work, she still made a lot of efforts to learn and could recite about ten poems when she was in kindergarten. I still remember how impressed her kindergarten teacher was by that. . . . Later on, when she was in elementary school, we explained to her the meaning of those poems. Some are about the beauty

of nature, some are about the fun of a leisurely life, and some are about the pleasure of learning. . . . She started to appreciate these poems and like to read poems and literature in general.

Yicheng's parents began to teach her Chinese characters when she was in kindergarten. Her mother pointed out that a little child would never feel interested in learning characters if he/she found it useless. So, her strategy was that after she taught Yicheng a new character, she would look for it in a newspaper and then show it to her daughter. It always made little Yicheng feel excited because she could read a word from a newspaper or a magazine. This strategy really encouraged Yicheng to learn. By the time she went to elementary school she had learned a lot of Chinese characters. The first day in elementary school, she got her textbook for her Chinese class and started to read it immediately. "Within two days," her mother recalled, "she read the whole textbook from page to page and didn't encounter any new word." The ability to read and comprehend the text helped Yicheng learn not only Chinese but also other subjects in elementary school. Because Yicheng's early education experience put her well ahead of many other students when she started elementary school, her teachers paid a lot of attention to her, frequently called on her in class, and praised her for her homework and her performance in class. Yicheng said,

> I remember being called to the platform to read for the whole class. I wasn't like a lot of kids, who could only murmur or stutter in front of the class. So, teachers liked me a lot and very often asked me to go to the platform to read.

Teachers' attention and praise gave Yicheng motivation to learn more and try to do better. Her father added that it was the same strategy he used to teach Yicheng English. Because she started learning English ahead of her peers, Yicheng knew much more other students in the English class and immediately won the teacher's attention and admiration.

Predisposition Stage

When Yicheng graduated from elementary school, her family was faced with two choices for middle school. For one, she could go to the school where her mother was teaching senior classes. The school was very close to where they were living, and Yicheng knew a lot of teachers there personally through her parents' social network. However, her mother did not want Yicheng to attend her own school. As a teacher, she is quite aware of the differences between an ordinary middle school and a key middle school in terms of the quality of teachers and students. Although they would not have to pay anything for tuition and fees if Yicheng went to her mother's school, Yicheng's parents did not think that they should fail to provide Yicheng with the best education because of financial reasons. As a provincial key high school, Fuzhong was permitted to have a special admission policy. In the year when Yicheng was going to middle school, Fuzhong admitted one-third of its freshmen by lottery and the other two-thirds by charging extra tuition and fees. Yicheng's mother contacted some of her friends who were either teaching in Fuzhong or working in the local Bureau of Education a few months ahead to make sure that if they did not win the lottery, she could get her daughter on the list to pay her way in. Not surprising, Yicheng was not lucky enough to win the lottery. However, Yicheng's parents got her on the list early enough that they did not have any trouble gaining the seat in Fuzhong. All they needed to do was pay an extra 5,000 yuan each semester for Yicheng to have the opportunity to study in Fuzhong. When recalling the event, her father said,

> We were lucky that we started talking to people early enough and acted quickly after the results of lottery came out. We learned later on that the waiting list was incredibly long and a lot of kids didn't get into Fuzhong although their parents were more than happy to pay the additional tuition and fees. . . . She [Yicheng's mother] knows a few people who were key in the admission process, so we made sure that Yicheng wouldn't get kicked off the list. . . . The list was not open to the public, so if you didn't have any network, your kid might be replaced by someone else and you wouldn't know it until the last minute when nothing could be changed.

Of course, sending Yicheng to Fuzhong middle school was not the ultimate goal. The reason why Yicheng's parents thought it was important to pay the extra money to get her the chance to go to Fuzhong middle school was that Yicheng could be well prepared academically and thus could go on to Fuzhong high school and then a good college. Undoubtedly, her parents' decision influenced Yicheng's self-expectation, and attitude toward a college education. As Yicheng pointed out, since the day she went to Fuzhong middle school, she knew for sure that she would continue her education beyond high school.

As noted previously, Yicheng was an early reader. She continued to like reading in middle school and developed a special interest in world classics. Yicheng recalled,

> It all began in the summer before I was going to middle school. My parents bought me a pack of books as a gift for the long summer. They were very easy to read, with short texts and many pictures. They sort of looked like comic books, but they were actually adapted from world classical novels. I was crazy about them. I could sit there for hours just to finish reading one story . . . and then I would chase my parents around the house to tell them the story.

Yicheng's parents also recalled that she became very interested in reading novels from that summer and spent most of her pocket money on collecting classical works from British and Russian writers since then. Those masterpieces in literature helped Yicheng with her Chinese composition class. She stood out among all the students in that class because of her excellent composition-writing ability. "I don't really know how I did it," Yicheng said. "But I never had any problem with writing an essay. Beautiful and powerful words just flew into my mind. And, because I'm familiar with many poems, sometimes I cited quotes from poems in my essay. Teachers are always impressed with that." Besides reading, Yicheng also practiced calligraphy in her leisure time. She started to learn calligraphy in third grade. At the beginning, she found it tedious and preferred reading much more. However, her parents insisted that she study it because it is a precious traditional art. Yicheng practiced calligraphy for six years and stopped taking calligraphy classes since high school because course work was getting really intense and she needed more time to study for school. But, in her leisure time, she still sometimes practiced calligraphy. Interestingly, she began to like the practice and found it very beneficial in the way that it could set her mind at ease. Yicheng also plays erhu, a traditional Chinese instrument. Yicheng said that most of her friends play piano or violin, but her parents always emphasized the preciousness of traditional Chinese arts, so they sent her to learn erhu. Yicheng had her heart in it because she found the music incredibly beautiful and touching. "My parents were right," Yicheng commented. "Nowadays, not many people can play erhu. But, it would be such a loss if the traditional music got lost in the young generation."

Yicheng's parents also provided her a very stimulating environment for learning at home. They talked about what happened in school over dinner, and then watched the national news on TV for half an hour. After that, they would all sit around a big table, with Yicheng doing her homework and going over what she had learned in school and her parents reviewing their students' homework or reading papers. Her parents both subscribed to journals in their fields. They sometimes showed her some interesting articles, which they thought were simple enough for her to understand. If Yicheng encountered any difficulty with her homework, she could simply ask for help from her parents. Both of her parents would stop their work and discuss with her different approaches to solve the problem. "Maybe because they are both teachers," Yicheng speculated, "they know how to lead you to think." Overall, Yicheng did not have any difficulty with school and was at the top of her class until senior high.

Search Stage

Because of her outstanding performance in the high school entrance examinations, Yicheng was not only admitted to Fuzhong but also assigned to the advanced science class. In that class, teachers finished teaching the whole high school curriculum in three semesters, and then focused the last one-and-a-half years on training students for competitions and preparing them for college entrance examinations. Yicheng's parents noticed that because of the intense curriculum and the severe competition, Yicheng got discouraged from studying. She had been the top straight-A student since elementary school. However, since she came into this advanced science class, she was not No. 1 anymore. Her ranking was in the middle of the class, which terribly disappointed her and hurt her self-esteem. Her parents were very concerned and wanted to pull her out of the advanced science class. Her father commented that because she was in the provincial key high school, they did not think she would have any problem getting into a key university, so it was pointless to unreasonably push her. Her mother added, "Competing with all the top students was really tiring. . . . I felt that she was defeated in spirit and was losing interest in study." So, they went to talk to her homeroom teacher about their concerns. However, Yicheng finally decided to stay in the advanced class because she still wanted to be one of the best and she did not want to be defeated. Yicheng's parents commented that the good aspect of staying in the advanced class was that everybody in the classroom talked about going to prestigious universities and shared with one another their college plans. Under this positive influence, Yicheng never set her college goal lower than a key national university.

Yicheng always assumed that she would go to college. "It is just one of those things that people assumed would happen," she said. "College is the only viable path after high school." When she was in elementary school and middle school, she dreamed of going to Beijing University or Qinghua University, "you know, just like everybody else." However, since the start of high school, she came to realize that her grades would put her out of reach for either of those two most prestigious universities in the nation. "I've always been at the top of my class, so I always thought I'd go to Beijing University or Qinghua University," Yicheng said. "But then I came to this advanced science class and realized that the competition was more severe than I imagined. . . . I'd be competing with all the top students across the country, and I just don't think I'd make it. . . . It's not pessimism. I'm just being realistic." Therefore, she ruled out these two universities. Naturally, the University of Science and Technology in China then came into her sights because it is among the top three science universities across the country.

Yicheng's mother has an older brother working as a faculty member in the Department of Mechanical Engineering at the University of Science and Technology in China. She called up her brother constantly to ask for information regarding early admissions, academic programs, and opportunities to study abroad during or after undergraduate programs. Her second summer in high school, Yicheng was sent to her uncle's place and spent two weeks there. During her stay, she went to visit her uncle's lab and observed some of the projects his students were working on:

> It was a fantastic experience. I think I would like it if I finally decided to attend that university. However, my uncle told me about the general undergraduate curriculum, and it sounded boring. It is all about science and engineering. Except for English and politics, no other arts and humanities courses are required.

Yicheng believed that even though she would definitely major in science, she still preferred to study in a university that embraces both the arts and sciences, like Fudan University where her father was pursuing his Ph.D. Fudan University was founded in 1905. The literate meaning of its name is "heavenly light shines, day after day," which indicates inexhaustible and industrious exploration in humanities and science. It has also become the university motto and the central goal of its education. Fudan University is one of the most elite universities across the country, and it especially enjoys a high reputation in eastern China. Fudan is a comprehensive university that consists of seventeen schools, which include solid programs in arts and humanities and science. Yicheng's father did a lot of research on different academic programs offered at Fudan University for her. Moreover, he took Yicheng to Shanghai for weekend trips several times. He showed her around the campus and took her to different lectures on culture, arts, and history and to campus concerts. Yicheng loved these cultural events and plays. Her father also believed that cultural activities were very important for one to lead a holistic life:

> Participation in extracurricular activities instills confidence. . . . While money enables one to lead a comfortable life, cultural activities enable one to live a meaningful life. In addition to professional skills, I'd like to see my daughter develop a liking for cultural activities. I think that Fudan University is a better place in terms of cultivating interests in literary and cultural activities.

Choice Stage

From the second year of her high school, Fudan University and the University of Science and Technology in China became two competing choices for Yicheng. She did not make up her mind until the last semester of her senior year when her father was offered a well-paid job at an international computer company in Shanghai. Since then she and her parents discussed her college choices together several times. At that time, her average score in the previous two simulative college entrance examinations was 600. She and her parents were confident that her academic achievement score would get her into either of these two universities. Although the University of Science and Technology in China has slightly stronger programs in science and engineering, the cultural environment at Fudan University was more attractive. The final decision was that they would all move to Shanghai.

Like most of her peers, choosing a college major was a critical yet difficult issue for Yicheng. She planed to pursue her graduate study abroad after obtaining her bachelor's degree. To keep her opportunities open, she did not want to major in any particular discipline in science and engineering. From her parents' college experiences, she learned how important mathematics is in the whole science curriculum:

> My dad told me that math is really important in every major in science. For example, he majored in computer science. He said that a student with a math major could transfer to computer science and would not experience too many difficulties to catch up. I am not very sure which area of specialization I would like to be in yet. . . . I definitely want to go abroad for advanced study. I want to major in math so that when I am applying for graduate school abroad, I will have more choices.

Because of her uncertainty about which major she wanted to take, Yicheng's father suggested she major in mathematics. He pointed out to her that mathematics is the quantitative language of the science world and that it underpins computer science, engineering, and the physical sciences and also plays an important role in the biological and medical sciences and economics:

> Every student who majored in science and engineering understands the significant role of mathematics. Since my daughter is still too young to make up her mind about the profession she wants to be in, I suggested she take mathematics as her undergraduate program. . . . With a degree in mathematics, you can continue on to graduate studies in mathematics or in a broad range of other fields such as computer science, statistics, or finance. . . . It will be easier for her to adjust to other majors if necessary.

Yicheng did not consider money an issue when it came to applying for universities and choosing majors. She emphasized that although their family had been living on her mother's single salary for three years, they had quite a lot of savings before her father quit his job and went for his Ph.D. Her parents explicitly told her not to think about money, "All you have to worry about is your academic achievement." So, she believed that she could go to any university where she was accepted. She happily attended Fudan University.

RUAN WEI

Family Background

Ruan Wei's father holds a baccalaureate and a master's degree in architecture, specializing in architectural and urban design. Wei's mother has a B.A.

in economics and a master's degree in architecture, with her interest focusing on history, theory, and criticism of art and architecture. Both parents are senior researchers at Wuhu Architecture Research Institute, whose mission is to promote cross-disciplinary research in design and urban planning. Wei's father is also doing some consulting work for private architectural firms. The family income is about 300,000 yuan per year.

Early Influence Stage

Wei's parents began to teach him Chinese characters and poems when he turned three. Like a lot of middle-class parents, they started with a set of rhythmic poems from Tang Dynasty. They usually taught him to recite one poem, and then picked up a couple of simple characters from the poem and taught him how to recognize and write the characters. Wei started to read picture books at about the same age. His grandparents and aunts all liked to give him "wonderful books" as presents. His mother recalled,

> We started very early. Most kids don't know how to write before they go to preschool. But our son could write his name the first day in kindergarten (when he was three years old). In preschool, when other kids just started to learn how to read, my son could read chapter books. He could read and comprehend and remember what he's read. . . . He's always been a big reader since he was little.

A year later after he started learning Chinese characters, Wei's parents sent him to a calligraphy class on the weekends. Both of Wei's parents practice calligraphy themselves as a hobby, but they wanted Wei to learn from a professional calligrapher. His parents took turns accompanying him to the class and supervising him to practice it, and sometimes practiced with him. According to his parents, Wei made good progress in calligraphy pretty quickly and also showed interest in drawing. From age five, Wei started to have three classes during the weekend—calligraphy, drawing, and piano. His father indicated,

> Calligraphy is a good way to discipline a child, especially a boy. He not only learned about the art but also the discipline carried by practicing the art. To practice good calligraphy, you also have to pay attention to details. Using brush can be slow or quick. Lifting and pressing brush can be both light and heavy. The structure is either open or close. The posture is both motive and quiet. . . . He learned about all of these in calligraphy. It provided him with the basic skills he needed for his drawing class.

His mother added that because neither her husband nor she plays an instrument and both of them always regard it as a pity, they decided to send Wei to learn to play piano. Wei did fine with his piano class, but he was not very interested. In contrast, he showed real talents in calligraphy and drawing. According to his parents, he began to practice running script and grass script in elementary school, both of which have more powerful expressive force of rich rhythms and tunes than regular script and are therefore more difficult to practice. Two of his scripts got picked for the local calligraphy exhibition when he was only at the age of nine. During the years in elementary school, his calligraphy scripts and watercolor paintings kept being sent to different exhibitions. His works also won quite a few local and provincial competitions.

Wei indicated that he spent a lot of time and energy on practicing calligraphy, drawing, and other extracurricular activities in elementary school and that studying was not his number one priority. His parents did not set any ground rules about schoolwork or ranking in class. "Elementary school was easy," Wei said. "It was so easy that sometimes I'd skip homework. My parents sometimes would ask me, 'Did you do your homework?' And if I said yes, they believed me." Instead of drilling him in school subjects, Wei's parents encouraged him to participate in all sorts of extracurricular activities. Wei attended aircraft modeling class, in which he learned the art of building fine aircraft models. He was also a member of the Chinese chess club and liked to challenge his grandfather to a game. He also played soccer and ping-pong.

Wei read a lot and read widely. He had a broad interest in reading. He read comic books and novels. He read about science and philosophy, arts and history. "I read everything I could get," Wei said, "and my parents subscribed to a whole lot of magazines and journals, and most of them were for me, such as *Youth Science, Chinese Youth, Reader*, and *We Love History*." Surprisingly, despite the fact that Wei spent very little time on learning the school subjects, he still did quite well in school.

Predisposition Stage

The summer when Wei graduated from elementary school, his aunt invited him to go to Beijing to spend the summer break with her family. Wei's aunt is a professor at Beijing Foreign Language University, and they live in a beautiful community close to the campus. His cousin, who is three years older than he is, showed him around Beijing. They visited Forbidden City, Tiananmen Square, Summer Palace, Temple of Heaven, and Temple of Earth. For most of the time, however, they traveled on their bicycles from one university to another in the college district where they were living. There are ten national key universities located in this northwestern suburbs of Beijing. Wei has heard about all of them, but that was the first time he had the opportunity to visit them one by one. Wei was impressed by every one of them.

They are all so beautiful. My parents talked to me about them a long time ago, maybe even before I went to elementary school. I've also visited Beijing before. But that was the first time that I visited all of these universities. . . . Only then I began to have real feelings about these famous universities.

Qinghua University was Wei's favorite. The campus of Qinghua was built on the remains of several former royal gardens of Qing Dynasty, surrounded by a few historical sites. The garden-like landscape, the Wanquan Creek meandering through the campus, and the famous "lake of lotus" that inspired a renowned Chinese writer's best-known prose all amazed Wei. Tsinghua University was established in 1911 originally as "Tsinghua College," a preparatory school for students who would be sent by the government to study at universities in the United States. Therefore, the campus also has several Western-style buildings. "That was amazing," Wei commented. "The very Chinese artistic architectures and some baroque-style buildings can accommodate each other so well and contribute equally to the beauty of the campus." Wei was so impressed by everything he had seen.

When Wei returned to Wuhu, his parents already got admission to Fuzhong middle school for him by paying the extra tuition. Wei was not surprised because he had always assumed that Fuzhong was where he would be going for middle school. He shared with his parents his feelings and opinions about the different universities he had visited in Beijing. His parents were very happy to find out that he showed a strong interest in architecture. They encouraged him to set his goal on the school of architecture in Qinghua University. They also pointed out to Wei that to accomplish that goal he had to take the schoolwork more seriously. Wei agreed:

I always paid attention to the teachers' lectures. I just didn't always finish my homework, and that's only because it was too easy for me. But middle school became a little bit difficult and thus more challenging. I kind of liked it.

In the first year of middle school, Wei's academic performance ranked in the top 10 percent of his class. According to his parents, Wei still did not give 100 percent of his effort, but they did not want to push him too much. They had confidence that he would work hard enough to make his college dream come true.

When Wei was a junior in middle school, his father was invited to work at the University of Greenwich in London as a visiting scholar for one year. He asked Wei if he would like to study in England for a year. Wei jumped at this wonderful opportunity. His mother said,

Before we talked to him about this possibility, we had been hesitating about this idea for a long time. It's easy to pull him out of the school and take him to London, but it would be extremely difficult to bring him back and try to put him back in the Chinese educational system. . . . So, we decided to talk to him and just see how he would respond. To our surprise, he was very excited and absolutely certain that he wanted to go.

Wei also recalled that moment. "I've read so much about Europe, especially the art and history of architecture in Europe. I wanted to go there and to experience it myself, so of course I said yes." Because of Wei's strong desire for this opportunity, his parents finally decided to let him go to England with his father. In the winter of Wei's junior year in middle school, Wei and his parents and he worked out a plan for his education in England. They bought all the textbooks for the next year according to the curriculum of China. Wei's father planned to teach him math and physics. Wei was going to learn Chinese by himself. Moreover, Wei's parents had a conversation with the principal of Fuzhong about this temporary withdrawal from school. The principal agreed to keep Wei's record in school, but Wei's parents still had to pay the tuition and fees for that year. They signed the agreement and began to prepare for this big trip.

It was the first time for both Wei and his father to visit England. Everything was foreign, exotic, but also interesting to them. In the middle of chaotic excitement, however, they still managed to find a middle school for Wei as soon as possible with help from the Chinese community at the University of Greenwich. Not unexpectedly, Wei had some difficulty with school at the beginning.

> It was mostly the language problem. I've learned English since fifth grade, but when I went to school in London I felt that I'd never learned anything useful in my English class. . . . Math and science were fine. Actually, I already learned in China most of what they taught [in math and science] in eighth grade.

Wei's father turned out to be very busy with his research at the University of Greenwich and did not have much time to teach Wei math and physics. Mostly, Wei studied on his own. Since the school in England has a rather short school day compared to the Chinese school, Wei had a lot of time after school to work on the textbooks he brought from China. It was the most challenging time for Wei, but he still cherished the experiences and learned a lot from the school and the life in London.

A year later Wei came back to China with his father and continued his education at Fuzhong. Although he had learned all the school subjects on his own during the year he was in London, Wei could hardly catch up with the class. In addition to the textbooks, teachers at Fuzhong used a lot of supplementary materials that Wei did not have. Wei's father explained the whole situation,

Often, teachers at Fuzhong asked students to buy additional learning or testing materials and trained students to be familiar with different types of questions. Since students had done a lot of exercises, once they saw a similar question in an exam, they could quickly figure out a solution. . . . Of course Wei hadn't been trained this way, so generally he needed more time to work out one question. Usually he didn't have enough time to finish the exams.

Wei's grades began to slip. He had to cut back on the time he used to spend on drawing or playing piano in order to "drill [himself] in exercises and testing." He made some progress within the half a year left in middle school; however, it was not enough to get him high scores in the high school entrance examinations. He missed Fuzhong's admission score by 15 points. Without any hesitation, his parents paid the extra 7,000 yuan per semester to get him into Fuzhong high school.

Search Stage

After graduating from middle school, Wei realized the need to dramatically change his attitude toward achieving academically, especially the need to improve his grades. Therefore, since the start of high school, Wei stopped going out to play soccer or basketball with his friends, ended his private piano lessons, reduced the time for extracurricular reading, and began to spend most of his time on learning school subjects.

I got up at five in the morning to memorize English vocabularies and texts. . . . I studied until 11 at night. . . . In addition to the large amount of homework assigned by the teachers everyday, I completed a lot of exercises and testing my parents could find for me from bookstores. . . . I didn't have a life. . . . What I wanted the most at that time was sleep. I was totally sleep deprived.

While Wei was trying his best to catch up in terms of academic performance, his parents were collecting information about different universities and their architecture schools for Wei. They looked up information online, went to consult with Wei's homeroom teacher regarding enrollment rates to different colleges, and made a chart representing all the information they collected. On the left side of the chart, they had four universities listed by the rank of their architecture schools. They are Qinghua University, Tongji University, Tianjin University, and Southeast University. Across the top of the chart were the five years from 2001 to 2005. In each cell, they put in the enrollment quota each university had for the Anhui province in one specific year and its admission score. In the winter of Wei's junior year, his parents showed him the chart and a pile of national college entrance examination papers from the previous five years. "Here," they said, "take the test and see which university you could get in." Wei recalled that during the whole winter break he had been working on all of those test papers. He usually locked himself up in his study room, set an alarm clock to time the testing, and then did the previous college entrance examinations. After he finished one set of testing that included five subjects—Chinese, math, English, physics, and chemistry—Wei would take his testing papers to his teachers and ask them to score for him. The results were not very encouraging. Comparing his own scores with the admission scores listed in the chart his parents gave him, Wei found that he only reached Tongji University's admission score once and Tianjin University twice. His achievement was far from Qinghua University's admission requirement. His parents discussed his achievement scores with him and suggested he aim for Tianjin University. Meanwhile, Wei's parents began to search for information about applying to colleges and universities in Great Britain for him.

Choice Stage

The summer before his senior year in high school, Wei went to Shanghai to take a month-long heavy training class in IELTS, the International English Language Test System. IELTS is a part of requirement for college applications in Great Britain. Wei went to a private language school that provided comprehensive preparation for the exam. According to Wei, the courses were demanding and boring. He attended 80 classes over a four-week period and was challenged with extensive homework assignments that reinforced the concepts and methods presented in each class. Later that year, Wei took the IELTS test and got 7.5 out of 9. He and his parents were very happy about his achievement score. "When we saw his score in IELTS, we became more confident that Wei would be going to Great Britain for his college education. . . . He had a pretty good GPA from high school, an impressive collection of his paintings and calligraphy works . . . and then a high score in IELTS to approve his language ability."

Wei continued to prepare for the national college entrance examinations but felt more relaxed about it. He also spent part of his time and energy on writing his personal statement and preparing the collection of his paintings. His parents talked to his homeroom teacher about their alternative plan for Wei. The teacher was very supportive and agreed to write a recommendation letter for Wei. In the end, Wei's homeroom teacher and his English teacher wrote a strong recommendation letter together for his application to the British universities. His parents did more research on the British universities and their architecture programs. They made a list of twenty universities that have strong programs in architecture. They helped Wei pick ten of them to apply to. Although University of Greenwich was not on that list, Wei still applied to it because of the positive experiences he had there a few years ago.

In March 2006, Wei went to Qinghua University, Tongji University, and Tianjin University to participate in the talent test on drawing, which is mandatory for students who apply for architecture programs. Wei successfully passed the tests required by all three universities. About the same time, Wei sent out all his applications to the universities in Great Britain. In early June, Wei took the national college entrance examinations. He performed fairly well in the exams, yet his total achievement score was still a few points lower than the admission score to Qinghua University and Tongji University. In early August, he received the admission from Tianjin University. A week later, he also received a couple of admission letters from British Universities. After a few discussions between Wei and his parents, they all concluded that it would be better for Wei to go to Great Britain for his undergraduate study instead of living with his third choice—Tianjin University.

The total expense of attending a British university is almost ten times the expense of a college education in China. According to Wei's parents, they needed to provide financial evidence that they had at least a savings of 600,000 yuan in order for Wei to get his student visa to Great Britain. "It was not very easy for us," Wei's mother admitted. "We didn't have that much cash in the bank, so we sold some of our stocks and an old apartment we had been renting out for a few years. . . . We all believe that studying abroad is a precious experience and will help Wei with his career in the future. So, as long as we could afford it, we'd go for the best choice for him."

ZHANG PENG

Family Background

Zhang Peng is a well-behaved, cheerful student with superior academic achievement. He is from a working-class family. His father, with a high school diploma, is working on a boat for a local river transportation company. Because of the nature of his job, Peng's father does not have a regular work schedule. Generally, he can spend five days at home every month. His mother, who is also a high school graduate, is working at a large automobile factory in the suburbs.

Early Influence Stage

Before going to elementary school, Zhang Peng was taught a few Chinese characters by his mother. However, Peng's parents were not very serious about teaching him to learn Chinese characters because they believed that if he had already learned what teachers were going to teach in class, it would bore him and he would lose the interest to learn in class. "We taught him a few, just for fun," Peng's mother said. "He could recognize about ten words before going to school, but he couldn't write at all." Peng went to a kindergarten at age four and spent two years in there before going to elementary school. He learned to count from one to a hundred in kindergarten and also finally learned how to write his name. "Those were the only two characters I knew how to write when I started elementary school," Peng recalled. "I still wasn't good at it, and my teacher couldn't recognize what I wrote, so she mispronounced my name."

Zhang Peng was not an outstanding student in elementary school. "I did pretty well. I wasn't top of the class of anything, but I wasn't too bad. My grades were pretty average." He spent a lot of time playing soccer and did not care much about schoolwork. Peng could not recall any ground rules made by his parents about schoolwork. "My parents sometimes scolded me for not doing my homework," Peng said, "but there was not much they could do about it." However, Peng's mother said that they did have rules about schoolwork and homework for Peng. It had to be done before other activities, like playing with friends or watching TV, were allowed. The problem was that his father was not much around because of his job and his mother got back home pretty late at night because of the long commute, thus no one was at home to supervise Peng.

Nobody mentioned college to Peng before he went to middle school. Neither his father nor his mother had a college education, so any talk or discussions about their own college experiences were nonexistent. The first time going to college came cross Peng's mind was when he was in middle school.

Predisposition Stage

Upon graduating from elementary school, Peng won the lottery to Fuzhong middle school. He regarded it as the most important turning point of his life so far.

> Sometimes when I look back, I would have this fear that what if I didn't get the lottery and went to an ordinary middle school. I guess my life would be totally different. And, college might not be an option for me. . . . You might think going to college is the key for a person's course of life, but I feel that . . . for me, it's such a natural thing to go to college since I came to Fuzhong, where everybody talked about colleges. . . . The real turning point was winning the lottery. My life has completely changed since then.

Peng recalled that the first day in middle school the homeroom teacher asked everybody to stand up to share their college dream with other students. Peng had no idea about colleges at that time, so he picked one community college that he knew because it was close to where he was living. Other students were staring at him like he was from "another planet." He still remembered the teacher's comment, "I bet you'd do better than that." When recalling that event, Peng laughed at how ridiculous he was.

As he progressed through middle school at Fuzhong, he was constantly surprised by how often teachers and his classmates talked about a college education. It seemed that going to college was the only viable path that every student in Fuzhong should take, and that not going to college was such a shameful thing. Under the influences of his teachers and classmates, Peng began to seriously think about going to college and wanted to do better in school so that someday he could go to one of the prestigious universities that other students presented in class as their dream schools on the first day.

Peng had his hard work rewarded—he began to catch up academically and started to show his talents in science. He especially excelled in chemistry and participated in the special training program for chemistry competitions. He won two championships in chemistry, one in the school district and the other citywide. However, his achievement in Chinese and English was still below the average, and he especially struggled with his Chinese written composition class. Peng never developed a love of reading throughout his school years. Actually, the first book he remembered reading in its entirety was in high school. Occasionally, he would borrow some Japanese comic cartoon books from his classmates, but he never did any serious extracurricular reading. His mother also said that both she and Peng's father did not read for enjoyment,

> Normally, his father worked on the boat for three weeks per month and then could stay at home for five to seven days. When he was at home, he liked to go to his friend's place to play poker or mahjong. I sometimes went with him. Most of the time, I was so tired after work and I'd just relax and watch TV. . . . We didn't subscribe to any magazine or newspaper. . . . We were not very interested in reading. . . . But, we bought all the textbooks and supplementary learning materials required by the school to make sure that Peng had things to read.

Because of Peng's low achievement in Chinese and English, he sometimes had doubts about his ability to go to college. Therefore, when it came close to graduation from middle school, he was still very hesitant about whether he should continue his education in a general high school or go to a specialized secondary school:

> I truly appreciated the opportunity to attend Fuzhong middle school, so I really worked hard and I was among the top ten in my class. So, I thought if I applied to a specialized secondary school, I could get into a very good one.

... I had Nanjing Transportation School in mind. My parents had a few friends who graduated from there were working on the railroad. They got decent salaries and good benefits. . . . At that time, college still seemed to be far away from my life.

Peng communicated his idea about going to a vocational school with his parents. They were supportive of his idea because they also felt a college education did not seem to be very practical. However, Peng's homeroom teacher paid a visit to Peng's family after he saw Peng's application form. He persuaded Peng to continue his education in a general high school and he showed his strong confidence in Peng's ability to pursue a good college education afterward. "He gave us a lecture on the importance of a college education and all the possibilities for life that can only be achievable with a college education. . . . So, he won me over. . . . My parents are always supportive of my decision, so they had no problem with the change of the plan."

In 2003, Peng successfully passed the high school entrance examinations and was admitted to Fuzhong.

Search Stage

From the minute he made his mind to go on to high school, Peng knew that he would try his best to go to college. Still concerned with his achievement in Chinese and English, Peng began to spend more time on reading. He bought a few composition books to learn how to write an essay. He found a trick that was helpful to his written composition. He recited quite a few sample essays provided in the composition books, which he claimed really improved his writing skills. "I know it sounds stupid," Peng said, "but it worked well for me." Meanwhile, Peng continued to shine in science class. In the junior year of high school, Peng participated in a provincial-level chemistry competition and won.

In high school, college turned into a taken-for-granted reality for Peng. Talking about prestigious universities became part of his daily conversations with his teachers and classmates. "Everybody dreamed about Beijing University or Qinghua University," he claimed, "but not me." Peng was very aware of the fact that he would not be going to Beijing for his college education. It is too far from home. He was not comfortable with the idea that he would not be able to come home if and when he needed to. Moreover, he has never been to the north and he had no idea how life would be in Beijing: "I'm not sure if I'd get used to the cold weather and the northern diet. I don't know. I've never been there. It could be hard." Peng then added, "And people there speak perfect Mandarin. It could be intimidating." Therefore, from the very beginning of his college choice process, he narrowed the location down to the Anhui province and a few big cities in the neighboring provinces. He had a strong preference to stay in the Anhui province. Within the Anhui province, the University of Science and Technology in China is the best, thus Peng listed this university as number one on his list of choices. Peng had three universities in mind. Anhui University was the second on the list, which is a provincial key university. The third was Anhui Normal University.

Choice Stage

As previously noted, Peng's father was not around the house much and Peng's mother usually had to leave home early in the morning and got back quite late at night because of the long commute from home to work. Moreover, because neither of his parents had college experience, they were not very much involved in Peng's college decision-making process. Basically, Peng forged his own way in sorting through college choices for himself:

> My parents were both really busy with their work and seldom had time to discuss the issue [college choice] with me. I'm not complaining about it. I understand that now without a college education, it is tough to keep your job. I heard them talking about their companies laying off people all the time. They were constantly worried about their jobs . . . so, I just made the decision all by myself. . . . Maybe I have talked to my friends a little bit about it, but basically it was just me . . . and I knew, whatever I decided, my parents would be 100 percent supportive, because they always were.

As noted earlier, Peng was a star student in chemistry and won a championship in a provincial-level chemistry competition in the second year of high school. Therefore, in the fall semester of his senior year, he got a chance to choose between the participating in the early admission examinations to Fudan University and the University of Science and Technology in China. It did not take long for him to choose the University of Science and Technology in China. First of all, in Fudan University's early admission exams, students had to take three subjects. Math was required for every student. The second subject could be either physics or chemistry. The third part was called "gift demonstration." Students could either choose to give a speech in Chinese or English, play an instrument, practice calligraphy, or draw. Peng's achievement in Chinese or English writing was about average. Moreover, he never learned any instrument and had no experience with calligraphy or drawing. So, the so-called gift demonstration part could be hard for him. In the University of Science and Technology in China's early admission exams, the subjects included math, physics, and chemistry. Peng found it much easier for him. Moreover, the University of Science and Technology in China is located in Hefei, the capital city of the Anhui province.

It is much closer to Wuhu compared to Shanghai where Fudan University is. When talking about his decision making over which college to attend, Peng expressed his concerns about his mother. Because his father was not at home very often, Peng was worried that his mother might feel very lonely after he went off to college. Therefore, he would like to come home reasonably often. Moreover, the living expenses in Hefei are similar to Wuhu, while Shanghai, the largest city in China, is notorious for its extremely high living expenditures.

Money was not only a factor in Peng's college choice process but also a substantial variable that influenced his decision about college major. When he went to Hefei for the early admission examinations, Peng talked to people in the student office about the tuition and fees charged by different departments. He first considered choosing information system or computer science as his undergraduate program because these two majors currently have a very good job market in China. A graduate from these two fields can expect to find a well-paid job rather easily. However, he found out that information system charged tuition of 8,000 yuan for a year and computer science charged 6,500 yuan. He believed that his parents had probably saved enough money for his college education, or at least for the first one or two years. However, Peng could not bear the thought that he might use up all of his parents' savings for his college education. According to Peng's observation, his parents were very restricted when spending money for themselves. They very seldom bought nice clothes for themselves and never went out for a nice meal or any other entertainment. They always told Peng that sending him to college would be the biggest and the only luxury they would like to enjoy. His parents were getting old, and once they retired their pension would decrease to only two-thirds of their current salaries, which would make their not-so-good situation even worse. "I have to worry about all of these things, although my parents told me not to," Peng said. Therefore, after all of these considerations, he chose chemistry as his major, which cost only 4,000 yuan for a year.

However, Peng did not share his concerns about money with his parents. His parents had no idea that Peng had struggled among different possibilities for his undergraduate program. His mother indicated that college decision making depended entirely on Peng himself. She and her husband felt incompetent when it came to discussions about colleges and majors. They had absolute trust in Peng and believed that he would be able to make the best decision for himself. They tried to ensure Peng that they had some savings for his college education so that money should not be an issue when he was making his choice for college.

We always tried to squeeze some money out of our daily expense and put it aside in case of an emergency. We began to save specifically for Peng's education after he went to Fuzhong middle school and showed some interest in going to college. . . . Neither of us had a college education and thus could not help him with his schoolwork. So, the least we could do is to be supportive of his decision and not let money bother him.

Obviously, money still played a large role in Peng's college-decision process. The reason Peng did not communicate his concerns with his parents is that he did not think it would be helpful. He expressed concern that his parents might feel guilty that they were unable to pay for him to go to the ideal program. Or, they might decide to borrow around in order to support the best choice for him. Either way was not what Peng wanted. Peng said that choosing chemistry as his major might turn out to be a good decision because he was actually interested in chemistry and confident that he would do well in this major. He was hoping that his outstanding performance in chemistry would bring him some merit-based scholarships.

Peng passed the early admission examinations and became one of the chemistry freshmen of 2006 at the University of Science and Technology in China.

SHI JUAN

Family Background

Both of Shi Juan's parents are high school graduates. Her father is working at a textile factory as a mechanic, and her mother is working at the tobacco factory as a packaging worker. They are living with Juan's grandfather in his apartment. Her grandfather used to be a middle school teacher at Fuzhong, and the apartment was provided by the school as part of his retirement settlement.

Early Influence Stage

Juan and her parents moved in with her grandfather while she was in second grade in elementary school and when her grandmother passed away. Before that, Juan and her parents were living in a rental apartment, which was close to her mother's factory but about one hour's bus commute to her father's working place. At age four, Juan's parents sent her to a kindergarten that was owned by her mother's factory. The kindergarten was located inside of the factory, and the teachers were actually employees the factory. Different from other kindergartens that were sponsored by the community or the local government, the teachers were not certified kindergarten teachers. Juan's mother explained that usually those teachers were wives or daughters of some experienced and skilled workers. They were hired by the factory as a benefit provided to their husbands or fathers, who were highly valued workers; however, since they lacked skills for other positions, they were put in this kindergarten and became so-called teachers. Juan's mother was aware that this kind of kindergarten would not provide her daughter with valuable preschool experiences. Nevertheless, she did not have a choice.

> Because our factory is a tobacco factory, it's located in the suburbs. Other nice kindergartens were all very far from our factory. If we sent her to another kindergarten, transportation and time would become a problem. . . . We just needed someone to look after her when we were at work.

Juan's mother decided to teach Juan herself. The year before Juan went to elementary school, Juan's mother started to teach her Chinese characters. It usually took her half an hour to teach Juan a couple of characters, and then she would make her copy the characters 50 times each in order to make her memorize them. "She was not a fast learner," her mother recalled, "but she did learn quite a few characters before going to school."

Juan usually spent her weekends in her grandparents' place. Her grandfather had some knowledge about calligraphy and used to teach her to exercise it. Juan's parents were very supportive of Juan's calligraphy practice. Juan's mother specified the importance of practicing calligraphy:

> I think having beautiful handwriting is very important. I remember when I was in school, our composition teacher used to tell us that good handwriting could easily impress the teacher who was grading the composition. You might get a high grade for your composition not because of what you wrote but because of how your handwriting looked. . . . It's also important when you are looking for a job. You will give the interviewer a really nice first impression if you have neatly written your resume. [When I pointed out that nowadays people usually print out their resumes, she responded that, "Yeah, but you get the idea. It's a very useful skill."]

By the time she went to elementary school, Juan had learned quite a few Chinese characters and some simple math. Juan's mother continued to oversee her schoolwork at night and set up rigorous rules about homework and grades. Juan's mother shared that, "Juan was raised in a very disciplined home. I was there every day after school. She'd come home and immediately start to do her homework. Only after she finished her homework, we'd let her watch TV a little bit. In fact, we didn't allow her to watch any TV drama series the whole time she was growing up. She could watch cartoons and the program the 'Animal World,' and that's about it."

Juan's parents had high expectations for her, and Juan did not disappoint them. She was doing very well in school and graduated from elementary school as one of the top ten students in her class. However, unluckily, Juan did not win the lottery to Fuzhong middle school. It was the first time that her family was facing such a difficult choice about where she should go for middle school.

Predisposition Stage

Having learned that Juan was not one of the few lucky winners of the lottery to Fuzhong middle school, her parents' initial response was that they had no choice but to send her to an ordinary middle school in their community. However, Juan's grandfather insisted that they should try everything to get Juan to Fuzhong. Usually, Juan's grandfather did not interfere with Juan's parents' decisions about her education, but this time he stepped in and lectured them on the importance of sending Juan to a good middle school. Although her grandfather had already retired at that time, he still had a few friends in administrative positions at Fuzhong. So, he paid some visits to his friends and used his network to get Juan into Fuzhong middle school. Her parents had a big argument with her grandfather when they learned about the fact that in addition to mandatory fees and textbook costs they had to pay an extra 5,000 yuan every semester for Juan's admission to Fuzhong. Juan offered her observations and comments about this issue:

> It's not like they didn't care about my education. They actually cared a lot. It's just that they didn't know how important it was to go to a good middle school. They thought I could go to an ordinary middle school and then go to Fuzhong for high school. It's not impossible, but it would be extremely hard. And my grandfather knew all about it.

Finally, Juan's grandfather offered to pay the extra tuition. However, Juan's parents did not sincerely appreciate the choice he forced them to make until the year Juan graduated from middle school. Juan's parents learned that not a single student in the middle school in their community reached the admission score to Fuzhong in the high school entrance examinations that year. Juan's father said,

> The old man was right . . . it was not about money. We just wanted to save the money for her high school and college education. We didn't want to spend the money so early on . . . but, he [Juan's grandfather] was right. If we didn't pay to get her into Fuzhong middle school, she probably wouldn't need the money we've been saving for her college education—she might not be able to get into one.

Juan's parents both agreed that Juan could not have gone so far on the path to college if it were not for her grandfather.

During her time in middle school, Juan was continuously exposed to the idea of going to college. Fuzhong is a school with a college culture that expects its students to attend college and whose students share the goal of continuing their education beyond high school. Immersed in such a school culture, Juan began to consider a college education. Her parents also had high expectations for her. That is, she could obtain a college degree someday in the future. However, although both Juan and her parents had developed the preference for a college education when she was in middle school, they never clearly discussed a college plan until Juan's second year in high school.

Since Juan's parents could get some financial help from her grandfather, they did not feel their budget was too tight even though they were both workers with low to medium salaries. They were always willing to spend money for Juan's education more than anything else. Juan continued to study hard in middle school; however, she was not in the top rank anymore. To encourage her to work even harder, Juan's parents set up a reward policy, by which they would reward Juan with 50 yuan if she could get into the top ten in her class in any semester or semi-semester examinations. There was also a punishment for not achieving the average score of the class. They would not let her watch TV for a long time until she showed some progress in the next exams. "They were very strict with my schooling. They never let me go out to play with other kids," Juan complained, "not even in the weekend. They made me do extra homework during the weekend." Her mother said that they had tried their best to help Juan with her education. Since middle school, Juan's parents had sent her to a variety of afterschool classes, such as a math class, an olympic science class, and an English class. All of her afterschool classes were related to her schooling. Juan's parents did not think that it was a good idea to send her to a real extracurricular class, such as a dance class or a drawing class, because they thought it would only distract her from her schoolwork and therefore would do no good for her. Juan agreed with her parents on that; however, she also complained that going to afterschool classes was not helpful and it simply drained her energy for studying. For the same reason, Juan's parents did not subscribe to any extracurricular readings for Juan. Nevertheless, they bought a lot of supplementary materials for Juan's schooling every semester.

Overall, Juan's academic achievement in middle school was about the average. Since Fuzhong has much better qualified teachers and better facilities and learning environment, graduates from Fuzhong middle school are generally better prepared academically and therefore there is virtually no competition from outside when it comes to the high school entrance examinations. Therefore, although Juan was not a top student in her middle school class, she did not have any difficulty passing the high school entrance examinations and to gaining admission to Fuzhong.

Search Stage

Although Juan's parents had been paying close attention to her education from elementary school, they never talked to Juan about a college plan. It only began in her sophomore year in high school, when her parents encouraged her to start thinking about college. Over the years Juan had heard her teachers and classmates talking about going to college. However, she never thought of discussing this topic with her parents until her second year of high school. She was surprised when her parents brought up this topic, but since then she would sometimes discuss her thoughts about colleges and possible majors with her parents:

> I knew I would go to college. Every student in Fuzhong high school is supposed to go to college. That's what they say, "Once you get into Fuzhong, you get one foot into college already." I didn't think of talking to my parents about my college choices until they asked me about it, like, "Where'd you want to go? What do you see yourself doing?"

Neither of Juan's parents had college experiences. They were generally supportive of Juan's education, but not very knowledgeable about what they could do to help with her college choice. Thus, Juan did the initial search for college information by herself.

Students in Fuzhong are highly encouraged to attend college. Teacher-student interactions, course content, and a variety of testing are all directed at supporting college preparation. Juan heard classmates talking about colleges in middle school, and began to think about her college choice once she started her high school. Like a lot of her peers, Juan regarded Beijing University and Qinghua University as her dream schools. However, since her sophomore year, she began to think about her college choice more practically:

> I think that everybody dreamed of going to Beijing University or Qinghua University once in their lives. I know I did. And then once you see what your scores are, you become more realistic as time goes on. . . . New schools come into the picture after you realize the limitations.

Juan was still ambitious enough to apply to a national key university. To find out the most appropriate school to apply to, Juan consulted with her homeroom teacher, who provided her with a list of first-tier universities and their entrance scores in the previous year. After processing the information given by her teacher, Juan found out that a few key universities located in the far north generally had lower entrance scores for high school graduates in the Anhui province.[1] Juan figured that it could be because not many people want to go that far for college. Given her academic achievement, the chance for her to get into a national key university around the east cost area was rather small. Therefore, she decided to take the advantage of that and applied to Jilin University, which is more than 2,000 kilometers away from Wuhu. Juan has never been in the north. She did not think she would like to live in the north because of the weather and the diet. However, she believed that "living an easy life is not the reason for one to go to college," and that she was "choosing the college for a right reason." She thought that a degree from a well-known key university would definitely help with her career. "Nowadays life in the work environment can be very hard without a good education from a good university," Juan said. "The better school you get in the better off your life will be."

Choice Stage

When she had finished her initial research on college information, she talked to her parents about her idea to go to a key university in the north. Unfortunately, her parents did not support her idea of going to a university so far away. As her mother said,

> She didn't know what she was doing. She was still a child, and we didn't think she was making the right choice. We didn't want her to go there only to find out that she simply could't get used to the environment and got sick of the foods, while nobody is around. . . . We felt obligated to make the right decision for her when she was too young to think things through. . . . We knew how much she wanted to go to a key university, and that's why we suggested she apply to Nanjing University.

Nanjing University is in a neighboring province that is only a two-hour drive away. It is one of the oldest universities in China and enjoys a high reputation in the east coast area. Juan was afraid of the competition for Nanjing University and had the fear that putting Nanjing University as her first choice might ruin her whole college application. Nevertheless, under pressure from her parents, she still applied to Nanjing University. Unfortunately, she missed the entrance score by only 15 points. She ended up going to her backup school, Anhui Normal University. It was heartbreaking. She refused to talk to her parents for a week after she received the rejection letter from Nanjing University. She also bitterly found out that if she insisted on her original plan, she would have been accepted to Jilin University. However, her parents did not quite understand her frustration. Her mother's comments were,

> Anhui Normal University is not a bad school. Officially, it's also a key university. It's just not that prestigious. But, it's here, in Wuhu. She can come back home for meals, just like when she was in high school. And, we can save a lot of money on transportation, boarding, and food. . . . She will understand it eventually.

Although ending up in a college distant from her own choice made Juan severely disappointed, the rather low tuition charged at the normal university relieved Juan's parents of financial burdens to some extent. Juan was aware that paying for her college education was a great expense for her family, but she did not want to apply for financial aid. She thought that financial aid is only for those from extremely poor families, and she did not think she would be eligible. Even if she was, she added that she still did not want to apply for financial aid because she thought that it was shameful to depend on financial aid, which she took to be like a social welfare. She commented that people usually looked down on those students who relied on financial aid, and it would make one's college life really difficult. "You'd become one of those poor students, and nobody wants to socialize with you. College life, which is supposed to be the most beautiful time in your life, would be totally ruined." She could not explain where she had gotten these feelings about financial aid and referred to it as "a general impression" that she got from reading some news published in the mass media.

LI QUNHUAN

Family Background

Qunhuan grew up as one of two sons in a peasant family. His family is living in the rural area about 50 kilometers away from Wuhu city. Qunhuan went back to visit his family once per semester during his high school years in Wuhu. Both of his parents are farmers. Qunhuan's father has an elementary school education and can speak some Mandarin with a heavy accent. His mother is illiterate and speaks only the local dialect. The understanding of Qunhuan's childhood experiences and his college decision-making process is mostly based on the interview with Qunhuan.

Early Influence Stage

Qunhuan could not recall any early educational experiences at home before going to elementary school. Instead, he began to help with chores around the house when he was five years old. When he turned seven, he had already become a good helper in farming.

The village where Qunhuan's family was living had a small elementary school. The school used to have two teachers. One taught Chinese and math for the first, second, and third grades. The other taught Chinese and math for the fourth, fifth, and sixth grades. The year when Qunhuan reached the age to go to school, one of the two teachers quit and left the village. The only teacher in the school had to teach more than 30 students across six grades. Thus, the teacher worked out a schedule that half of the students came to school in the morning only and the other half came in the afternoon. This situation continued for a year until the village found a new teacher for the school.

Unlike the elementary school in the city that provides a variety of classes including drawing, music, and physical education classes, the school Qunhuan went to only offered Chinese and math classes. More important, because neither of the two teachers was able to teach English, no English class was offered in the village school. In contrast, in the city English class was required from fourth grade. This gave Qunhun a difficult time later when he went to middle school.

Qunhuan studied really hard and was the best student in school. At that time, he already showed his talents in mathematics. "I like math very much," Qunhuan said. "In the elementary school, we didn't have any supplementary materials other than textbooks. So, I did every exercise in the math textbook. After I finished going through the whole book, I didn't have anything else to work with, so I'd sometimes make up math questions for myself. . . . I'd play with the math question provided in the book, and then thought 'what if I took out this variable, what would happen?' or 'what if I changed this condition, how the result would change?' I had a lot of fun studying math." The teacher thought highly of Qunhuan's academic ability and encouraged him to go on to middle school after graduation. "My parents didn't have any problem with that," Qunhuan recalled. "They have high expectations for me, and they wanted me to finish middle school." Upon graduation from elementary school, Qunhuan became the only student who continued his schooling in the county seat. Another three classmates of Qunhuan went to a neighboring village for middle school and none of them went on to high school.

Predisposition Stage

The middle school in the county seat that Qunhuan was admitted to was a local key school. Most of its student population was from the county seat, but it also admitted a few outstanding students from the villages around it every year. It provided room and board for those students who were not local. However, Qunhuan did not become one of the boarding students because the expenses were too high. Therefore, Qunhuan had to travel on a bicycle one-and-a-half hours to reach the school in the morning and then to come back home at night. "I had to get up at five in the morning in order to be on time for school [which began at seven]," Qunhuan said. "It was fine in spring and fall, but very difficult during the winter. When weather was bad, I had to get up even earlier in order to get to school on time." However, when Qunhuan recalled the three years in middle school, traveling between home and the school everyday was not the hardest part. The issue that bothered him the most was the English class. Most of Qunhuan's classmates had already studied English for two years in their elementary school, while Qunhuan had to begin with the 26 letters. "I was left behind from the beginning," Qunhuan said, "and I never really caught up." In contrast to his struggle in the English class, Qunhuan began to shine in math, physics, and chemistry. In his second year of middle school, Qunhuan came in second place in a provincial chemistry competition. In his senior year, Qunhuan won the championship in a provincial math competition and came in third in physics. In the last semester of middle school, Fuzhong's special recruiting crew came to Qunhuan's middle school and persuaded him to go to Wuhu, a city 50 kilometers away from his village, to continue his high school education. His homeroom teacher also had a talk with him and encouraged him to take the opportunity to go to Fuzhong high school because it would give him a better chance to go to college. That was the first time that someone talked to Qunhuan about going to college.

Qunhuan always wanted to be a good student and never lacked the motivation to learn. However, the idea of going to college never occurred to him. He just thought that he should try to get as much education as possible because he knew it is important to be educated. He witnessed his parents' lives as farmers, and he thought that was miserable. His dream has always been about getting out of the small village and becoming a city resident. His homeroom teacher assured him of the importance of education and pointed out to him that getting a college education was the best way to get away from a farmer's life. Qunhuan became excited about the whole idea of going to Fuzhong high school and then going to college. He went back home to share this exciting news with his parents. Qunhuan stated,

> It was a shock to my mom. She expected me to go back home after middle school and become an accountant in our village. . . . Every village has only one accountant, who works at the office of the head of the village. It's an honorable position in the village, and it pays rather well in the countryside. . . . Generally, the monthly salary is around 500 yuan. . . . Everybody in my village knows that I'm good with numbers, so the head of our village already promised my parents that he would offer me the accountant position if I went back. . . . So you can see, it was a huge disappointment to my mom.

Fortunately, Qunhuan's father was fine with the idea of sending him away for high school. Nevertheless, money was a huge issue for his family. His parents had some savings for family emergencies, and his father decided to take out the money to pay for Qunhuan's high school education. "My mom thought my dad was going crazy. They had fights about it," Qunhuan sadly recalled. "It was a mess. But, my dad finally got the money."

In the fall of 2004, Qunhuan went to Wuhu for his high school education, and become one step closer to going to college.

Search Stage

Although he decided to accept the offer from Fuzhong high school, Qunhuan was still not sure how far he could go on the path to college. After spending the whole summer break contemplating the possibilities for his future, Qunhuan went to Fuzhong high school the following fall and surprisingly found that everybody there was college bound. Teachers constantly talked about college preparation in class, and his peers shared their college dreams with one another. Immersed in this kind of atmosphere, the college dream seemed not too distant and unreachable. Qunhuan realized that it was absolutely possible for him to go to college given his outstanding academic performance; however, he was not sure he could actually afford a college education. Before he allowed himself to really dream about going to college, he thought he needed to have a talk with his parents regarding the financial issue given that the drama about him going to Fuzhong high school was just in the recent past. In the summer break of his freshman year in high school, he went back to his hometown. For the first time, Qunhuan sat his parents down and discussed with them the possibility for him to go to college. The tuition and fees for the three years in Fuzhong high school were 4,800 yuan. The total expenses of room and board, books and supplies, and transportation were around 4,500 yuan per year. It meant that Qunhuan's high school education would have exhausted his parents' total savings of 18,000 yuan. Once again, Qunhuan's mother was strongly against the idea of going to college. His father became reluctant as well when informed by Qunhuan of the average cost of college tuition and fees. After learning that his parents would not be able to pay for his college education, Qunhuan was overwhelmed by the huge disappointment and the fear that he might end up going back to the village after so many years of hard work. "I kept asking myself what's the point of studying hard," Qunhuan recalled of that difficult time. "I'll just become a farmer like my parents and my life will be forever trapped by inescapable rural poverty." After a couple of weeks of struggle, Qunhuan persuaded his father to go to the head of the village to talk about the possibility of a loan. Although Qunhuan decided to go to Fuzhong high school and consequently turned down the offer to be an account for the village, the head of the village still thought highly of Qunhuan. He promised to lend them money if Qunhuan made his way to college.

When Qunhuan returned to Wuhu for the second year of his high school, he felt obligated to work even harder because he knew that he was shouldering the hope of his whole family. The ultimate motive for Qunhuan to be diligent in his studies was that he had witnessed his parents' lives in the countryside, which was the kind of life he would not want for himself. Qunhuan explained his feelings,

> I was very precocious. When I was little, I already decided that my dream was to get out of the village and settle down in the city and to become one of the pretentious city residents . . . yes, pretentious. I don't think they are better people than us, but they feel rather good about themselves. I actually like that kind of attitude. . . . I worked really hard to get into Fuzhong. None of the city residents would understand how difficult it could be for a rural kid to get into a key high school in a city. But, I'm here, and I won't stop here. I'll fight my way to college.

Qunhuan was ambitious about his college plan. His overall academic rank is right in the middle of his class. He knew that every year more than 50 percent of the graduates from Fuzhong went to national key universities. Therefore, he set his college goal on a key university in a metropolitan area, although he did not have a specific university in mind until his senior year.

Qunhuan did not do well in Chinese and English classes, but he was a star student in mathematics and physics. He won two championships in provincial-level mathematics competitions in high school and joined the national olympic mathematic team for several months. Therefore, in the spring semester of his senior year, he got a permission to take the early admission exams for Fudan University. He went to Shanghai to participate in the examinations. It was his first time out of the Anhui province. The trip was a wonderful experience for him and expanded his horizons. "Shanghai is such a beautiful, exotic, and awesome place to be," he exclaimed. "After the trip, I knew I absolutely wanted to live my life there." Unfortunately, he did not get early admission to Fudan University. Although he performed pretty well in his math and physics exams, he failed terribly in the "gift demonstration" part. It was not a surprise to him because he had no experience with any extracurricular activities, nor was he good at Chinese or English oral composition. It did not defeat his spirit though. When he returned to Wuhu, he began to search for a national key university in Shanghai that suited his strong science background. After a month's research, he set his goal on Shanghai Transportation University, whose naval architecture and ocean engineering, automatic control, and electronic engineering programs have high reputation in the nation.

Choice Stage

After his decision to make Shanghai Transportation University his first choice, Qunhuan began to contemplate which program he wanted to major in. Although he liked mathematics very much, he did not think a math major would lead to a well-paid job. For Qunhuan, who wished to go into the job market right after graduating from college, a good salary is the most important element when considering an undergraduate major. Qunhuan stated,

> If I didn't have to worry about paying the tuition, the only factor I would consider when choosing the major was the job market. I had to get a job with decent salary so that I could pay back my family, especially my brother. . . . I owed him so much and money was the only thing I could give him to thank his sacrifice for my education.

Qunhuan had a brother who is four years younger than he is and was about to go to high school at the time when Qunhuan was graduating. This meant that Qunhuan's brother would be in high school when Qunhuan went to college. Since high school is not a part of compulsory education in China, every high school charges tuition and fees. For a family like Qunhuan's, it was impossible to pay for both his college education and his brother's high school education at the same time. One of them had to make the sacrifice for the other. Qunhuan's father finally decided to fully support Qunhuan to go to college because he had gone so far on the path to college and was very close to his goal. "My brother wasn't very good in school, so he didn't care too much about it," Qunhuan said. "Nevertheless, I still feel guilty about the fact that he had to quit after middle school and went to do labor work in a city in the south."

After serious consideration, Qunhuan chose material engineering as his major, which cost a third of the tuition for electrical engineering. The tuition for electrical engineering was 8,000 yuan per year at Shanghai Transportation University, which was nearly the total amount of his family's annual income and thus was just not a feasible choice.

Qunhuan successfully passed the national unified college entrance examinations in June 2006 and was admitted to his first-choice college, Shanghai Transportation University, in August. As promised, the head of the village loaned him 10,000 yuan for his first-year tuition and fees. Qunhuan was also hoping that because of his outstanding performance in science, he might be able to get a scholarship. Although Qunhuan was from a low-income family and was desperately in need of money, he knew nothing about financial aid and student loans.

Even after Qunhuan had already filled out the whole college application form, his parents still had no idea about which universities he was applying to. They did not know exactly what kind of university Shanghai Transportation University was. They consistently referred to it as "the university in Shanghai" and to them that was good enough. Qunhuan's admission to college has certainly brought them joy. They were so proud that Qunhuan was the first one in their village who was going to a "real" university; however, college tuition and fees brought them a huge financial burden. They did not even know whether their family could survive or Qunhuan could persist in college.

NOTE

1. Every university has different entrance scores for different provinces.

8

Nancheng High School Students

The senior class in Nancheng High School had 313 students, and class size averaged around 60 students. The majority of the class chosen for this study had working-class parents, with only seven students from farming families. In this graduating class, 68 percent of the students directly went on to college; however, only 9 percent of them went to four-year colleges and none of them attended out-of-province universities. The ten students interviewed for the study had a wide range of academic achievement, from A students to low-performing students. Among these ten students, six went to Anhui University, Anhui Normal University, Wuhu Mechanical College, Wuhu Normal College (2), and Wuhu Traditional Medicine College. One student interviewed for the study did not get accepted into any college but decided to repeat the senior year in high school. The other three students decided not to continue their education beyond high school.

ZHANG HUIFENG

Family Background

Zhang Huifeng's father has a high school diploma and is working as a mechanic at a Wuhu machinery factory. His mother is working at the same factory as a machine operator, with only elementary education. They are living in the suburbs. The house they are currently staying in is about to be torn down by the government in order to build a new apartment complex. However, the whole process is taking a long time, three years up to the interview time. The house is very small and shared by three families. Huifeng's family has two rooms and shares a bathroom with another family on the second floor. Some of the houses in the neighborhood have already been torn down, so the whole community looks like a construction site, covered in mud and dust.

Early Influence Stage

Huifeng did not recall any early educational experience at home except that his parents taught him to count from one to a hundred before he went to elementary school. Nevertheless, he liked school and did fine in elementary school. Huifeng's parents had rules about doing homework before he could watch television or play with other children. They usually looked through his homework to make sure that he had actually done the work. "We didn't really think of a college education at that time," his father said. "We just wanted him to do well in school. Everybody knows that education is important. So, we wanted him to receive as much education as he could."

Unfortunately, after graduating from elementary school, Huifeng did not win the lottery to the key middle school, Fuzhong. A close friend of his father told them that they could pay an extra amount of 5,000 yuan per semester to get Huifeng in Fuzhong. Although they were very hesitant about the choice because it was a large amount of money that was more than two months of his parents' combined salaries, Huifeng's parents still went to Fuzhong to talk to the person in charge. They were put on a waiting list. After one month of waiting, they were officially informed that the admission quota was full and Huifeng did not get in. Huifeng's parents had no idea that besides the money, they had to get in contact with those people who were in charge or to have some sort of inside connection. When they found that out, it was too late. So, Huifeng ended up going to an ordinary middle school in their community and gradually trailed far behind those who went to the key middle school.

Predisposition Stage

Huifeng is a self-motivated student. Although he was disappointed at the fact that he did not get to go to Fuzhong middle school, he continued to study hard and mainly received As for his schoolwork. Therefore, it really puzzled him that although he was one of the best students in his middle school, he still missed the admission score to Fuzhong high school by ten points. "I don't understand." Huifeng said, "I did all the homework. I did well in every test in school. I was really serious about my achievement, and so were my parents. . . . I performed normally in the high school entrance examinations, but I still failed to get into Fuzhong. . . . I was really wondering what kind of people could get in."

At that time, Fuzhong had a policy that within 30 points below the cut-off score, students could buy into Fuzhong high school by paying an extra amount of 7,000 yuan per semester. This additional charge and the normal tuition and fees added up to the shocking number of 8,500 yuan per semester for a high school education. Although Huifeng's parents had enough savings to pay for the total expenses, they did not think a high school education was worth it. Huifeng's father said, "We talked to Huifeng about this issue. We asked him if he wanted to go to college one day. He said yes. So, we said, 'Well, then we had to save the money for your college education.'" Huifeng's parents believed that if Huifeng continued to perform well in high school, he would be able to go to college even though he was not in a key high school. Huifeng doubted this point. His experience in the high school entrance examinations scared him. He became suspect of the chance for him to go to college if he could not go to a key high school and desired to go to Fuzhong. However, he did not know how to deal with the financial barrier his family was facing.

> I guess I could have insisted on going to Fuzhong. They probably would have let me. I'm sure I'd be able to go to college if I went to Fuzhong. . . . Fuzhong has almost a 100 percent college enrollment rate. . . . I knew it because it was published in *Wuhu Daily* every year . . . but the question is, how could we pay for my college education if we had already used up all the savings? So, I came to Nancheng. I don't think I had a choice.

In the end, Huifeng went to Nancheng high school and decided to devote himself to hard work in order to go to college. He even quit playing soccer after class, which was his only hobby. He did not visit the bookstore on a regular basis and went there only when there were some supplementary textbooks or examination exercise books he wanted to get. He did not read for fun. He and his parents thought that extracurricular reading would distract his attention from his study, so their family did not subscribe to any magazines or newspapers. He sometimes watched television for entertainment. "But it was only during the weekend," his father said. "We wanted him to spend 100 percent of his time on studying to secure the opportunity to go to college."

Search Stage

Huifeng had been determined to go to college ever since the moment he decided to come to Nancheng high school and saved the money for his college education. Nevertheless, not until in senior year did he begin to think seriously about his college choices. He wanted to go to a four-year institution, which he referred to as "a real university." His parents thought that

he was too ambitious about his college plans and suggested he start with a
two-year community college. His father said,

> We know that people with an associate degree earn a whole lot more than
> people with only a high school diploma. But, there is no big difference [in sal-
> ary] between an associate degree and a bachelor's degree . . . and it takes only
> two years [to earn an associate degree], so we think it is a better choice.

Moreover, Huifeng's parents were also concerned that a four-year university
would cost too much and they would have to borrow to pay for Huifeng's college education. "We are not comfortable with taking a loan. We never borrow
money from other people," Huifeng's father indicated. Regarding the college
cost, Huifeng thought of doing some part-time work while enrolled in college
or taking some summer jobs to help with paying for the tuition and fees. He
also learned about a student loan from the daughter of his neighbor, who
went to a four-year college two years ago and took a loan from the government. Huifeng did not know about it in detail yet, but he thought that when
the moment came, he would go over to his neighbor to ask about it.

Huifeng stopped communicating his thoughts about colleges with his
parents when he learned that they preferred a community college to a four-
year institution. "I know they are worried about money," Huifeng said. "I
just need them to pay for the first two year's costs. After that, I'd come up
with something, a loan or a part-time job." Huifeng turned to his homeroom teacher to seek for information about different four-year institutions
in the Anhui province. The teacher recommended three universities to him.
Two of them are located in Hefei, the capital of the Anhui province. One
is Anhui University, and the other is Anhui University of Technology. The
third one is Anhui Normal University, which is located in Wuhu. Huifeng
ruled out Anhui Normal University immediately because he did not want
to become a teacher and he also did not want to stay in Wuhu for college.
"I wanted to get away from my parents," Huifeng admitted. "They're too
strict with me and sometimes make me depressed. I want to go somewhere
else for college, but not too far from home. So, Hefei is a good place to go."

During the same period of time, Huifeng's parents also asked around
about choices for community colleges in Wuhu. They found out that Wuhu
Mechanical Engineering College is relatively good among all the community colleges in Wuhu and that its graduates have easy access to technician
positions in a lot of factories in Wuhu. "I asked several engineers I worked
with in my factory. Two of them graduated from Wuhu Mechanical Engineering College. So, I thought this could be a good choice for Huifeng,"
Huifeng's father said.

Therefore, Huifeng and his parents had different college choices in
mind until the last moment when Huifeng was filling out his college application form.

Choice Stage

Huifeng's parents finally gave in and decided to support Huifeng's choice of college. "We didn't think he would get into a four-year institution, so we said, 'Well, if you can get an admission [to a four-year college], we'll support you.'"

Huifeng was not sure of his academic skills and was not clear about his career interests, he therefore had no idea which program he wanted to major in. He actually did not care about his college major. All he was concerned about was to getting into a four-year institution. Although Huifeng was one of the best students in his class, he was clearly aware of the fact that the percentage of students in his high school going to four-year institutions was very low and he feared that the nightmare he had with the high school entrance examinations would repeat. Therefore, to secure his chance to get into one, he thought of applying for programs in agriculture, a department that very few students would like to go as their first choice. Once again, his parents disagreed with him on this idea. This time, they had very strong opinions. They would like him to major in mechanical engineering. They knew how much technicians working at their factory got paid. They thought that was a decent salary, and they wanted Huifeng to be able to work as a technician and to have much less financial stress than they had been experiencing. They emphasized that this was the whole point of them paying for Huifeng's high school and continuing to support his college education. They would not let him choose agriculture as a major, even if it would mean to deprive him of the only chance to go to a four-year university. To them, there was not much difference between a bachelor's degree and an associate degree. The most important thing was to be able to get a well-paid job after graduation. Prestige of universities was the last thing they cared about. Because of his parents' strong opinions about the choice for his major, Huifeng finally chose mechanical engineering for his preferred undergraduate program.

Fortunately, Huifeng performed exceedingly well in the national college entrance examinations and became one of the ten students at Nancheng high school who were admitted to a four-year institution in 2006. Huifeng became a freshman at Anhui University.

GAO MANYUE

Family Background

Gao Manyue's father is a middle school graduate. He used to work at the largest nation-owned textile mill in Wuhu but got laid off in the mid-1990s when the factory was carrying out a reform and trying to cut back on the expenses by laying off all the employees without a high school diploma. He is now working for a small hardware factory. Her mother used to work in the same textile mill as her father and got laid off around the same time. She is now staying at home and taking care of her own parents. Her mother's siblings therefore pay her a small amount of cash every month for being the primary caregiver to their parents. The total family income per month is about 1,000 yuan.

They are living in the suburbs. It is a very old-style apartment building. It only has two restrooms on both ends of the corridor, which are shared by eight families. Manyue's family has two rooms. One is her parents' bedroom. The other one is used as living room, dining room, and Manyue's bedroom.

Early Influence Stage

Before going to elementary school, Manyue spent most of her time at her grandparents' place. Because her parents were both working outside the home and could not take care of her, they dropped her at her grandparents' place in the morning and picked her up at night. The only thing Manyue could recall for that period of time was that her grandparents often told the best stories.

Manyue's father indicated that his wife and he both cared about Manyue's education a lot and their family began to save for Manyue's education from the very beginning.

> We didn't send her to a kindergarten or preschool because there were no good ones in our community and kids didn't learn much there. So, we thought why don't we just let her grandparents take care of her and save the money for later? . . . I sometimes taught her some Chinese characters at night. That was about it. . . . I didn't want to force her to study too early and make her lose the interest to learn even before going to school.

However, Manyue never really showed any interest to learn. She said, "I've hated school since I was little." She recalled that in the first few days in elementary school, she cried all day at school and sometimes the teacher had to order her to stop. "The teacher threatened to throw me out of the classroom if I continued crying, but I just couldn't stop myself." It took her a couple of months to slowly adjust to the school environment.

Manyue began having some problems with math in first grade. "I've never been very strong in math. It's just a bad subject for me," she indicated. Manyue said her father sometimes tried to get involved in helping her with math homework, and they would argue about it.

> We've had a lot of arguments about that because I'd try to do it one way and try to figure it out, and he'd come in and try to tell me another way to do it. That wouldn't work at all and he insisted it was right and we just had a lot of fights over it. I gave up after a while and simply copied what he said.

Other than math, Manyue was doing fine in elementary school. She was about the average in class. In her spare time, she liked to read storybooks. She used to borrow them from her classmates and "just sit there and read for hours to finish one story." Her parents were fine with her extracurricular readings until her last year of elementary school. She got caught reading storybooks in math class several times. Her homeroom teacher reported them to her parents. At home, her parents also caught her covering her storybooks with her math textbook and pretending to study but actually reading the storybook. "I got really angry at her," her father said. "I told her that if I ever found any nontextbooks at home, I'd tear them apart. I know she borrowed them from her classmates, so she had to use her pocket money to pay them back. . . . She knew I was not just saying it, that I'd actually do it, so she stopped."

After elementary school, Manyue went to an ordinary middle school in her community. Her early school experiences were not happy, but her life in middle school became even more miserable.

Predisposition Stage

Like other students I interviewed in Nancheng high school, Manyue did not win the lottery to any key middle school, nor could her family buy her way into it after she graduated from elementary school. The extra 5,000 yuan tuition per semester was simply too high for her family to afford. Therefore, her parents sent her to the ordinary middle school in their community, which cost nothing other than about a hundred yuan per year for textbooks. Manyue began to have more problems with schooling about the time she started middle school. Her father was not sure of the reasons.

> In elementary school, she was doing fine except for math. She was not at the top of her class, but fine. Middle school became much more difficult. Besides math, she did poorly in physics and chemistry, too. Her grades began to slip; sometimes she got an F in her math or other science classes . . . even the composition class that she used to be good at became so-so. . . . I don't know, maybe lack of motivation, lack of interest.

Manyue's parents became really worried about her schoolwork. In the second year of middle school, her parents started to send her to her math teacher's home for tutoring during the weekend. It cost her parents 200 yuan per month, 20 percent of their family income. However, Manyue did not think it was helpful.

> Basically, my teacher just repeated what he said in class. It didn't make sense in class, and it didn't help when he explained it for the second time.

. . . I don't know where the problem is. Maybe I just don't have the talent in math or science.

Upon graduating from middle school, Manyue was faced with two choices: going to a vocational school or going to an ordinary high school. On one hand, she did not want to go to a vocational school because she did not know what her interest was and could not pick a specialization. As Manyue put it, "I couldn't decide which program to go into and tell myself with confidence that 'this is it. This is what I want to do for my life.'" On the other hand, she was not sure if she could handle the course work in high school because she has already been struggling a lot in middle school. It was her father who insisted she should go to an ordinary high school. Her father did not have a clear college plan for Manyue at that time; however, he thought that she should at least obtain a high school diploma and keep the option of going on to college open. Therefore, in Manyue's case, although she did not develop an aspiration in middle school to attend college, because of her father's insistence, she chose an ordinary high school over a vocational secondary school to keep the chance for a college education open.

Because her family was living in the suburbs, the middle school in her community was poorly equipped in terms of facilities and teachers. In the high school entrance examinations, only the top student passed the admission score to Fuzhong high school. Most students went to the vocational school. Manyue was not good with any test. In the high school entrance examinations, she did not pass the admission score for Nancheng high school, which was the only ordinary high school in the community. Since her father made the decision for her to go on to an ordinary high school, Manyue's family had to pay an extra amount of 2,000 yuan per year to get her place in Nancheng high school.

Search Stage

Although Manyue sometimes had fights with her parents over schoolwork, she still understood and appreciated how much her parents had sacrificed for her education. She indicated that for years, her parents had never bought any new clothes for themselves and never went out for dinner or any entertainment. They saved every penny they earned to pay for her education. She always felt guilty for not being a good student. She tried very hard and did not understand why she could not succeed in school.

Manyue's parents usually went out to play mahjong with neighbors to relax after work. Manyue indicated that her parents were very concerned about her study, so they never invited any friends to come over to play mahjong. They always went to other people's places and left a quiet room for her to work on her schoolwork. Sometimes she found it difficult to control herself when her parents were away. Her mind sometimes just drifted off to other things, such as a TV drama. She very carefully controlled herself so as not to spend too much time on reading books other than textbooks. She was proud of herself for being disciplined since starting high school and never wasting time on any "irrelevant" reading materials. Nevertheless, very often when she was studying and encountering something she did not understand, she had nobody to talk to and she got stuck and could not move on. "My life continued to be miserable in high school," Manyue complained. "I can't wait until the day when I don't have to study."

In their sophomore year of high school, every student has to make a decision between two different tracks: the science track or the arts and humanities track. Manyue's father planned everything for her. He decided that Manyue should choose science not humanities as her major despite that she did poorly with all science subjects and had no interest in them at all. He reasoned that because there were more colleges and programs in science than in humanities, there would be a better chance for his daughter to get into college if she chose the science track. In fact, he was right about that. Generally, the science track has a higher college enrollment rate than the arts and humanities track. Manyue was fine with her father's decision. "I'm not good at history and politics either, so I don't really care," Manyue said. "My parents talked to me about college a couple of times in the first two years of high school. I wasn't very excited about the idea of going to college, so they didn't mention it very often. But I guess my dad never gave up the idea for me to go to college."

Manyue's father played a major role in her college decision-making process. He actually somehow decided the college and major for her. Manyue did not think about which college she should apply to until the last semester of her senior year when her homeroom teacher asked the whole class to think about this issue. Manyue told her father about it and surrendered the decision to her father immediately and completely. Her father began to ask around to his co-workers and got two colleges for his daughter to pick. One was Wuhu Traditional Chinese Medicine College and the other was Wuhu Mechanical Engineering College. Both are two-year community colleges. Given Manyue's low academic achievement, she and her parents never thought a four-year university could be a possible choice.

Choice Stage

In early June 2006, Manyue participated in the national unified college entrance examinations. Unfortunately, she failed again, and her total achievement score did not reach any admission score for any college. Consequently, she was turned down by both Wuhu Mechanical Engineering College and

Wuhu Traditional Chinese Medicine College. Because of his own negative experiences with lack of adequate education, Manyue's father placed great importance on a college education. Although disappointed at her achievement in the college entrance examinations, he still encouraged Manyue to repeat the senior year of high school and to try again the next year. Manyue had no choice but to accept her father's arrangement. She repeated her senior year at Nancheng high school.

Manyue's father was also very aware that his own educational level limited his ability to help his daughter with her study. To compensate for that, he decided that he would give his daughter full financial support. He was trying to quit smoking in order to save a bit more money because of the unexpected cost from his daughter having to repeat the senior year of high school. Manyue's parents have almost exhausted their savings to pay for all of her educational expenses over the years. Her father did not know about financial aid. He mistook financial aid for merit-based scholarship and thought that his daughter's academic performance was not good enough to earn any scholarship. Her father said that they probably would have to borrow from relatives or friends to pay for Manyue's college education if she can make it to college after repeating her senior year of high school.

HUANG XIAOMIN

Family Background

Huang Xiaomin's father is a high school graduate working as a boilermaker at the Wuhu steel factory. Her mother has only elementary school education. She used to be a farmer and recently moved to the city. She is now a part-time housekeeper. Xiaomin grew up in the countryside with her mother until she graduated from middle school. When she turned 17 years old, her father brought her to the city in order to send her to high school and later moved the whole family to the city. Xiaomin has a younger brother, who has mental disabilities and did not finish his elementary education.

They were living in a poor community in the suburbs of Wuhu. They only had two small rooms in a two-story house and shared a kitchen and a bathroom with other three families. Xiaomin's father made a small loft for her in the roof. The loft was tiny and could only contain one small bed. Xiaomin usually studied in the living room, which was also used as her brother's bedroom.

Early Influence Stage

Like most children in the countryside, Xiaomin did not have any kindergarten or preschool experience. Before going to elementary school, she spent most of her time helping her mother with household chores, doing some simple work in the field, and taking care of her brother, who is two years younger.

Xiaomin's parents had been separated since the beginning of their marriage and were not reunited until recently. Her father worked in the steel factory in the suburbs and came back home every two weeks. Her mother stayed in the village, taking care of the farm and two kids. Xiaomin did not go to elementary school until she turned eight. Her mother was simply too busy with farming and housework and did not notice that Xiaomin had reached school age. Therefore, Xiaomin went to school at a slightly older age than other kids.

Xiaomin was a well-behaved and cheerful student with a positive attitude to life. Although she started school a bit late and did not receive any early education at home, she did fine in elementary school.

> A lot of kids in my class had already achieved a higher level and knew how to write their names and count numbers. I knew nothing, and I'm older than most of them. So, I tried to make friends with them and study with them, just kind of absorbing what they were doing. . . . School was fun. It's definitely more exciting than working in the field, feeding pigs, and making meals. . . . I still had to do most of the work at home, but school was a good place to escape, so I liked it a lot.

As mentioned before, Xiaomin's brother has mental disabilities. He went to the same elementary school a year later but could not keep up with the class. He had to repeat first and second grades. The teacher lost patience with him and suggested her parents take him out of school. Her brother never received any formal or informal education since then and has been helping her mother with farming. In contrast, Xiaomin successfully passed the middle school entrance examinations and went to the neighboring village for middle school.

Predisposition Stage

As a girl growing up in the countryside, Xiaomin was among the fortunate ones, and she was very aware of it. Although her parents could not help her with her homework, they encouraged her to get an education. Grateful for her parents' supportive attitude toward her education, Xiaomin studied very hard in school and was one of the best students in her class in middle school. Her score in the high school entrance examinations passed the admission point for the high school in the nearest county seat. Xiaomin was very excited about it and was ready to go. In the following weekend, her father came back home and learned the news that she did quite well in the entrance examinations. Given that the quality of teaching in the village's middle school was significantly lower than the schools in the county seat or in the city, her father was surprised that she could pass the admission score. For the first time, her father sat her down and asked her, "Do you want to go to college?" Although Xiaomin had been working hard in school, she never really thought of what she was trying to achieve. Nevertheless, she was so excited about the very word "college" and she jumped and responded to her father with a firm "yes." A month later, her father came back with the news that shocked everyone in the family—he would bring Xiaomin to the city for high school.

> Honestly, I've never paid much attention to my daughter's education. I knew she was smart and diligent, but because she is a girl, I didn't really expect her to achieve anything. . . . But at that moment, I suddenly realized that she might have a chance to go to college and therefore completely change her life. So, I thought I had to help her.

Nancheng high school was in the community where her father's factory was located. Her father went to the admission office at Nancheng with Xiaomin's academic performance reports from middle school and her score in the high school entrance examinations to see if they would admit her. The admission administrator approved of Xiaomin's academic achievement. However, since Xiaomin did not have the city residence certificate, Nancheng school would charge them an extra amount of 3,000 yuan every year in addition to tuition and fees. Her father agreed to pay all the additional expenses and went back to the countryside to announce the big news.

In the fall of 2003, Xiaomin came to the city of Wuhu for her high school education. It was an eye-opening experience for her. Even though Nancheng high school is only an ordinary school, it is still much better than what she had seen in the countryside.

> My village does not have its own high school. Middle school graduates from my village have to walk five kilometers everyday to the nearest county seat for high school . . . no school bus or anything like that. . . . You have to leave home at five in the morning, and get back home eight at night. . . . Still, the high school has nothing to compare with Nancheng. . . . I'm really lucky to be here, and I promise myself I'll make as much use of it as I can.

Search Stage

Because of her positive attitude and high motivation to study, Xiaomin has been among the top of her class in high school. Generally, her peers from the city often figured that they were in an average high school with a low enrollment rate to college and therefore did not bother to study hard.

In contrast, Xiaomin felt she was among the privileged few who could make it from a small village to the second largest city in her province and get the chance to study in a city high school. She very much appreciated the opportunity and believed that once in the city, a college education was not something impossible.

In her second year of high school, a neighbor's daughter went to a normal college in another city in the Anhui province. They began to talk about college life when they ran into each other in the public kitchen shared by their families. Xiaomin began to search for information about different colleges and universities in Anhui. After a lot of research, she set her heart at Anhui University, a provincial key university located in the capital city, Hefei.

> I know I'm ambitious. But I thought I had to come to Wuhu from a small village for high school. I could as well go to the capital city to attend the college. Who knows, from my experiences, everything is possible.

Xiaomin wanted to major in marketing and dreamed of finding a well-paid job in business after graduation. "I worked even harder in the next two years of high school," Xiaomin said. "I never had any spare time. I was always studying, studying, and studying."

Choice Stage

In the last semester of high school, Xiaomin was satisfied with her academic performance and quite confident that she would be able to achieve her ideal college choice—Anhui University. She did not talk to her parents about her ideas because she thought they had no experience with college application and probably would have no knowledge about which university would be good for her either. But she still wanted to talk to someone about her plan just to make sure it was reasonable. "So, I decided to go to talk to my homeroom teacher, although I hated to talk to the teacher after class. . . . somehow it's just so intimidating." The conversation she had with her homeroom teacher disappointed her at the beginning. For the first time, Xiaomin realized that academic achievement could get one into a college, but he/she still had to have the financial ability to pay for it. She learned from the teacher that the business school usually charges much higher tuition than other departments. "It was a huge disappointment," she said. "I knew instantly that I had to change my choice, at least for the major." She was very aware of her family's financial situation and knew for sure that there was no way for her family to afford more than 5,000 yuan for tuition every year, which was almost half of her family's annual income.

Her teacher understood the financial difficulty that her family was facing. He told her that normal colleges and universities usually charge relatively low tuition and even provide monthly subsidies to students. He recommended Anhui Normal University to Xiaomin. "My teacher said it's a good university, too. And, it also has a business department but charges lower tuition because after all it's a normal university. So, I decided to stick to my preference for major, but change my college choice."

Money was definitely a concern in Xiaomin's college decision making. She knew that her parents did not have much savings and they also had to take care of her brother financially. So, apparently going to a normal college was the best choice for her family, even if it was not for her. Her parents were completely absent in her college choice process. She mentioned it once to her parents, and her parents were fine with whatever she had decided. "I believe she has the ability to decide whatever is the best for her," Xiaomin's father said, "My job was to give her the chance to receive a high school education in the city. Now her fate is totally up to herself."

Xiaomin successfully passed the national college entrance examinations, and became a freshman in business at Anhui Normal University in fall 2006.

XIE ERPING

Family Background

Xie Erping's father is a graduate from Wuhu vocational secondary school. He used to work as an assistant chef at the Wuhu textile factory. Erping's mother is a middle school graduate and used to be a worker at the same textile factory. In the mid-1990s, both of Erping's parents were laid off when the factory was carrying out a reform to cut production expenses. Erping's family is now running a food stand in their neighborhood. His parents do everything from ordering meat and vegetables, to selling, cooking, and cleaning dishes. They usually work more than 14 hours per day, covering food for breakfast, lunch, and dinner.

Early Influence Stage

Erping did not have any experience with kindergarten. His grandparents had been taking care of him until the year when he was sent to a preschool. Erping did not remember much from that period of time. "Nothing serious," he recalled, "just playing with other kids." He did not learn how to read or write before elementary school. The two Chinese characters for his first name are very simple, but not the character for his last name. Erping told me as a joke that he could not write his last name on his homework assignments for a long time, so the teachers had to call him without his last name, which is very awkward in the Chinese culture.

In his second year in elementary school, Erping's parents both lost their jobs. The family went through a very difficult time. After the first emotional wave of shock, sadness, and anger, his parents began to look for new jobs. According to Erping, his father had been a janitor, and his mother had been a cleaning lady. However, since neither of them had a fixed income and both of their salaries were very low, they could hardly support the family. A year later, they got this idea of opening a food stand. Erping's family was living in a two-bedroom apartment on the ground floor. Their balcony was facing to the main street in their neighborhood. Thus, they had their balcony and living room reconstructed into a small food stand. During the two months of renovation, Erping had to stay with his grandparents. Erping recalled that he began to be truant from that time.

> My grandparents didn't set any ground rules for homework. They didn't even know if I went to school or not. I'd sometimes go somewhere with other kids during the school day, and they never found out. . . . I don't think the teachers cared. And at that time my family didn't have a telephone, so getting in contact with my parents was not easy for the teacher anyway.

According to Erping, his academic performance was always below the average. His parents' bottom line for his achievement was that he should not fail any subject and should not repeat a grade. "I didn't like school," Erping said, "but I still tried. I almost never failed any test in elementary school." Erping's parents think that Erping is not "school material." Erping's mother said,

> He didn't like to study. We didn't have any rules for him. . . . I think a kid would study hard if he wanted to, and he wouldn't need any supervision. My son doesn't like school, and we don't think he would have been a better student if we pushed him.

Since Erping's parents opened the food stand, they have been completely occupied by the business. Generally, they had to get up at four in the morning to start the preparation, and busied themselves with providing breakfast, lunch, and dinner through the whole day until ten at night. They did not have any weekends and holidays. Because of the intense work, Erping's parents had no time or energy to care about his study. Sometimes the food stand was so noisy at night that Erping could not concentrate on finishing his homework. Oftentimes he would take his homework to his classmates' homes in order to finish the assignments, but he ended up spending the whole night playing video games somewhere on his way. Sometimes when his parents were too busy, Erping had to help with washing vegetables and dishes.

Predisposition Stage

In middle school, Erping's grades began to drop dramatically. He continued to go to school, but he mainly wanted to hang out with his friends. Erping said, "I wasn't really interested in doing the work. I just wanted to pass it and get it over with." However, upon graduation, Erping chose to go on to an ordinary high school. He had a big fight with his parents over where he should go for school. His parents wanted him to go to his father's alma mater, Wuhu vocational secondary school, and to take cooking as his specialization. The business of the food stand was getting better, and Erping's parents felt that they could not handle all the business by themselves, but they did not want to hire help. They wanted Erping to get a certificate in cooking and help with their business. However, that was not what Erping wanted for his life.

> I hate the food stand. It smells, and it's so greasy. . . . They never had any weekends or holidays because during weekends and holidays business was always better. . . . They worked more than 14 hours a day but made very little money—so little that they had to do everything themselves and couldn't hire help. . . . I don't want to spend my life like that.

Although Erping was very clear about what he did not want to do, he was not sure what really interested him either. Vocational secondary schools require students to indicate the specific vocation they want to major in when they are applying. For this simple reason, Erping went to an ordinary high school so that he would have three more years to think about what he was interested in and willing to pursue in his life.

Choice Stage

Finally, Erping went to Nancheng high school. He continued to do inadequate work in school and could hardly catch up with the class. Students who are at risk for academic problems and failure are not new to faculty at Nancheng high school. Their expectations for students are that they graduate from high school so that the school can keep its 100 percent graduation rate. "I don't think the teachers cared. As long as I didn't fight with anyone and could pass the test, they'd leave me alone."

Erping never thought a college education could be an option for him. His parents never discussed a possibility for a college education with him. Although teachers sometimes encouraged them to study hard in order to prepare themselves for the college entrance examinations, Erping did not feel that was something relevant to his life. "Teachers were really just talking to those good students," he said, "not to someone like me. Plus, even those good students probably wouldn't be able to get into college. You know, we are in a pretty bad school." So he did not even bother to think about it. His parents wanted him to help them with the food stand after he graduated from high school. However, he had no interest in their suggestion. Instead, he preferred to be a construction worker. He commented,

> I want to become a construction worker. It's manly . . . and I can at least learn some skills. That might be helpful and bring me some other chance in the future.

When asked if going to vocational schools would be more helpful given that those schools provide professional training for some construction work, he admitted that it would be, but "nobody told [him] about it" before he made his choice to go to high school.

Erping did not find any job after he graduated from high school. Unfortunately, despite his strong dislike of the food stand, he is currently helping his parents with their business.

LIN CONGBO

Family Background

Lin Congbo's parents are both farmers, and both have a middle school education. Congbo has an elder sister, who is two years older and a middle school graduate. They are all living in the countryside 40 kilometers away from Wuhu. The family income is around 20,000 yuan a year. Congbo lived with his uncle in Wuhu city for three years in high school.

Early Influence Stage

Congbo lived a typical life for a child born in the countryside. He began to help his parents feed pigs, hens, and ducks when he was four. He started to work in the field when he turned seven. Oftentimes he accompanied his mother to the county seat during the weekend to sell eggs and some fresh vegetables. Congbo did not receive any early education at home, nor did he have any preschool experiences.

Congbo went to elementary school in his village at age seven. His village was a rather large village in that area, therefore it had relatively better school facilities. The school had a two-story building and a small playground. The elementary school occupied the first floor, and the second floor was for middle school. The school had ten teachers altogether. Quite a few children in the neighboring villages also came to this school for their middle school education. Congbo liked school in general and did fine with schoolwork.

> I was not a star student in any class, but I did fine with every subject. . . . My parents didn't have any rules for homework. . . . I went to school with my sister and came back home with her. She kind of supervised me, making sure I was not hanging out with other kids after school but going back home immediately and that I was doing my homework.

Congbo never had any difficulties with reading, but did not really enjoy it either. His family did not subscribe to any magazines or newspapers. When asked, he laughed and said, "The postman comes to the village only once per week," and indicated that people use the post office only for really important things, "like someone died or got a college admission or something."

Predisposition Stage

Congbo did not give a thought to his future until middle school when his father brought up the topic. "My dad asked me what I wanted to do when I've grown up, and I said, 'I don't know.'" Congbo's father then explained his plan for him. His father wanted him to finish high school and then join the army. It was the first time that Congbo's father expressed his expectation for Congbo's education and his future. It was also the first time that Congbo began to contemplate what he wanted to do in the future.

From the mid-1990s when Congbo was in elementary school, more and more young people in his village went to the city to become migrant workers. According to Congbo, almost every family in the village had at least one member who become a migrant worker in the city. They toiled mostly on the construction sites in the urban areas, working long hours every day but being paid very little, usually around 20 Chinese yuan per day. Many of them had very bad experiences working in the urban areas. Some of them never got paid for the work they did for their temporary bosses, who often ran away with their salaries after having finished one project. They were often treated as second-class citizens in the city, where locals looked down on them and government officials frequently harassed them for not being able to get a working permit. Because most of the peasant workers had no official working contract, no insurance, and no benefits, all sorts of tragedies happened to them. One of Congbo's relatives lost his left leg in construction work. He not only did not get any insurance coverage from the company but also was denied half a year's salary. Congbo commented:

> It was too sad. . . . His family spent a lot of money on his medical treatment. He survived, but his family was broke. And now, he is handicapped. A handi-

capped man is totally useless in the countryside. Every time I saw him, I just felt life was so miserable. . . . If he died in the construction site, maybe his family would be able to get some money. Both he and his family would be better off that way.

Congbo decided that he would never become a peasant worker and live his life on the edge. His parents did not want him to take that kind of risk either. His father had a strong opinion that Congbo should not spend his whole life in the countryside and just be a farmer, and he conveyed his thoughts to Congbo. "My dad felt his life was kind of wasted, so he had a huge hope for me. He wanted me to become a city resident," Congbo said. "In the countryside, you need to work really hard in the field, but still can barely afford the basic living." Although Congbo's parents wanted him to get rid of a village life amidst wheat and paddy fields, they did not expect him to go to college. Congbo did not see that a college education was a possibility for him either. He thought that "only the smartest kid in a village could go to college." Since he thought himself an average student, he did not have the ambition for a college education. According to Congbo, people in the countryside all know that there are only three ways to move to the city. The first choice is to go to college. The second choice is to become a migrant worker. The third choice is to join the army. Since he ruled out the first two choices, he was left with the only way out—joining the army.

Choice Stage

Although for a rural youth, fighting his/her way to college is unspeakably difficult, it is not very easy to go into the military either. First of all, one has to have a high school diploma to be recruited into the army. Moreover, there is a quota for recruitment each year. Generally, a city gets a larger recruitment quota, and the county and its villages are assigned a relatively smaller one. From the discussions with his uncle, Congbo's father learned that most city residents do not want to send their children to the army because military life can be hard and the salary is quite low. Therefore, Congbo's father got this idea to send Congbo to the city for high school so that he could be easily recruited to the military from a city high school. Congbo's father consulted with his brother, who is a taxi driver in Wuhu, and decided that Congbo should go to Wuhu for his high school education.

As a taxi driver, Congbo's uncle had a good network to get Congbo into Nancheng high school. Nevertheless, Congbo's parents had to pay an extra amount of 3,000 yuan per year in addition to tuition and fees because Congbo was not a city resident. The total cost of Congbo's high school education was about 25,000 yuan.

Congbo's academic performance in high school was about average. If he would have participated in the national unified college entrance examinations and submitted his application, he would have had a chance to go to a two-year college. However, when asked if he had ever considered a college education as an option, Congbo responded that the idea never occurred to him. Nobody in his family had any college experience. Even his cousin— his uncle's son who was born and raised in the city—did not make it to college. So, Congbo never thought college was an option to him. Moreover, his family had already spent a significant amount of money on his high school education and living expenses in the city, thus he did not think his parents would be able to pay for his college education anyway. Congbo had no knowledge about the financial aid system. At the end of June, Congbo got his high school diploma and went to the army, as he wished to.

9

Cross-Case Analysis

EARLY INFLUENCE STAGE

According to cultural capital theory, children from higher socioeconomic backgrounds are born into home environments in which they are exposed to socially valued knowledge and cultural cues much earlier than children from lower social strata (Bourdieu, 1977a; Bourdieu & Passeron, 1977). Therefore, children from families of higher socioeconomic status already possess more cultural goods and media, such as works of art and instruments, and also develop the ability to understand and appreciate those cultural goods by the time they enter school than do children from families of lower socioeconomic status. More important, the educational system that values certain types of cultural dispositions cannot reduce or eliminate the initial differences in cultural capital. Instead, the school reinforces the initial differences. Students from higher social strata who have more valuable cultural capital to begin with thus do better than their peers with less valuable cultural capital.

The research on the importance of early childhood education also confirms that the earlier children are exposed to language, the better their long-term academic achievement will be. Researchers (Fisch, Smith, & Phinney, 1997; Tokuhama-Espinosa, 2001) point out that from what we've learned about children and their brain development, there are critical windows of opportunity for children to learn language, which unlocks learning puzzles in their future. The family environment and exposure to language are the biggest factors in cognitive development, which translates into achievement success in later years.

From the interviews with students from different family backgrounds, we can see a clear pattern of early childhood family education. All of the students from middle-class families received some kind of education from their parents before going to elementary school. Generally, the parents placed an emphasis on teaching Chinese characters and developing their children's reading abilities. In addition, calligraphy practice and poem recitation were important cultural activities emphasized by middle-class parents. In the following, I will discuss the early family education received by students with different socioeconomic status and analyze the relationship between cultural capital accumulated in early childhood and academic performance in school.

Teaching Chinese Characters

The three middle-class students reported in the previous chapter, Cai Shuang, Wang Yicheng, and Ruan Wei, all had learned to read and write Chinese characters before they started elementary school. Shuang began to learn Chinese characters when she was five and could recognize 100 characters and write at least half of them before elementary school. Yicheng started even earlier, when she was only age four. Yicheng had learned so many Chinese characters that, as her mother claimed, she could read textbooks from the first grade without any problem while she was still in kindergarten. Similarly, Wei's parents taught him Chinese characters before they sent him to kindergarten at age three, thus he could write his name the first day in kindergarten, which really impressed his kindergarten teacher. As a nonalphabetic language, Chinese has a completely different writing system from English. Unlike English, a word in Chinese is represented by distinct symbols that represent meaning instead of sound (Wang, Perfetti, & Liu, 2003). Because of this distinctive feature, writing Chinese is particularly difficult for children who have just learned to speak. Yet, reading and writing Chinese characters, together with math, are the most important skills taught throughout elementary school. Therefore, by teaching their children to read and write Chinese characters, middle-class parents prepared their children at an early age for formal schooling.

This common educational practice is not taken by most of the working-class parents. Among all the working-class students, Shi Juan was an exception. Juan's parents have always placed a great emphasis on their daughter's education. As mentioned earlier, because of the transportation issue, Juan went to the kindergarten that was owned by her mother's factory. It was a poorly equipped kindergarten with underqualified teachers. Therefore, Juan's mother decided to teach her Chinese characters at home. By the time she was going to elementary school, Juan could recognize quite a few Chinese characters and could also write them. Other working-class students interviewed in the study did not have any early family education. Two male students from the working-class families mentioned that they had difficulties writing their names when they started elementary school. In contrast to Wei's case, in which he could write his name at the age of three, Peng shared that the only two words he learned to write in kindergarten were his name, but he still could not write them well so his teachers kept mispronouncing his name. Erping also told as a joke that he could not write his family name because of its complexity, and had to skip his last name whenever he had to sign his name for the first few weeks in elementary school.

None of the students from farming families learned to write or read at home before going to the elementary school. However, different from the argument of cultural capital theory, theses students did not find the school environment hostile. Their unique experiences will be discussed later in this chapter.

Developing Reading Abilities

Since spoken Chinese is highly homophonic, writing has been a practice used in school to help children learn Chinese characters. A Chinese character usually comprises two parts: semantic radicals and phonetics (Cheung & Ng, 2003). The semantic radical represents meaning, and the phonetic component represents sound. Through writing, children learn to deconstruct characters into a unique pattern of strokes and learn both the sound and the meaning. Researchers (Tan et al., 2005) point out that English reading abilities rely more on listening skills, while Chinese reading abilities rely more on writing skills. The parents of the three middle-class students all purposefully connected writing Chinese characters with reading. Yicheng's mother indicated that when she was teaching Yicheng Chinese characters, she tried to find those simple characters in newspaper or magazine she had read and point them out to Yicheng. This strategy made Yicheng really excited about the fact that she could recognize a few Chinese characters in the adults' reading materials and thus felt more motivated to learn. Wei's parents also shared that they taught Wei poems the same time they started teaching him Chinese characters. Wei often felt excited when he found in a poem the Chinese characters he had recently learned. As we can see, their reading abilities developed with writing Chinese characters.

During the interview, the three students also consistently mentioned a love of reading. They were all early readers. Shuang and Yicheng both read a substantial amount of storybooks in kindergarten and preschool. According to his mother, Wei was already reading chapter books when other kids in the same kindergarten just started to learn how to read. In contrast, none of the working-class students or the students from farming families recalled any reading activities before starting first grade. This situation is not unexpected because without learning Chinese characters, it is impossible for someone to read. As some researchers point out (Snow et al., 2007), these differences in early literacy practices at home can contribute to later differences in reading practices and academic achievement in school. This correlation will be examined in the later analysis.

Calligraphy Practice and Poem Recitation

Bourdieu points out that family lifestyles and cultural consumption patterns are critical sources of children's cultural formation. Bourdieu (1977a) considers art, classical music, and literature "beau arts" and contends that beau arts play an important role in formal education. Art museum visits, concert attendance, and literature reading are all concentrated in the upper- and middle-classes families, which represents distinctive cultural traits, tastes, and styles from those of lower- and working-class families. In China, poetry, calligraphy, and painting are considered the three major forms of traditional fine art (Li, 2004). From the interviews, poem recitation and calligraphy practice seemed to be very typical cultural activities among the middle-class families. Six out of seven students from middle-class families interviewed in the study both practiced calligraphy and recited poems from Tang Dynasty in their early childhood.

Chinese poetry is the most highly regarded literary genre in China. As Lee (2000) indicates in his book about the history of Chinese education, poem recitation has been the most common practice used in traditional Chinese education to teach a child literary appreciation and to instill in him/her the sense of Chinese aesthetics. This practice is still commonly employed by Chinese middle-class parents to teach their children Chinese characters and to foster certain unique cultural dispositions. Poems from Tang Dynasty (618–907 AC) are generally accepted to be of good quality, and among them quite a few are regarded as masterpieces. Therefore, most middle-class parents chose poems from Tang Dynasty for their children to study. Yicheng's parents started to teach her to recite poems around age three. Yicheng could remember about ten poems when she was still in kindergarten. Later on when she was in elementary school, her parents began to explain to her the meanings of those poems that she had memorized. According to her parents, she started to appreciate the poems and became interested in literature reading in general. Moreover, middle-class parents also tend to connect poem recitation with word recognition. Certainly, reciting poems enriches a child's vocabulary. According to her mother, Shuang was attracted by the rhythmic and musical sound of the pomes picked by her parents, and she was quite motivated to learn. Her mother also taught her the meaning of those frequently used and rather simple characters in the poems. By the time she went to elementary school, Shuang could recite at least 50 poems and write more than 100 Chinese characters. Finally, poem recitation directly contributes to a child's academic achievement because textbooks for Chinese classes from elementary school to high school include many poems from the ancient historical periods, especially from Tang Dynasty. Reciting poems and explaining their meanings are one of the most common testing items in examinations. Therefore, poem recitation at an early age prepares those middle-class students for formal schooling and for taking examinations.

Chinese calligraphy is a highly sophisticated form of art and widely recognized as bona fide fine art. According to Li (2004), in ancient China calligraphy served more than an artistic or linguistic purpose, it was the passport to the successful official career. Today, the importance of calligraphy in government official career development might have decreased, but it still represents a national taste in art. During the interviews, practicing calligraphy was found to be another popular cultural activity that was concentrated in Chinese middle-class families. First of all, practicing calligraphy is believed to contribute to the development of cognitive and linguistic skills. In ancient China, Wenyen Wen is the literary language used for law, administration, and works of art (Ridgway, 2003), and it is completely different from modern Chinese. In practicing calligraphy, one has to be conversant in the classics, which were written in Wenyan Wen. Studying and copying those poems and prose in the masterpieces of calligraphy are believed to cultivate reading skills and strategies (Tang, 2006). Being familiar with China's rich poetic tradition is also one of the prerequisites for practicing calligraphy (Li, 2004). Therefore, practicing calligraphy can also develop linguistic skills and cultivate aesthetic faculties. Second, practicing calligraphy is also a way for middle-class parents to teach their children to discipline themselves since the practice is an arduous process and requires a lot of patience and attention to detail. Shuang, Yicheng, and Wei all started practicing calligraphy in their early childhood and carried it through middle school. Both of Wei's parents practiced calligraphy as a hobby. They sent Wei to a weekend calligraphy class when he turned four and very often accompanied him to the class and supervised him practicing it. His father indicated that practicing calligraphy is a good way to discipline a child because it requires serenity and fortitude. Shuang's father also pointed out that sending Shuang to learn calligraphy was to cultivate her serious attitude to do things. Since practicing calligraphy is very detail oriented and requires patience and hard work, Shuang's parents believed that it helped Shuang form a good attitude toward studying. Compared to Wei and Shuang, Yicheng started to learn calligraphy a little bit late—in third grade. Her parents insisted that she study calligraphy because it is a precious traditional Chinese art. Yicheng first found the practice tedious and tiring, but she learned to appreciate it later on and claimed that whenever she was anxious about some issues, practicing calligraphy could set her mind at ease.

Shi Juan's parents were not college educated, yet they also regarded calligraphy practice as an important activity. Instead of emphasizing the preciousness of the art, her parents had more practical reasons for encouraging her to practice calligraphy. They thought that if one practiced calligraphy, he/she would naturally have beautiful handwriting, which is important in many aspects. For example, in the test for the subject of Chinese, composition is always the biggest part, which usually takes up 35 percent of the total score. Good handwriting can easily catch the attention of the teacher and make the otherwise average composition stand out, while bad handwriting can wipe out the uniqueness of an excellent piece. Although this point of view was not mentioned in the interviews with the middle-class parents, middle-class students could definitely benefit from this positive effect of good handwriting.

Although Peng and Qunhuan were never sent by their parents to learn calligraphy, they both practiced it because of their high school Chinese teacher. "He was really into calligraphy and asked everybody in the class to practice it," Peng recalled. "He told us how important it is to have good handwriting and asked us to turn in one piece of work every week. . . . So the year he taught us the whole class practiced it." Qunhuan admitted that his handwriting was "unreadable" before the practice and that he really appreciated the teacher's efforts to help him improve. The other working-class students and those from the farming families did not have any experience with practicing calligraphy.

Although the impacts of the school on students' cultural capital and academic achievement are not the focus of this research, we can clearly see from Peng's and Qunhuan's experiences that a good school certainly exerts positive influences on students' cultural capital accumulation.

Early Family Education and School Achievement

Cultural capital theory implies that the family provides a child's first and most significant learning environment and that parents are a child's first and most important teachers. The ability of the parents to provide the best possible environment for their child's learning and growth is very important to the child's academic performance later in school. For those children who have grown up in a home climate in which reading is emphasized, it is much easier for them to adapt to classroom learning once they enter schools (Lamont & Lareau, 1988). In Yicheng's case, the fact that she could read well made her an outstanding student in her class, which cultivated in her high self-esteem and made her more confident and motivated to learn. Yicheng shared her experience of being constantly called by the teacher to the platform to read for the whole class because she could speak clearly and distinctively while most of her peers murmured or stuttered in front of the whole class. Her parents also mentioned how much her teachers adored her and how that made Yicheng always try to do better.

In contrast, for those children who have not learned to deal with certain cultural practices, such as reading, school experiences could be shocking and frightening. Most of the working-class students interviewed in this study went to kindergarten and preschool. In the five cases of working-class students presented in the previous chapters, four of them at least went to preschool, and three had both kindergarten and preschool experience. However, with only one exception, they received no early childhood family education from their parents. And, the kindergarten and the preschool were just places to play with other kids but not a place where they were prepared for formal schooling. During the interview, Manyue's father expressed strong concern about his daughter's education and claimed that Manyue's education was always the number one priority in his family. A lot of events he mentioned that happened later on in Manyue's educational career actually proved that he did care a lot about her education. However, Manyue's parents did not realize how important early childhood family education is. In fact, Manyue was the only one who did not have any kindergarten and preschool experience among the five working-class students. Before going to elementary school, it was her grandparents who were taking care of her. She hated school from day one. During the interview, she recalled how she cried in school from being taken away from her grandparents. Because of her lack of experience with kindergarten or preschool, she could not get used to the classroom environment and hated being seated in a class for 45 minutes straight. The school environment was hostile to her, and she started to struggle with her schoolwork from the very beginning.

Like Manyue, none of the students from farming families had early childhood family education or kindergarten experience. However, they did not find the school environment as unfriendly as Manyue did. The main reason can be that in the rural area, almost none of the students have received any kind of education before attending elementary school. Therefore, they felt more comfortable in such a school setting where nobody had any educational experience beforehand and had to start from the very beginning. However, later on when the best of those students from a village elementary school were admitted to a middle school in a county seat, they experienced a more hostile environment where they were penalized for lacking certain social and cultural habits.

Besides emphasizing the direct effects of early cultural socialization, cultural capital theory also points out that while moving through the educational ladder, for those who begin with more initial cultural capital, cultural capital accumulates at a faster rate than does the cultural capital of those from lower classes. During the interviews, of the six students who positively mentioned elementary school experiences, three were middle-class students.

The three middle-class students, Shuang, Yicheng, and Wei, all did very well in elementary school. Shuang was a straight-A student. She recalled that schoolwork was easy for her in elementary school and she did well in every subject. Besides the schoolwork, Shuang read widely in different fields. She was also very active in extracurricular activities and participated in the school's play club and the literature club. Shuang's parents also pointed out that Shuang absolutely loved school from the very beginning and that she was very self-motivated to learn. "We didn't exert any ground rules for schoolwork or grades," her mother said. "Shuang always wants to be the best, so we figured that there was no need to establish any rules for her regarding her schooling."

Similar to Shuang's experiences, early education received at home also put Yicheng well ahead of her peers when she went to elementary school. Normally, students begin to have foreign language classes in fifth grade. However, Yicheng's father started to teach her English before she started elementary school. At the beginning, her father liked to point out things around the house and told her their names in English. She learned quite a few English words this way. Her father then taught her the letters and instructed her to spell the words for which she had already learned the pronunciation and the meaning. "It was fun," Yicheng said, "I learned it effortlessly. . . . I built my confidence early on, so I never had any problem with my English class, even in high school." Yicheng's parents also indicated that they did not have specific rules for Yicheng in terms of schoolwork and grades. However, Yicheng said, "The rules are always there. . . . They don't emphasize them because they don't want to be pushy, but I know a B will definitely disappoint them. . . . I have a high expectation for myself, too, so I never feel too much pressure from my parents."

Compared to Shuang and Yicheng, Wei's experience in elementary school was quite different. Both Shuang and Yicheng were among the top three students in their classes, while Wei's school achievement was only about the average. Wei shared that the course work in elementary school was so easy that he never really put in much time and energy into school learning. Instead, he engaged himself actively in all sorts of extracurricular activities. He continued to practice calligraphy and drawing. Additionally, he learned to play violin, attended the aircraft modeling class offered by some afterschool programs, and participated in the school's Chinese chess club. He was also a member of the school's soccer team. Wei's parents were highly critical of the test-driven schooling system in China. They indicated that since they felt cramming textbooks down the throats of students was not the way they wanted to teach their son, they did not drill him in school subjects. Instead, they encouraged him to read widely besides textbooks and believed that the extracurricular reading and other activities could "inspire him and let his creativity run free." Therefore, in elementary school, although Wei was not an outstanding student, both he and his parents believed that he actually had more potential and was more capable of learning than most of his peers and that he truly understood what he had learned.

Shi Juan was the only working-class student who mentioned positive school experiences on the elementary level. Juan recalled that the schoolwork in elementary school was not too difficult for her. "My parents had taught me a few Chinese characters and some simple math before I started formal school education. So, Chinese and math, these two main subjects in elementary school were not difficult for me." Juan also recalled that when she earned full scores for her Chinese and math classes in the first final exams in first grade, her parents established their high expectations for her academic achievement. Juan graduated from elementary school as one of the top ten students in her class.

In contrast with Juan's case, Manyue was the only working-class student who had no kindergarten or preschool experience before elementary school. Since the very beginning, the school had been a hostile place to Manyue. It took her a long time to get used to sitting through the 45-minute classes, to learn how to socialize with other children in class, and to understand the teacher's authority. Manyue's comment about the beginning of elementary school was that it was "totally another world." Although Manyue's father did not provide her with any early family education, he still expected her to do well in school. His logic was that "she is not stupid, she does not slack off, and we've always been emphasizing that a good education is important. I just can't see why she can't do well in school." While Manyue was struggling with the school subjects, her father tried to get involved by helping her with her homework, especially math. However, Manyue did not respond to her father's help very well. She complained that her father always came in and told her a way to do it while she was trying to figure out another way herself. They fought about it all the time. Manyue said, "I gave up after a while and simply copied what he said." With this kind of help from her father, Manyue's performance in school did not improve by much. Especially after she graduated from elementary school, when her father could not help with her schoolwork anymore, Manyue could hardly catch up with her class.

Interestingly enough, although none of the three students from the farming families received any early family education, elementary school was a positive experience for all of them. They all lived a typical childhood in rural China before going to school—helping parents with work around the house or in the field. They did not learn any Chinese characters or math from their parents; however, when they went to school, they found the school to be a novel and exciting place for them. As Xiaomin indicated,

> School was fun. It's definitely more exciting than working in the field, feeding pigs, and making meals. . . . I still had to do most of the work at home, but school was a good place to escape, so I liked it a lot.

None of their parents made any specific rules for them regarding school-work or grades. However, both Qunhuan and Xiaomin were very self-motivated to study. According to Xiaomin, the school was a much nicer place compared to home. Their shabby house in the village was dark and dirty. Her mentally handicapped brother required constant care and attention. Her mother, who had to take care of all the work in the field and around the house, was irritable and always complained about little things. Xiaomin sometimes would try to stay in school a bit longer after school was over in order to get her homework done or just to "enjoy the atmosphere there." Qunhuan also liked school a lot from the very beginning. He felt that naturally he was attracted to numbers, so he spent a lot of time studying math and gained a lot of fun from it. Later in elementary school, he realized that being a good student in school was the only way to change his life. "I didn't know how it was going to change my life," Qunhuan recalled, "but somehow I knew a good education was the only way for me to get rid of a farmer's fate." It also gave him strong motivation to learn and to do better in school.

PREDISPOSITION STAGE

As previously indicated, Hossler, Braxton, and Coopersmith (1989) found that the three-stage process of college choice generally begins around seventh grade and ends upon college enrollment. The predisposition stage is in large part dominated by the development of educational aspirations and intentions to continue education beyond high school (Cabrera & LaNasa, 2001; Hossler, Schmit, & Vesper, 1999). In this study, I found that students' expectations for a college education mostly depend on three elements: school culture, students' own academic performance, and parents' expectations.

Opportunities to Enroll in a Key Middle School

In the context of China, the predisposition stage starts with an exceedingly important choice faced by parents and students—which middle school to enroll in. There are three key middle schools in the city of Wuhu.

Before 1998, all elementary school graduates had to take the middle school entrance examinations to compete for the very limited seats in these three schools. Since summer 1998, the policy makers in Wuhu have introduced a voucher system into the middle school enrollment process. Different from the voucher systems in the United States, which are typically based on financial, educational, or geographical need, the voucher system in Wuhu is based on pure luck. Every elementary school graduate is assigned a series of numbers. Lottery is used to determine which students get the vouchers. Students with vouchers can go to the key middle school in their districts. However, each key middle school only enrolls one-third of their freshmen through the voucher system. The other two-thirds of freshmen have to pay additional tuition and fees to get into any of the key middle schools, although a public middle school education is supposed to be free. There is no minimum testing score requirement for admission.

Among the students interviewed in this study, only two out of 25 obtained the voucher to get into Fuzhong middle school. Among the eleven cases studied in more detail, Peng was the only one who won the lottery. During the interview, Peng mentioned a couple of times how important it was for him to gain the chance to go to Fuzhong middle school. He regarded this event as "the turning point" in his life. Peng had never thought of going to college before middle school. However, on his first day in Fuzhong, his homeroom teacher asked everybody to share his/her college dream with one another. It struck him how important a college education seemed to be to everyone. Since then, Peng began to think that a college education might be an option for him. Like Peng, Huifeng was also a male student from a working-class family who was smart and hard working. Peng and Huifeng both did fairly well in elementary school; however, Huifeng was not lucky enough to win the lottery and ended up going to an ordinary middle school. Although Huifeng continued to study hard in middle school and did well in school, he still trailed far behind those who went to the key middle school. Therefore, we can see that in the predisposition stage, which middle school a student can enroll in plays an important role in his/her educational career. Middle-class parents are clearly aware of this fact.

Yicheng's mother was a physics teacher in an ordinary secondary school. When Yicheng graduated from elementary school, she could go to the school where her mother was teaching senior high school classes. As part of the staff's benefit, Yicheng's family would not have to pay any tuition or fees if Yicheng went to her mother's school. However, as a teacher, Yicheng's mother was quite aware of the differences between an ordinary middle school and a key middle school in terms of the quality of teachers and facilities. She said, "We wanted to give her the best education. Money was not a consideration." Yicheng's father agreed with her on this issue. A few months before Yicheng's graduation from elementary school, her parents contacted a few close friends who were either working in Fuzhong or in the local Bureau of Education in order to put Yicheng on those people's private lists. As soon as the results of the lottery came out and they learned that Yicheng did not win the voucher, Yicheng's parents went to those people and made sure that Yicheng's name was on the top of the waiting list. Since they prepared well and acted early, Yicheng was admitted by Fuzhong without any trouble.

I learned from the interviews that every year the waiting list to get into Fuzhong is incredibly long. Without a strong social network, it is almost impossible to buy into Fuzhong middle school. Huifeng's parents were the only working-class parents interviewed in the study who were willing to pay the extra $5,000 each semester to buy the opportunity for Huifeng to go to Fuzhong. However, Huifeng's father told me that they were put on the waiting list for a month but finally did not get in. I learned from Yicheng's father that the waiting list is not open to the public so that those people who have strong networks can squeeze their children's names in and those who are just passively waiting are much less likely to get seats for their children.

Although neither of Juan's parents had a college degree, they both thought highly of education and wanted Juan to go to college. As mentioned before, Juan was the only working-class student in this study who received a fairly good early education before going to school. During her years in elementary school, her parents had high expectations for her and set specific rules for schoolwork and grades. Juan did really well in elementary school; however, she was not one of the few lucky winners of the lottery to Fuzhong middle school. Her parents' initial response to it was that they had no choice but to send her to an ordinary middle school in their community. However, Juan's grandfather, who was a retired math teacher from Fuzhong, insisted that they had to try their best to send Juan to Fuzhong middle school. He used his network to get admission for Juan. Juan's parents were at first upset by the fact that they had to pay $5,000 in extra fees every semester for Juan's admission. According to Juan's father, they wanted to save every penny they could to pay for Juan's college education, so they did not want spend this big amount of money so early on. However, Juan still went to Fuzhong middle school under the condition that her grandfather would pay the additional fees. Juan's parents only learned to appreciate her grandfather's decision three years later when they found out that not a single student in their community middle school reached the admission scores to Fuzhong high school, while Juan passed it without any difficulty.

Among the working-class parents interviewed in this study, Manyue's father and Juan's parents struck me by the importance they placed on their children's education. However, like Juan's parents, when facing the choice about which middle school to attend, Manyue's father chose to send Manyue to an ordinary middle school in order to save the money for her college education later on. This decision showed that although they knew how important a good education is, they did not understand that every single step in their children's education career path is critical. A choice made then can influence their chances to go to college six years later.

Home Environment and Academic Achievement

According to cultural capital theory, a particularly important aspect of family background is the educational resources parents can provide to their children (Bourdieu & Passeron, 1977; Coleman, 1988; DiMaggio, 1982). Valuable educational resources, such as books, newspapers, and computers, can cultivate and foster children's motivation to learn and shape orientations to school. The participation in cultural activities at home makes children become acquainted with cultural cues in formal school education and also leads to the development of knowledge or skills, which both in turn enable students to succeed in school (DiMaggio, 1982, 1985).

The middle-class students interviewed in the study all pointed out that their families subscribed to certain kinds of newspapers and journals. Some of them also emphasized that reading together and sharing what they had read was an important family activity. As indicated previously, the three middle-class students all consistently mentioned a love of reading. Shuang, Yicheng, and Wei all read a significant amount of books before they went to school and continued to read for fun in their spare time after they started formal schooling. Shuang developed a special interest in science and history in middle school, thus her parents subscribed to several magazines in these two fields for her. Both of her parents also liked to read for fun. Shuang indicated that one of her favorite family activities was reading with her parents:

> We all crowded in my dad's study room and read after dinner. Sometimes it would be silent for an hour or so, but then one of us would burst into laughter and read out the funny part to the other two people . . . and we sometimes commented on each other's readings, or argued about issues brought up by one article. . . . It was really fun and I learned a lot from both the books and my parents.

According to cultural capital research (DiMaggio, 1982, 1985), the parental effort found to be most critical to school success is active encouragement of literacy activities, such as reading and writing activities, in the home. Middle-class parents, who are more likely to read books and newspapers regularly at home, have better linguistic skills and can pass these educational skills on to their children. As indicated before, Yicheng developed a special interest in reading literature, especially those masterpieces from British and Russian writers. Reading world classics was also a habit of Yicheng's mother. In fact, Yicheng's first set of world classics was a gift from her mother for elementary school graduation. Since then, she began to buy classical novels with her pocket money. Her parents were very supportive of her extracurricular reading. Yicheng shared that reading those great novels did not distract her attention from formal schooling. Instead, the extracurricular reading in literature and poetry significantly improved her writing skills, which helped her with her Chinese classes and made her stand out in the written composition class,

> Beautiful and powerful words just flew into my mind. And, because I'm familiar with many poems, sometimes I cited quotes from poems in my essay. Teachers were always impressed with that.

As one middle-class parent interviewed in this study commented, "Few children learn to love books themselves. Someone must lure them into the wonderful world of the written word, someone must show them the way." Evidently, middle-class parents are more likely to establish a stimulating learning environment at home and act as role models for their children. The learning environment at home must contribute to the overall higher academic achievement of middle-class students.

In contrast, working-class students did not have an easy access to books and newspapers at home and were also not encouraged to read by their parents. Although they always placed an emphasis on their daughter's education, Juan's parents thought that only formal schooling was important and that extracurricular reading could distract Juan's limited time and energy from studying textbooks. Like Yicheng, Juan was also interested in literature reading. Usually she borrowed from the school library. However, her parents did not allow her much time for extracurricular reading. She recalled that her mother used to say, "For the time you spent reading those novels, you could have done your math exercise," or, "You could have memorized a lot of vocabulary for your English class." This kind of parental behavior is not uncommon among working-class parents. Manyue had a similar experience. Manyue's father recalled how much it upset him when he found out that Manyue was using her math textbook to cover her novels. Her father then forbade her to read anything other than textbooks.

Some other working-class students mentioned the lack of reading materials at home or a lack of interest in reading. Erping particularly mentioned that his home was turned into a food stand by his parents, which was dirty and noisy and there was no room for quiet reading. Peng also shared that his parents tried to make sure he got all the textbooks and supplemental learning materials required by the school, but they had no spare money to spend on subscribing to any newspapers or journals for him, although he "might enjoy reading" them if he had the access.

Qunhuan, the only student from a farming family who finally went to a national key university, particularly mentioned his lack of interest in reading and how he thought it handicapped his ability in written and oral compositions. That was one of the reasons why he failed the early admission exams and did not get to go to a prestigious university, Fudan University. As indicated in the case description, Qunhuan got admission to participate in Fudan University's early admission exams because of his outstanding achievement in math and science. However, besides math and physics, the exams also consisted of an oral Chinese composition. It included selecting a subject assigned by the examiner, compiling information and experiences appropriate to the topic in ten minutes, and presenting a clear argument about his/her statements or positions. Qunhuan could only "murmur or stutter during the exam" and "failed terribly." Qunhuan was not the only one who had a problem with reading and writing. The other two students from farming families also indicated that there was not much reading material available at home and that they did not develop an interest in reading during their childhood. In fact, this is a problem existing universally in rural China. According to statistics from the National Department of Culture (2005), only 45 percent of farming families have any reading materials and only 1 out of 100 young peasants (ages 15 to 30) reads in their spare time.

The problems those students had with reading and writing skills could considerably harm their academic performance in school. The Chinese class is the most important course from elementary school to high school that is all about linguistic skills. In both high school entrance examinations and college entrance examinations, the subject of Chinese plays an important role in deciding final achievement scores.

Research conducted in Western countries has consistently indicated that socioeconomic status and academic performance have a joint effect on students' decisions about college participation (Alexander et al., 1978; Elsworth et al., 1982; Jackson, 1978; Tuttle, 1981). Using data from the 1980 *High School and Beyond Study*, Tuttle (1981) finds that socioeconomic status can explain 7 percent of the variance in students' college plans. He particularly points out that the effect of socioeconomic status on college plans is not direct but mediated by students' achievement. In China, academic performance might play a larger role in students' decisions on whether or not to continue their education at the postsecondary level because of the college admission policy. Unlike the college admission policy in the United States, which includes SAT scores, extracurricular activities, community service, and essay writing for consideration, Chinese colleges and universities choose their students mostly based on academic achievement, principally their achievement scores in the national unified college entrance examinations. Therefore, when considering whether or not to go to college, Chinese students make their decisions largely based on their academic performance. The three middle-class students all indicated that they were completely sure they wanted to go to college in the predisposition stage. One of the important reasons for their decisions to go for a college education is that they were confident that their academic performance in school made access to a college education possible. For the same reason, some of the working-class students did not want to continue their education beyond high school. Manyue mentioned quite a few times in the interview that she hated school, she did not enjoy studying, and she always felt humiliated by the teacher because of her low achievement. She did not wish to go to college because "I can't wait until the day that I don't have to study." Other students decided not to continue their education beyond high school because they had no confidence that they could succeed in the college entrance examinations. As Erping said, "Given my poor performance in school, it would be a joke if I could make it to college. . . . I only wish I could graduate from high school." The interviews reveal that academic performance plays an important role in the model of students' college planning.

Parental Expectation and Students' College Planning

According to some researchers (DiMaggio & Mohr, 1985; McDonough, 1997), cultural capital also refers to the value placed on obtaining a college education. Prior research indicates that a family's socioeconomic status is highly associated with parental encouragement for the student's educational attainment (Hossler, Braxton, & Coopersmith, 1989). Therefore, parental expectation can be regarded as an indicator of the initial stock of cultural capital possessed by the student, which conditions his/her attitudes and aspirations (Bourdieu & Passeron, 1977; McDonough, 1997). Several studies (Ekstrom, 1985; Soper, 1971; Tillery, 1973) examine the impact of parental educational expectations and encouragement on the postsecondary aspirations of their children and found positive relationships between parental expectations and students' educational aspirations. Consistent with the findings from prior research, this study found that students from different family backgrounds consider a college education at very different ages.

According to Hossler and Gallagher (1987), the predisposition stage refers to the phase in which students make a tentative decision about whether or not they want to pursue a college education. In their model, this stage covers the third year of middle school or the first year of high school. Nevertheless, Hossler points out in a later study that students whose parents have received a high level of education might consider a college education earlier (Hossler, Schmit, & Vesper, 1999). In this study, the earliest age at which the student began to aspire for a college education is 11. It was Shuang whose parents both had master's degrees. Shuang's parents began to talk to her about colleges and universities even before she started first grade. She started to seriously think about a college education after her parents took her to visit several prestigious universities in Beijing when she was in fifth grade. From then on, going to college had become the only viable way for her. In her own words, "I can't think of myself without a college education." Both Yicheng and Wei also made their decisions to attend a college upon entering middle school.

Peng and Juan also began to think about a college education in middle school; however, it was mostly due to the impact of their school culture. The key middle school, Fuzhong, is a school with a college culture. The college culture cultivates in its students' aspirations and behaviors conducive to preparing for and applying to college. During her time in middle school, Peng and Juan were encouraged to achieve strong academic performance and were continuously exposed to the idea of going to college. Immersed in such a school culture, they began to consider a college education. However, Peng was still not sure if his college goal was practical upon graduation from middle school and almost opted to continue his education at secondary specialized school if his homeroom teacher did not try to persuade his parents that he had a very good chance to go to college.

Manyue's father had high expectations for her and saw himself as encouraging and helping Manyue achieve success at school. Nevertheless, he never clearly communicated with Manyue which educational level he hoped she would attain. As he put it,

> I always encourage her to work hard and make sure she's not distracted from studying by anything else. . . . There is no use to just talking [about a college education]. She has to be a good student first, and then we can talk about the possibilities for her to go to college.

Manyue also admitted that a college education never came across her mind when she was in middle school. For her, she never considered whether or not she should continue her education at the tertiary level. "It's all my dad's decision," she said. "I don't care." In contrast, Erping's parents busied themselves with the small family business and did not involve in his schooling at all. Erping said he never pictured himself going to college simply because "I'm not good in school" and "no one went to college in my family."

For the two students who were from farming families and eventually went to college, their college plans started only in high school. Qunhuan's parents did not expect him to attain a college education. In fact, he even had to fight for the right to go to high school. As Qunhuan said, he was not sure how far he could make it on the path to college because of the financial situation in his family. When he started to seriously think about the possibility for a college education, his middle-class peers had already made their list of choices, which I will discuss in the following section.

SEARCH STAGE

In Hossler and Gallagher's model of college choice (1987), the search stage refers to the process during which students consider different higher education institutions to which to apply. This stage extends roughly from tenth grade to the middle of twelfth grade and is heavily focused on the development of a student's college "choice set" (Hossler, Braxton, & Coopersmith, 1989). In this section, I am going to look at actions taken by students that are related to their college plans, which include enrolling in the right high school, choosing a major in high school, and college visits.

Opportunities to Enroll in a Key High School

The three-tiered examination system in China refers to the entrance examinations to middle school, high school, and college. The entrance examinations to middle school divert elementary school graduates into key middle schools and ordinary middle schools. Because key schools in China are given priority in the assignment of teachers, equipment, and funds, their students generally can achieve better academic performance and therefore have a better chance of enrolling in key high school. Recently, the entrance examinations to middle schools were abolished in many places. The underlying rationale is that these examinations determine children's educational fate so early on and thus are not fair. However, the entrance examinations to key high schools still universally exist in China. Key high schools are allowed to recruit students who have the best achievement scores in the examinations. The three key middle schools in Wuhu constitute only a small percentage of all regular middle schools (three out of 85) and funnel most of their students into their own high school sections, largely on the basis of entrance scores. In contrast, students from ordinary middle schools have a very small chance of passing these key schools' admission exams. In addition, the provincial key high school, Fuzhong, enjoys the privilege of recruiting outstanding students from other cities in the Anhui province. Fuzhong has a special recruiting team that visits many local key middle schools in different cities in the spring semester, locates those outstanding students, and brings them to Fuzhong high school in the fall.[1]

Shuang's family was living in a city that is a two-hour drive from Wuhu. Shuang was picked by this special recruiting team from Fuzhong not only because she had outstanding overall achievement but also because she had won two championships in biology competitions on the provincial level. She was thus recruited to the gifted science class at Fuzhong high school. Although it meant that she had to become a boarding student for three years in high school, Shuang believed that a provincial key school would give her a better chance to get into her dream college—Beijing University. "I know being a boarding student could be really hard—being far from parents, taking care of little things in life, and having to eat terrible foods from the school's cafeteria," Shuang shared her feelings about coming to Fuzhong. "But, going to Beijing University is my dream, and to make my dream come true, I'm willing to do everything I can."

In comparison, Yicheng's decision making was easy. As a top-three student in her class at Fuzhong middle school, Yicheng passed the entrance score to Fuzhong high school easily. Because of her high achievement in the high school entrance examinations, she was admitted to the gifted science class as well.

Wei's situation was a bit more complicated. As presented in the case description chapter, when he was a junior in middle school, Wei's father got a chance to go to the University of Greenwich in London as a visiting scholar for one year. He brought Wei with him in order to give him the opportunity to "see more and learn more about the world outside of China." Although Wei learned the school subjects on his own with help from his father, he still could hardly catch up with his class when he returned to Fuzhong middle school. In the high school entrance examinations, Wei did not reach the admission score for Fuzhong high school. However, Fuzhong was permitted by the local bureau of education to admit a certain number of students who did not reach the cut-off score by charging extra tuition and fees. Without any hesitation, Wei's parents agreed to pay the extra 7,000 yuan per semester to get him admission to Fuzhong.

Peng and Juan were two working-class students who went to Fuzhong middle school. Upon graduation, Juan's decision making was easy and straightforward. Her parents always had this pity that they did not have a college education, so they wanted to support Juan going to college. Juan, influenced by her classmates and teachers, also thought a college education was the only way to obtain a good job and the type of job that will allow for a comfortable lifetime income and a secure future. Therefore, Juan applied to Fuzhong high school without any hesitation. Although Juan's achievement was only about the average in her class at Fuzhong middle school, she still passed Fuzhong high school's entrance score easily because students from Fuzhong middle school are generally much better prepared academically compared to students from ordinary schools. Using one parent's words, there is almost "no competition from outside [of Fuzhong]."

Since Peng won the lottery to go to Fuzhong middle school, he had been working hard and was among the top ten in his class. However, upon graduation, he was uncertain about the idea of going on to a general high school. Both he and his parents thought that a specialized secondary school would be a good choice since he could get into any of these schools because of his high academic achievement. Peng had been thinking of a college education since he started middle school, yet when facing the choice of which type of senior secondary school to attend, he was still very hesitant. The influences of Peng's parents were very weak. They basically agreed with anything Peng had decided. Peng thus put several specialized secondary schools in his application. When his homeroom teacher found out, he paid a visit to Peng's family. "Basically he (the homeroom teacher) told us that a college education is far more important today than it was ever before," Peng's mother said. "Fifty years ago, college education was only for the elite. We did fine in life without any college education, but it's not going to be the case for Peng's generation." Peng finally decided to continue his education in general high school after thinking over his homeroom teacher's words. His parents had no problem with his decision. Peng passed the high school entrance examinations with flying colors and got admitted to Fuzhong high school.

As discussed previously, because of the lack of a social network, the working-class student Huifeng did not get into Fuzhong middle school. However, it did not defeat him. He thought he could work hard in an ordinary middle school and go to Fuzhong for his high school education. Although Huifeng had been a good student in school and performed normally in the high school entrance examinations, his total achievement score was still ten points lower than the cut-off score for Fuzhong high school. This fact really puzzled him and his parents. Huifeng said, "I was really wondering what kind of people could get in." At that time, Fuzhong had a policy that within 30 points under the entrance score, students could pay an additional 7,000 yuan per semester to get admission to Fuzhong. His experience in the high school entrance examinations scared Huifeng so much that at that point he desperately wanted to go to Fuzhong high school to secure his chance to receive a college education. However, since high school is not part of a compulsory education in China, every high school charges certain tuition and fees. Therefore, the total expense for Huifeng to go to Fuzhong would be 8,500 yuan per year, which was more expensive than tuition charged by a lot of colleges. Huifeng's parents did not think a high school education should be worth that much, so they did not want to pay for it. Although Huifeng preferred to go to Fuzhong, he also understood that his family was not able to pay both a high school education at Fuzhong and a college education. Huifeng finally gave in and went to Nancheng high school.

The Rural Education Research Institute at the Northeastern Teachers' University conducted a survey in 14 counties across six provinces regarding middle school graduation rates (Peng, 2004). Although these rural areas are not considered particularly poor, survey responses from the teachers there revealed only about a 60 percent graduation rate. Among middle school graduates, the number of those who continued to receive a high school education is even smaller. Having these statistics in mind, the experiences of the three students from farming families in this study were quite unique.

Qunhuan was admitted to Fuzhong by its special recruiting team. His achievement in science was outstanding. Qunhuan came in second in a provincial chemistry competition in his second year of middle school, a championship in a provincial math competition, and third in physics in his senior year. In the last semester of middle school, Fuzhong's special recruiting crew came to Qunhuan's middle school and offered him admission. Qunhuan was very excited about the idea of going to a key school in a big city for his high school education. However, because his mother was strongly against that idea, his father had to fight for his opportunity. According to Qunhuan, his parents had many arguments and fights over this issue. Finally, his father took out the whole family's savings to pay for Qunhuan's high school and living expenses in the city. Xiaomin's and Congbo's experiences were less dramatic. Xiaomin could come to the city for high school because her father was a worker in the suburbs and had some network in the city. Congbo was from a relatively wealthy family in the rural area. His admission to Nancheng high school came from his uncle's network in the city and the extra tuition his family agreed to pay.

Choosing the Major in High School

In their second year of high school, Chinese students have to choose between a science major and an arts and humanities major. Students in these two majors will have a different curriculum and be tested on different subjects in the national college entrance examinations. Compared to the American educational system, the Chinese system has much less flexibility in terms of switching majors. Changing majors in high school is relatively easy, but once the student gets into college, it is almost impossible for him/her to switch his/her major between science and arts and humanities. Therefore, making a decision about his/her own major is very critical to a high school junior.

Three elements play a role in the students' decision-making process about which field to major in. First, it is personal interest. All three middle-class students mentioned in their interviews that personal interest played a key role in their decision making about majors. Shuang had a strong interest in biology. Wei became interested in architecture during his childhood. Yicheng had a general interest in science, including math, physics, and chemistry. Therefore, all three students chose to attend the science class. Their decision-making processes were relatively easy and straightforward. To most of the working-class students, however, the other two elements seem to be more important. One is the expected earnings of a certain field, and the other is the possibility for them to get into college. Later on, I will discuss how these two variables also largely influence working-class students' decision making about which major to choose in college. Manyue's father made a every important decision in her educational path for her. When facing the choice to enroll in the science or the humanities class, Manyue's father decided that Manyue should go to the science class despite the fact that she hated almost every science subject. He reasoned that because there were more colleges and programs in science than in humanities, there would be a better chance for his daughter to get into college if she chose the science class. Manyue did not protest, although she felt that she might be more comfortable in a humanities class. Manyue expressed her appreciation for what her parents had done for her education. "They literally saved every penny for my education," Manyue said. "My dad always said that if I could obtain a college degree, it would be the only luxury possessed by our family." Therefore, she compliantly accepted her father's decision for her with a wish that the decision would make a college education more reachable. Compared to Manyue, Peng was a very independent student, and he made his decision without consulting his parents. Peng shared that it was an easy choice for him. "I like science in general," he said, "and the job security and expected salary are also better for science students. So, there was no reason I would choose the humanities class." Juan struggled a little bit when facing the choice since she did not have a strong interest in science like Peng did. Nevertheless, she still chose to enroll in the science class given that there was even more severe competition to get into college for humanities students. "I wanted to secure my chance to go to college. That's my ultimate goal. So, it seemed to me that the science class was a reasonable choice," Juan said. Similar to the working-class students, the three students from farming families also made their choices based on the prospective job market and salary. Qunhuan actually had a strong interest in math, but the reason for him to choose the science class was not his personal interest but that "it would be easier to get into college and find a job with decent pay after graduation." Xiaomin also admitted that she did not really have a preference between science and humanities and that the chance to be admitted to college and the expected income were the main reasons for her to choose the science class.

College Visits

College visits are a prevalent practice in the United States. Most colleges and universities have open houses and offer organized campus tours. Many students make college visits during their junior and senior years in order to get a firsthand view of the colleges they are interested in. They go to open houses to talk to students, faculty members, and administrators, attend student-conducted campus tours, and sometimes stay overnight in a dorm to see what living at the college is really like. Moreover, they can also take the opportunity to talk to admission officers and ask questions about financial aid and other services that are available to students. In China, college visits are not very popular among high school students and their parents. Colleges and universities do not offer organized tours around campus. It is also impossible for high school students and their parents to have face-to-face interviews with financial administrators to get any clear idea about the financial aid available at certain college. Although college visits are not common practice for most of the high school students, middle-class parents are increasingly more likely to take their children to visit the colleges and universities to which they are considering applying.

In the United States, a campus visit is an opportunity for students to really get a feel for the schools that they are interested in. They walk around the quad, sit in on a class, and visit the dorms in order to determine whether the school is a good match for them. In China, many middle-class parents encourage their children to visit their dream colleges and universities with the intent of invigorating their spirit to get into their dream school.

Shuang's first college visit took place when she was on a trip with her parents to Beijing when she was in fifth grade. In that trip, her parents took her to visit the ten national key universities located in the college district in Beijing. Although she was too young to get any feel for what it is like to actually study there, the visits did boost her interest in colleges and universities. "They looked smart and awesome," Shuang said about her impression of the college students, "and I wanted to be one of them." Shuang went to Beijing several times throughout her middle school and high school time. For a couple of times, she was with her parents. And for the other times, she was with school teams attending national competitions in science. Every time she visited Beijing, she spent some time in the college district.

> That is my favorite part of Beijing. Being there, you can just feel the culture, the history, and the atmosphere that you can only find in those prestigious universities. . . . They are all very different from the colleges in my hometown [most of them are community colleges]. Compared to these key national universities, the colleges I've seen in my hometown are like, you know, like nothing. So, it's not very surprising that I want to go to Beijing for my college education, where I feel I can expect to become a bright and entitled thinker.

In the last semester of her high school senior year, Shuang was facing a choice between accepting admission from the University of Science and Technology in China with an exemption from the national unified college entrance examinations and going through the normal procedure to apply to Beijing University. It was the most difficult choice that she was ever presented. To help her make her decision, Shuang's father took her to the capital of the Anhui province, where the University of Science and Technology in China is located. As mentioned before, college visits are not well structured in China. There is no campus tour, no interviews, and no overnight stay in a dorm. However, Shuang and her father still went there anyway just to "get some feel" for that university. Shuang spent the whole day walking on campus, looking around for student newspapers, and checking out bulletin boards. The University of Science and Technology in China has a large and beautiful campus, too. However, Shuang felt that it lacked a sense of history, which at Beijing University had impressed her. She also had a feeling that the school's personality was not a good match for her. A couple of weeks after her visit, she turned down the offer from the University of Science and Technology in China and decided to go through the overwhelming college entrance examinations in order to go to her dream school, Beijing University.

Wei's first college visit happened when he was visiting his aunt in Beijing. The summer when Wei graduated from elementary school, his aunt, who is a professor at Beijing Foreign Language University, invited him to spend the summer break with her family. They lived near the campus of Beijing Foreign Language University, which is not far from the two most famous universities in China, Beijing University and Qinghua University. Wei and his cousin traveled on their bicycles from one university to another in the college district. Wei was very impressed by those universities. He went back to visit them again a couple of times during high school. In the winter break of his senior year, he went to Beijing alone to visit Qinghua University. This time, his father helped arrange a meeting with a professor in the architecture school for him. The professor was his father's colleague, so Wei felt fairly comfortable talking to him about his interests, concerns, and all sorts of questions regarding the admission criteria at Qinghua University. After the meeting, Wei felt more confident that Qinghua was the right place for him, although on the other side he felt the admission criteria were quite high at Qinghua and he might need to stretch to reach them.

The two universities Yicheng visited are the University of Science and Technology in China and Fudan University. Yicheng has an uncle teaching at the University of Science and Technology in China, so Yicheng has visited the campus several times. In the second summer of high school, Yicheng spent half of her summer break at her uncle's place. Her uncle is a professor in physics. This time her uncle brought her to his lab and introduced her to some of the ongoing projects in his lab. Yicheng also had chances to talk to his students about their programs and campus life. Yicheng was impressed by the lab and the research projects available to undergraduate students;

however, she felt that the general undergraduate curriculum was too science oriented and offered almost no courses in arts and humanities. The other university, Fudan University, which she had the opportunity to explore in certain depth, is where her father was pursuing his Ph.D. Compared to the University of Science and Technology in China, Fudan University's programs in science are not as strong, but its undergraduate curricula are more balanced in science and humanities. Yicheng went to Shanghai several times for weekends in her last year of high school. Her father brought her to different lectures, campus concerts, and student events. Yicheng admitted that if she did not have the chance to visit these two candidate universities in depth, she might have had a difficult time making her mind. But, after her few trips to Fudan University, she found "the right atmosphere" there and made her mind to apply.

As mentioned before, college visits are not a routine expectation in Chinese high school. Among the three middle-class students, two had relatives teaching at universities, which provided them with opportunities to visit certain colleges in some depth—meeting with professors, visiting labs, and attending lectures and concerts. Shuang did not have any family members working at universities. Therefore, although her parents thought visiting colleges was an essential step in the decision-making process about college application, all Shuang could do during her college visits was just walking around on campus and checking out some bulletin boards. Yet, she could still get some feel about a university by spending time on a campus and therefore determine whether the school was a good match for her or not.

Students from the working-class families and farming families interviewed in this study did not mention any college visits. To some of the students with high academic achievement, college visits were considered unnecessary. As Peng indicated, he knew he would not go to Beijing for a college education because it is too far away from home. He wanted to stay close to home for two reasons. First, the time and cost of transportation were prohibitive. Second, he wanted to be able to come home quickly in case of an emergency. Since the University of Science and Technology in China was the best science university in his desired distance from home, he was sure that it was his only choice. As Peng indicated,

> The atmosphere, the campus life, and the dorms' conditions . . . those are superficial things. The most important thing is a university's reputation. The University of Science and Technology in China has a high reputation for educating the best college students in science, and that's the only thing I care about. And I don't have to go to the campus to learn about that.

The students with low academic achievement also indicated that their only concern was to get into a college, and that whether the college was a good match for them or not was not something they worried about. Hui-feng put it this way, "To get college admission is the only important thing. Say, if you visited one college and you liked it, but it turned out that you didn't get admission, what's the point to visit it?" Huifeng's comments represented most of the students' attitudes from low socioeconomic status about college visits in the study. The majority thought that college visits were a waste of time and money and were also not expected or supported by their teachers and parents.

Choice Set and Information Resource

According to Hossler and Gallagher's model (1987), those students who have decided to pursue a postsecondary education begin to seek information about colleges and universities in which they are interested during the search stage. Students create a list of these colleges and universities, which Hossler and Gallagher refer to as a choice set. Using this choice set, students begin to examine certain attributes of these colleges and obtain information that will assist them in making their decision to apply to particular institutions. Researchers (Hossler & Gallagher, 1987; Litten, 1982) have found that a wide variety of colleges are chosen to create an applicant's choice set. The colleges usually differ in size, type (public or private), and cost. Once this choice set has been created, students begin to seek various resources to assist them with their information search. Matthay (1989) points out that the most common and helpful resources are college visits, college catalogs, parents, and high school guidance counselors.

From the case description chapters we can see that the search stage of the Chinese students' college decision-making process differs from Hossler and Gallagher's model (1987) on two aspects. First, the students interviewed in this study all had a very short list of colleges that they would like to apply to, usually including two competing colleges of the same type. This can be a result of the Chinese college application process. In America, high school graduates can apply to different colleges and universities, and their applications to different schools do not interfere with one another. As introduced in chapter 7, the college application process is quite different in China. Chinese students only need to complete one application form, which includes all the schools they want to apply to. The application form comprises four categories: military and specialty schools, national key universities, ordinary universities, and training schools and community colleges. Theoretically, students can put in four to six schools in order of preference for each category; however, they only have a chance for their first-choice school. Since colleges and universities all require much higher admission scores for those students who do not put their schools as the first choice, it is almost impossible for students to enroll in their second or third choice if they miss the admission score for their first choice. Responding to this kind of college application process, Chinese students usually have two colleges in mind and then seek information to compare the two candidates. For example, the two universities on Yicheng's list were Fudan University and the University of Science and Technology in China. Yicheng only visited these two universities, and all the information she sought was about the program, the curriculum, and campus life at these two universities.

Second, for Chinese students, the most common resources about colleges and universities seem to be parents, homeroom teachers, and peers. All the middle-class students reported that they first asked their parents about the possible candidate colleges and information concerning those colleges and their programs. Taking Wei as an example, his parents collected information about four universities and their architecture schools, took him for college visits to two of them, and put him in contact with professors at his first-choice university. Wei then sought advice from his homeroom teacher about his college choice set. For the working-class students and students from farming families at the key high school, Fuzhong, their homeroom teachers and peers were the two key resources. Peng's parents were completely absent from his college decision-making process. He learned about the University of Science and Technology in China from conversations with his classmates and then obtained more information about its programs from his homeroom teacher. His homeroom teacher also suggested that he look into Fudan University, which enjoys a similar reputation for its academic programs as the University of Science and Technology in China. Similarly, the working-class students and students from farming families at the ordinary high school, Nancheng, all predominantly relied on their homeroom teachers for college support. Some of them, like Xiaomin, communicated their college plans with the homeroom teacher by themselves. Others, like Manyue, were dependent on their parents to obtain information about colleges from the homeroom teacher for them. Conversations about college plans were less common among the students studying at the ordinary high school.

CHOICE STAGE

In Hossler and Gallagher's model of students' college choice process (1987), the search stage ends when students have decided on the colleges or universities they will apply to and have completed applications for those respective institutions. The final stage of the college choice process is the choice stage. At this stage, students are notified of their acceptance into certain colleges and universities, and they choose to enroll in a particular institution from the available alternatives. In the context of China, the choice stage actually ends when students have submitted their college applications. Because of the particular college admission process in China, students make their decisions about which college and which major they want to enroll in when they complete their applications. In the following, I will discuss how academic performance and financial resources influence students' college decision making.

Academic Achievement and College Choice

Prior research points out that a family's socioeconomic status is highly associated with school success (Cabrera & La Nasa, 2001; Coleman, 1988; McDonough, 1997; Perna, 2000; Swail and Perna, 2002). Achievement and ability in turn determine students' college choice. According to Hossler and Gallagher (1987), as academic achievements and abilities increase, students are more likely to attend college. This study also found that when students' achievement reached a certain point (e.g., examination scores and class rankings) that is college competitive, the college selection process becomes more formal. Students with higher achievement scores are more likely to aspire for a college education and to talk with teachers, parents, and peers about their college plans.

The middle-class students, Shuang, Yicheng, and Wei, all expected to attend a prestigious university. Besides the fact that their parents encouraged them to aim high and apply to their dream colleges, they also gained their confidence from the fact that their academic achievement would allow them to compete for a limited seat in national key universities. The working-class student, Peng, and the student from farming family, Qunhuan, also applied to national key universities. They were both high achievers in science and had little interest in arts and humanities. Therefore, different from Shuang and Yicheng, who applied to science departments in comprehensive universities, Peng and Qunhuan both chose to enroll in science and technology universities.

Huifeng and Xiaomin both had high academic rankings in their class. However, they were also aware of the fact that the percentage of students in the ordinary high school going to college was quite low. They both applied to four-year institutions, which was an ambitious college goal compared to most of their classmates. Nevertheless, they did not include national key universities in their college plans because they knew that as good students in a low-performing school, they could not compete with students from the key high school in the national college entrance examinations.

Students with low academic achievement, like Manyue and Erping, did not aspire for a college education. Erping even mocked at the idea of him going to college and said it would be a joke if he could make it to college. Under significant pressure from her father, Manyue claimed that she wanted to go to college; however, she also shared how much she disliked school and longed to be freed from studying. Not surprising, she did not have a college plan compared to other students with higher achievements and expectations for a college education.

Parents' Ability and Willingness to Pay for College

Some researchers (Steelman & Powell, 1989) argue that different types of capital have different impacts on children's schooling at various points of an educational career. Researchers suggest that social and cultural capital provided by the family have profound influences on students' academic development in childhood and adolescence, while financial capital's impact is more significant on their opportunities to obtain a college education. Compared to elementary and secondary education, equality of opportunity to obtain higher education is more problematic because in most countries higher education is only partially subsidized by the government and paying for a college education is largely the responsibility of students themselves and their parents (Fitzgerald & Delaney, 2002; Gladieux, 2002; McDonough, 1997).

Clearly, sufficient financial support from their families is important for students to be able to continue their education on the tertiary level. It is argued that since access is contingent on unequally distributed parental income and wealth, the better-off families are able to secure a college education for their offspring and therefore maintain advantageous positions in the occupational attainment contest (Steelman & Powell, 1989). In this study, I also found that the extent to which parents were willing to sponsor their children's college education was highly associated with their family income.

During the interview, parents of the three middle-class students all explicitly expressed that money was never an issue in their children's college decision-making processes. Shuang was hesitant between two universities; one is in Hefei, which is only two-hour drive away from home, and the other is in Beijing, which is more than a two-hour flight away. Although both of the two universities are prestigious and charge the same level of tuition and fees, the living expenses in Beijing and transportation costs are much higher. According to Shuang, those factors never came into her mind when considering these two alternatives. What matters are the reputation of the school, the ranking of the program, and the chance for her to pursue graduate study abroad. Shuang and her parents had many discussions about her college choice and about which major she should choose. However, during their conversations never once did they mention money. Shuang's understanding about college choice was that her choice was only limited by her academic ability. Shuang's father confirmed that it was also their belief that financial issues should not get in the way of their daughter's path to college.

Similarly, Yicheng was also considering two universities, one of which is in Hefei and the other is in Shanghai. Like Shuang, Yicheng was not very concerned with college cost. Financial issues did come up in one of the discussions Yicheng had with her parents. She was a little worried that her family did not have enough savings to pay her tuition and fees because they had been living on her mother's single salary for almost three years. She was then explicitly told by her parents that money was not an issue and it should not be one of the factors influencing her decision-making about which college to attend. During the interview, Yicheng's mother admitted that she and Yicheng's father were not very optimistic about their financial situation in the last year of Yicheng's high school. However, they did not want Yicheng to be bothered by the financial issue. They were ready to take a loan to pay for Yicheng's college education. Nevertheless, they did not want Yicheng to feel guilty about it and thus choose to settle for a second choice, so they kept it from her. Yicheng's father found a well-paid job a couple of months before Yicheng submitted her college application, which completely changed their financial situation. Without any worries about money, Yicheng chose to go to Shanghai and she happily attended Fudan University.

In Wei's case, the willingness of his parents to pay for a good college education for him was even more pronounced. As mentioned before, Wei did fairly well in the national unified college entrance examinations and received an offer from Tianjin University, which was the third choice on his list. However, Wei's parents finally decided to send him abroad for his undergraduate study because they believed that it would be better for Wei's future career development than settling for his third choice in China regardless of the fact that the total expense they would have to pay was ten times higher than the cost of a college education in China.

While middle-class parents were ensuring their children that their college choice should not be limited by financial issues, low-income families could hardly afford the tuition and the foregone earnings associated with pursuing a college education and had to make some compromises when making the choice about college and major.

In Juan's case, her parents forbade her from applying to a university in the far north because of the associated extra costs and the fear that she would be no longer under their direct supervision. Juan thus ended up going to Anhui Normal University, which is local but a distant college choice for her. Juan was very disappointed by the fact that she would not become a boarding student and would have to go back home for meals. "It would just be like in high school. . . . I wouldn't be able to fully enjoy the campus life. . . . It's just so disappointing." However, the fact that Juan was going to a local university gave her parents relief about the financial burden. Juan's mother shared that they probably still had to use all of their savings to pay for Juan's four-year college education, but at least they did not have to take a loan. According to Juan's mother, she and her husband always shielded Juan from worries about money in order to not distract her from her study. "'Just concentrate on your study. That's your only job,' we always told her," Juan's mother said. However, this strategy also sent Juan the wrong message that her parents did not have any problem paying for her college education, while in reality they did. During the interview, Juan expressed her disappointment about her parents not being supportive in her college application process, "They don't care about my education and my life. They just want me to stay with them." On the contrary, Juan's mother expressed how much they cared. Her mother's understanding was that because most of the students in Juan's class were from wealthy families, Juan did not really understand her own family's financial situation and her parents' dilemma.

Compared to Juan's parents, Qunhuan's parents, who were both farmers, were much less willing to pay for their son's college education. Qunhuan's mother was strongly against the idea of Qunhuan going to high school. Instead, she wanted him to become an accountant in the small village where they had been living for generations, while Qunhuan, full of ambition, wanted to get out of a farmer's life. With help from his father, Qunhuan finally managed to go to high school. When the time came for him to choose a college and a major, Qunhuan was explicitly told by his parents that they had used up all their savings for his high school education and simply could not afford his college education. Being clearly aware of the financial difficulty his family was facing, Qunhuan decided to choose material engineering as his major. Qunhuan shared that if he did not have to worry about tuition, he would have chosen electrical engineering, which he believed had a better job market. However, the tuition for electrical engineering was 8,000 yuan per year at Shanghai Transportation University, which was nearly the total of his family's annual income. Therefore, Qunhuan chose to settle for material engineering, which cost a third of the tuition for electrical engineering.

Johnstone (2000) points out that the willingness of students and their families to pay for a college education is a function of wealth as well as culture. China is a country in which education has an extraordinary role in the formation and preservation of its culture. John L. Stuart, U.S. Ambassador to China during 1942–1946, went so far as to suggest that "the history of Chinese education is almost the history of China, for perhaps in no other country has the educational process had such influence in shaping the national life" (cited in Galt, 1992, p. 16). In general, regardless of class-based differences in attitudes about education, " the Chinese parent, who probably has only one child to begin with, and who has probably always placed a very high value on education . . . is apparently willing to make considerable personal financial sacrifices for their child to go to a university" (Johnstone, 2000, p. 13). It is true that the parents interviewed in this study, no matter how much education they themselves had, all expressed that they valued a college education. However, since low-income parents apparently possessed much fewer economic resources to pay for it, their children had to make some compromises when it came to choosing a specific college and major. Yet, the personal financial sacrifices those low-income parents had to make for their children to go to college were incredible.

According to Peng, his parents had never gone out for a dinner or any type of entertainment since they began to save for his education when he was in middle school. They had been so careful with money that even meat and seafood were luxury foods for them and they always saved them for Peng. Peng's mother never bought new clothes for herself during all of these years. Peng's father used to enjoy a small glass of liquor with dinner, but he quit when Peng decided to continue his education at Fuzhong high school. Peng witnessed all of these changes in his parents' lives and felt guilty about it. Therefore, although his parents asked him not to take financial issues into consideration when making his decision about college and major, money still played a large role in Peng's decision-making. As in Yicheng's case, the University of Science and Technology in China and Fudan University were also two candidates for Peng. Yet, Peng made a different choice because of two reasons. First, a variety of cultural events and campus activities at Fudan University that strongly attracted Yicheng did not matter to Peng. "I'm going to college to study, not to socialize. . . . My only objective is to become an outstanding student and then to find a decent job easily after graduation." The second reason was the financial issue. The University of Science and Technology in China is located in Hefei, where the living expenses are not much higher than in Wuhu, while Fudan University is in Shanghai, the largest city in China, which is notorious for its extremely high living expenditures.

Money was not only a factor in Peng's college choice process but also a substantial variable that influenced his decision about college major. When he went to Hefei for the early admission examinations, Peng talked to people in the student office about the tuition and fees charged by different departments. He learned from the student office that the first two choices he originally had in mind, which were information system and computer science, were too expensive for him to afford. The information system department charged a tuition of 8,000 yuan for a year and the computer science department charged 6,500 yuan. Peng could not bear the thought that he might use up all of his parents' savings for his college education. Therefore, after all of these considerations, he chose chemistry as his major, which cost only 4,000 yuan for a year.

Similarly, Manyue also mentioned the considerable financial sacrifices her parents made for her education. As previously discussed, Manyue had been struggling a lot with her study since middle school. She failed the high school entrance examinations, thus her parents had to pay an extra 2,000 yuan per year to get her into Nancheng high school. She had no luck with the national college entrance examinations either. Since she did not get admission from any college, her parents had to pay 4,000 yuan for her to repeat the senior year in Nancheng high school in order to get her a second chance for college. Manyue indicated that her parents saved every penny they earned to pay for her education.

STUDENT LOANS, FINANCIAL AID, AND COLLEGE ACCESS

Finally, as Johnstone (2002) points out, for a culture that regards higher education as a public entitlement and is averse to debt, students and their families would be more hesitant to borrow for a college education. This is also true in China. Receiving a college education for free has been regarded as one of the privileges that socialist Chinese citizens could enjoy from the founding of the People's Republic of China. Because of the pervasive belief that higher education should be entitled to those who have proved themselves to have profitted most from education, it is a cultural challenge that a student's chance of continuing his/her education at the postsecondary level depends both on academic achievement and financial ability. In this study, I found that the discontent with tuition charging together with a cultural aversion to debt, students, especially the low-income students and their parents, did not want to borrow to pay the university bill.

Huifeng's parents had some savings for his college education, but only enough to cover tuition and fees at a community college. That was one of the reasons why they tried to persuade Huifeng to apply for only community colleges. As Huifeng's father indicated, their family did not feel comfortable with taking a loan. They were proud of themselves for "never borrowing money from other people." Similarly, to avoid taking a loan for her college education, Juan's parents did not want to send her to a university that was far away from home because they wanted to reduce the transportation cost and other expenses that were related to going out of town for a college. Juan's mother was one of the few parents who actually knew that there was a student loan program supported by the government. However, she made it clear that even if they had to take a loan, they would not borrow from the bank because it would give them too much pressure. They would rather borrow the money from relatives and friends. Manyue's parents have similar feelings concerning a loan. They had already spent most of their savings on Manyue's high school education. They must borrow to support her college education. Her father said that they probably would take small amount of loans from relatives and friends. Qunhuan's mother was scared of the fact that they had to take a loan to pay for Qunhuan's college education. To her, it was something unthinkable. She was not alone. Most people in their village thought they were crazy to borrow to pay for education and did not want to lend them the money because they thought there was too much risk that Qunhuan's family would never be able to pay it back. Qunhuan finally borrowed enough money for his first-year tuition and fees from the head of the village, who had more confidence in the payback of a college education than the majority in the village. He promised his parents that he would try his best to shine academically in college in order to get a scholarship.

As discussed in chapter 3, there are four different types of campus-based scholarships available at Chinese universities and colleges. Among them, the National Speciality Scholarship and career-based grants reflect the special commitment of the central government to favor students in areas of high priority for national development, such as education, agriculture, forestry, and maritime sciences (China Education News, 2001; Liu, 2002). However, we need to look at the distribution of financially disadvantaged students in these majors to understand the issue more completely. According to research conducted in the Shaan'xi province (Central Education Research Institute, 2001), the average percentage of low-income students enrolled in these fields of study is very high, ranging from 30 percent to 50 percent. As we know, these majors are less marketable and thus promise fewer economic returns and less mobility to city locations. Therefore, even though such a grant can relieve some financial pressures of needy students for a while, it eventually limits the professional choices of these students, whose primary concern is how to pay for their college education.

Among the students interviewed in this study, Juan, Huifeng, and Xiaomin all considered this type of grant as a way to lessen their family's financial burden. Juan's parents strongly encouraged him to apply to Anhui Normal University because students enrolled in a normal university with the promise to become teachers after graduation are eligible for the National Speciality Scholarship and also enjoy a certain amount of monthly stipend. Although Juan was not enthusiastic about becoming a teacher, she agreed with her parents that it was a compromise they had to make given their family's financial situation. Juan said that she would look for a non-teaching position after graduation, and if she could find one with a good salary package, she would not go into teaching. As a punishment, she would have to pay the school back for the amount of scholarships and monthly stipends she had received during her four years of college.

It is also common for normal universities to offer noneducational majors. Xiaomin is mostly interested in a business major; however, a business department generally charges a relatively higher tuition because of its popularity. Xiaomin consulted her homeroom teacher about choices for colleges and majors. She learned from the teacher that a business department at a normal university usually charges lower tuition and sometimes even provides monthly subsidies to students. After consulting with her teacher, Xiaomin decided to stick to her preference for major but chose a normal university to attend. However, it has to be noted that normal universities are generally considered inferior to regular key universities in China. Graduates from normal universities are thus treated as second-rate, especially graduates from noneducational majors from a normal university. Therefore, Xiaomin will receive fewer economic returns on her college degree because of her college choice.

Making the Final Decision

The final decision about which college to go depends on many factors, including high school academic performance, parental expectation and support, expected college costs (direct and indirect), prospective future earnings, and college characteristics. Clearly, these factors play different roles in their final decision making about which college to attend and which major to enroll in for students from different family backgrounds. For middle-class students, the right college often means a college that has the right academic and cultural atmosphere and matches their personalities. For working-class students, the right college usually means a college that is close to home and charges reasonable tuition and fees. When making the choice about academic major, middle-class students tend to consider the reputation of the particular program and the opportunities for advanced study in the future. In contrast, the pivotal factors that influence the decision making of students from working-class or farming families about which major to choose are the cost of the program and its marketability—that is to say, the foreseeable economic returns in the job market.

NOTE

1. Key schools compete with one another in terms of how many students they can send to key institutions at the next level. Key schools with higher percentages of their students going to key institutions at the next level are more likely to get more funding from the government and recruit better qualified teachers. Therefore, key schools try to recruit students with high academic achievement so they can funnel more students to key institutions at the next level.

10

Findings, Limitations, and Implications

Drawing on cultural capital theory, this study is aimed at exploring the various factors that influence the college choice process of Chinese high school seniors. The conceptual framework of this study is a derivative of Hossler and Gallagher's model of students' college choice process (1987). Using a case study method, the research investigates how a family's cultural capital and economic capital join hands to influence a high school senior's perception of his/her opportunity for a college education.

This last chapter is designed to present the main findings of this study, examine its limitations, and discuss implications for future research and educational policy making.

FINDINGS

As the previous chapter revealed, not all students face equal opportunities for a college education if they start out with different family backgrounds and school resources. The family's cultural capital, coupled with financial factors, affects the student's chance to enroll in college and his/her choice of college. The cultural capital element consists of academic preparation, parental preferences and expectations, and parental involvement. The economic capital element includes parents' willingness to pay for education and their ability to pay. The cross-case analyses in this study support the propositions of cultural capital theory by demonstrating that families of different social classes transmit distinctive values and cultural knowledge to their younger generation, thus creating a divide between children of upper- and lower-class families. Children from families with higher socioeconomic status usually perform better in school than those from families with lower socioeconomic status because of their possession of socially valued cultural capital before entering the school system. Moreover, parents with higher social positions place higher values on college education, have more information and knowledge about college access and choice, and are more likely to play a positive role in their children's college decision making. Students with well-educated parents therefore usually have higher educational aspirations and are more likely to choose to continue their education beyond high school. In addition, family income also has a great impact on the chance for a student to enroll in a key school on the secondary education level, while school resources and supportive school climate are powerful variables in the student's college decision making. Finally, family income also directly influences the student's chance to enroll in college and his/her final college choice. In short, the family's cultural capital and economic capital join hands to affect the student's college decision making. In the following I am going to discuss how each of the five constructs that make up students' cultural capital and economic capital shapes students' college enrollment behavior.

Academic Preparation

As discussed in the literature review chapter, cultural capital theory and research indicate that cultural capital plays a strong role in determining school success (Cabrera & La Nasa, 2001; Kuo & Hauser, 1995; Perna, 2000, 2002). Parental cultural capital and students' cultural participation have enduring effects on educational career. Consistent with the findings of prior research, this study also found that a family's socioeconomic status is positively associated with academic achievement, and academic achievement, in turn, has the largest impact on college attendance. Students with low academic aptitude are much less likely to plan for a college education and are also less likely to attend a national key university. To better examine the construct "academic preparation," I will break it into four variables: early family education, reading and learning environment at home, educational planning, and school choices.

First, middle-class children are more likely to receive early family education from their parents, while early family education is found to have a great impact on students' school experiences and academic performances. Chinese middle-class parents tend to teach their children Chinese characters, train them to practice calligraphy, ask them to recite poems, and cultivate their reading habits and skills before the start of formal schooling. All of these educational practices in early childhood are generally absent in working-class families and farming families. Undoubtedly, with more endowments of cultural knowledge and linguistic skills, children from middle-class families are better able to fit into the formal school environment and to further develop their academic skills. In contrast, students from working-class families and farming families lacking early exposure to certain cultural activities are more likely to find the school environment hostile and fearsome.

In addition to exposing their children to early cultural activities, middle-class parents continue to provide a more stimulating reading climate and learning environment at home throughout their children's elementary and secondary education. Some researchers (Crook, 1997; de Graaf et al., 2000) find that reading is associated with academic success because analytical and cognitive skills developed by reading significantly contribute to educational attainment. This study also found that middle-class parents are generally more supportive of their children's extracurricular reading and cultural activities. Good reading habits and skills have direct impacts on school performance, particularly achievement in the subject of Chinese. In recent years, some prestigious Chinese universities started to introduce early admission programs. In the examinations to these early admission programs, the performance on an oral Chinese composition often comprises a large percentage of the total achievement score. In this way, students' linguistic competence also directly influences their college choices.

Finally, educational planning and school choices are the other two variables found to be associated with academic achievement. With high expectations from parents, middle-class students are more likely to have early and formal college plans. Most of them form their initial college plans in the early influence stage or the predisposition stage and conduct in-depth research on prospective colleges and universities in the search stage. In contrast, students from working-class families or farming families start to think about their educational plans rather late. Only those with relatively good school performances begin to consider their college choices in the search stage, and their college plans are often tentative. Because they do not have clear educational goals and support from their parents, working-class students and students from farming families are less likely to choose to enroll in a key middle school. Since the Chinese government invests more resources (both financial resources and human resources) in the key middle school, students from a key middle school usually are better academically prepared and thus have a better chance to be admitted to a key high school. Middle-class parents generally make great efforts to have their children enrolled in a key middle school and then gain a higher chance for their children to be admitted into a good high school and, as a corollary, into the university. Therefore, the examination system in China actually reinforces and extends the initial cultural advantages that middle-class children have gained from their parents.

Parental Preferences and Expectations

Parental values and norms are among a variety of factors that influence an individual's decision to participate in higher education. Bourdieu and Passeron (1977; Bourdieu, 1977a) observe that parents with high socioeconomic status have a clear view of how much and what kind of schooling their children should have. They are quite aware of the importance of a college education and are willing to invest in time, effort, and money that higher education requires. Their high expectations have direct impacts on their children's educational aspirations. As the concept of habitus indicates, students' decisions to invest in their education, study hard, and go to college depend on their observations of other people's lifestyles in their communities, their view of themselves, and their reflections on other people's (parents, teachers, and peers) expectations of them. This study also confirmed that those students having well-educated parents tend to believe that they are entitled to a college education. In contrast, working-class students and students from farming families are often aware of the difficulties for a person from their class to get into college and sometimes self-select themselves out of the college-going track.

Some working-class parents interviewed in this study also claimed that they valued educational success and wanted their children to do well in school. However, those working-class parents still differed from middle-class parents in the level of achievement they wished their children could attain. Some of them preferred a local university, and some considered a community college is a good choice for their children.

In addition to the differences in the value that parents with different socioeconomic status attach to educational success, the way in which they promote their children's school achievement is also different. As Xiao (2000) indicates, well-educated Chinese parents are inclined to value children's autonomy, while parents with less education tend to desire children's conformity. In this study, most middle-class parents did not establish specific rules about schoolwork and grades, although they universally had high expectations for their children. They created a quiet and inspiring learning environment at home, provided a lot of reading materials, helped with schoolwork when requested, and acted as role models for their children. Working-class parents and parents as farmers in this study can be categorized into two groups. Some of them, such as Juan's mother and Manyue's father, had explicit rules regarding schoolwork and grades and even established some kind of rewarding rules, literally paying their children for doing well in school. They both overtly forbade their children to do any extracurricular reading and tried to help with their schoolwork, sometimes in a very negative way. As Manyue complained, her father's involvement with her math homework completely discouraged her from thinking independently and made her lose interest in math. Some other working-class parents were completely indifferent to their children's school performance, like Peng's and Erping's parents. In their cases, no specific rules about schoolwork from their parents is actually an indicator of their parents' low educational expectations for them.

Undoubtedly, parental expectation is highly associated with parental involvement in students' college decision making. In the following section I will discuss the class-based differences in parental involvement in students' college plans.

Parental Involvement

Prior research all consistently finds that parental involvement is positively associated with students' college attendance (Cabrera & La Nasa, 2001; Coleman, 1988; McDonough, 1997; Perna, 2000; Swail & Perna, 2002). Parents in a higher social class are more likely to involve themselves in their children's college planning and exert positive influences on the college choice process. Moreover, as indicated by Conklin and Dailey (1981), as parental involvement increases, the likelihood for students to attend more selective four-year postsecondary educational institutions increases. Certainly, parental involvement includes all sorts of parental activities, such as providing early family education, helping with homework, and establishing rules for schoolwork and grades, which were discussed in the previous section. In this section, I will look at three variables that are directly connected to students' college choice process: organizing college visits, assisting to form the "choice set," and helping make the final decision.

As indicated before, college visits are not routine practice among Chinese high school seniors. Nevertheless, the three middle-class students all had visited the colleges to which they were thinking of applying. Their parents played an important role in organizing their college visits. When Shuang was hesitant between two prospective universities, it was her father who suggested she visit the universities to figure out in which one she would feel more comfortable and get more out of her college years. The other two middle-class students both personally knew some professors in the universities that they were interested in through their parents' social network and thus were able to ask more questions about particular academic programs and got to know more about the campus life as well. The non-middle-class parents did not encourage or help their children make any visit to colleges. As one working-class student, Peng, indicated, getting into college was the most important thing, while which college to attend was secondary, and whether or not the college was a good match with the student's personality was the last thing to consider. This kind of thinking and behavior conveys an important message about non-middle-class students' college choice. Nowadays, more and more parents and students with low socioeconomic status have begun to realize the importance of a college education. However, most of them place an importance only on monetary benefits that investing in a college education can bring. Some of the parents, such as Manyue's father, learned from their own unhappy experiences with little education that a college education could improve knowledge and skills of an individual, which can bring higher income and higher social status. Although various studies (Bombach, 1964; Bowen, 1996; Cohn & Geske, 1990; Fagerlind & Saha, 1989; Harris, 1964) have shown that there are substantial indirect benefits of education to individuals in addition to these monetary and direct returns to educational investments and that these nonmonetary benefits seldom influence college decision making of the students with low socioeconomic backgrounds.

When students are making their final decisions about which college and which program to enroll in, parents with different socioeconomic backgrounds also act rather differently. Middle-class parents are all actively involved in their children's final decision making. When helping choose the university and the program, middle-class parents are more likely to emphasize the reputation of the university, the opportunity for advanced studies, and the chance to study abroad. Generally, their advice is considered valuable by their children. In contrast, some parents with low socioeconomic backgrounds were virtually absent from their children's college choice process, such as the parents of Peng and Qunhuan. Others, like Manyue's father and Juan's mother, overly participated in their children's college decision making so much that they either overwhelmed their children or they took over and made the final decision for their children. Moreover, parents with low socioeconomic backgrounds are more likely to take into account college cost when advising their children about their college choice and academic major, which will be analyzed in the next section.

Parents' Ability and Willingness to Pay for Education

As presented in Table 3.1, the two constructs representing economic capital are parents' ability and willingness to pay for education. As an important aspect of a family's socioeconomic status, family income is closely associated with college attendance (Fitzgerald & Delaney, 2002; Kane, 1999). By definition, low-income parents possess less financial capital. On the primary and secondary school levels, the lack of financial capital can limit low-income students' access to educational resources, such as books and other educational objects. As found in this study, low-income parents are less likely to subscribe to newspapers and magazines and also less likely to send their children to extracurricular activities and afterschool classes, which has negative impacts on students' academic achievement.

Another major issue highly associated with family income is the school choice made by parents concerning students' secondary education. As indicated in previous discussions, middle-class parents are much more likely to pay the extra tuition and fees to send their children to a key school. In this study, the provincial key high school, Fuzhong, charged an astonishingly high tuition to students who missed its admission score in the high school entrance examinations. The total amount of tuition and fees can be as high as the cost of a four-year institution of higher education. Unsurprisingly, none of the working-class parents interviewed in this study chose to pay the extra tuition and fees in order to send their children to the key high school when they failed the entrance examinations. Yet, as researchers (Hossler, Braxton, & Coopersmith, 1989; McDonough, 1997) point out, high school characteristics, such as culture and quality, are factors that directly influence students' college-going behavior. Certainly, students from the key high school have a higher chance to going to college and attending selective universities.

Finally, parents' willingness and ability to pay for a college education directly affect their children's college decision-making process. Low-income parents are more likely to take into account the expected college cost when considering prospective colleges and programs. For example, Juan's mother considered the tuition and various living expenses and thus limited Juan's college choice to the local universities, which made Juan end up in a far distant college choice. Some other low-income parents, such as Xiaomin's father and Peng's parents, could not afford to send their children to their first college choice or their choice for major, although they were willing to make significant personal sacrifices to pay for their children's education.

In conclusion, family income directly affects students' college choice because of their parents' willingness and ability to pay for their college education and also indirectly influences students' college planning by interacting with other factors, such as spending on educational objects and school choices for secondary education.

LIMITATIONS AND IMPLICATIONS FOR FUTURE RESEARCH

The Sampling

This study was designed to explore the role of cultural capital and economic capital in the patterns of higher education participation among different social groups. One key high school and one ordinary high school were chosen for the study in order to provide a diverse educational context. The original plan was to randomly choose students with different family backgrounds from the twelfth grade in each school. However, the first barrier I encountered in my fieldwork was that school officials considered the interviews with students big distractions from the intense preparation for the upcoming national college entrance examinations. The fieldwork was taking place in April, which was only two months away from the national college entrance examinations. To make sure that students would not be too distracted by this study, the principal of the key high school only allowed me to pick students from its science class, which consisted of advanced science students. The logic was that because these students were better prepared academically compared to those from average classes, the time spent on interviews would not lead to a failure in the college entrance examinations. Luckily, there were a few students from working-class families and farming families. However, they were all high achievers and college-bound students. Thus, they could be more motivated and determined to obtain a college education, and their college plans could be more formal than students with low socioeconomic backgrounds in average classes. Interviews with students from average classes might suggest more struggles and problems concerning students' college choice process.

Another limitation of the study was also associated with its sampling. The original goal of the research was to include students from middle-class families, working-class families, and farming families at both the key high school and the ordinary high school. To my surprise, I could not find any students whose parents qualified as "middle class" in the ordinary high school. One reason for this problem could be that the ordinary high school chosen for this study was located in a poor neighborhood and its students scored below the average in high school entrance examinations, even compared to other ordinary schools. This situation means that the student bodies in these two high schools are dramatically different in terms of social background and academic preparation, which makes comparisons across the schools rather difficult.

As pointed out in the cross-case analysis chapter, the three students from farming families studied in this research are quite special cases. The Chinese household registration system (hukou) divides China into two distinctive sectors: urban registration (urban hukou) and rural registration (rural hukou) (Wu & Treiman, 2002, p. 3). Individuals with rural hukou generally cannot attend primary and secondary schools in the city. Therefore, mere enrollment in the city high schools indicates the special status of the three students. One of them, Qunhuan, had outstanding academic achievement and was thus recruited as a gifted student by Fuzhong high school. Congbo, from a relatively wealthy farming family and with a family network in the city, paid extra fees to enroll in the city high school. The same situation was applied to Xiaomin, whose father actually had an urban hukou. Therefore, one suggestion for future research would be to include a rural high school in the research design, which would allow the researcher to examine more representative students from farming families.

Schools, Teachers, and Peers

This research was aimed at studying the college decision-making process of students with different social classes. In order to focus on the impact of family background on college access and choice, I intentionally excluded high school quality as a variable in the conceptual framework. However, during the data analysis, school quality and culture constantly emerged as factors anyway. First, school quality is highly associated with students' academic achievement. The students from the key high school had much higher average academic achievement than those from the ordinary high school, while academic ability was found to be one of the most important factors influencing students' college planning. Second, school culture also has a direct influence on the shaping of students' aspirations for college. The key high school had higher academic standards for its students and also expected all the students to attend college. Thus, future research should conduct some additional assessment of the school's role in students' college choice process.

A number of college access research studies conducted in the United States look at the role of counselors on students' college enrollment decisions (Cabrera & La Nasa, 2001; Hossler, Braxton, & Coopersmith, 1989; McDonough, 1988, 1997; Perna, 2000, 2002), and indicate their important influences. In the Chinese high school, there are no school staff memberss who work exclusively on providing individual guidance to students. However, homeroom teachers partially play the role of meeting students' needs in academic and personal development. In some cases examined in the research, homeroom teachers provided information about college costs and helped make the final decisions regarding colleges and academic majors. Homeroom teachers certainly exerted some impact on students' college decision making, especially for those students who could not get useful information and sufficient support from their parents. However, the teacher was not included in the conceptual framework as a variable, and his/her role was not examined in the study. Future research may include the homeroom teacher as a factor that affects students' college aspirations and planning.

Prior research (Hossler, Braxton, & Coopersmith, 1989; McDonough, 1997; Perna, 2002) also indicates that peers play an important role in the development of postsecondary educational plans. In her research regarding college planning, for each target student, McDonough (1997) also interviewed a best friend to study how the peer subcultures influence the motivation of a student to develop plans for college attendance. Yet, as a student collecting data independently, time and logistic constraints inevitably limited my sample size. Therefore, I did not have the capacity to examine peers' effects and suggest this variable be included in future research on students' college choice process.

POLICY IMPLICATIONS

The "Key School" System

One of the obvious conclusions of the study is that there is some overlap between cultural capital in families and schools. Those students who come from higher socioeconomic families with more effective cultural capital are more likely to attend a key school, which offers challenging academic courses, holds high academic standards for every student, and has a school culture promoting going to college. In Wuhu, the middle school admission policy truly puts families with higher socioeconomic status at an advantage by allowing the key school to charge exceedingly higher fees than the ordinary school. Moreover, as indicated previously, because limited seats are available in key schools, working-class students were very unlikely to get into a key school since their parents lacked the strong social network to get them in even if they were willing to pay the additional fees. The Chinese government invests more financial and human resources in key schools, so key schools can prepare their students much better academically and then ensure their success in the entrance examinations for the school at the next level. In Wuhu, key middle schools funnel most of their graduates to their high school sections, with very little competition from students from the ordinary middle school. Similarly, graduates from key high schools have a significantly higher chance of going to college, particularly the national key university. Therefore, in this way the Chinese examination system reinforces and extends the initial advantages that middle-class children have obtained from their family background and certainly limits the chances for students from a lower social class to receive a college education. The Chinese government needs to reconsider this educational policy, which places the priority on developing a small number of key schools, which considerably limits the resources available for basic education expansion. Although this research did not study a rural high school, the interviews with the students from farming families still gave us a glimpse on the poor school condition in the rural area. The inferior quality of ordinary schools and rural schools certainly places barriers in the path of academic routes to status attainment, which obstructs social mobility for urban children with low socioeconomic status and rural children.

The Early Admission Program

Second, college admission has been entirely dependent on the achievement score in the college entrance examinations since 1977. The examination system has been long regarded as impartial in deciding who gets the opportunity for a college education because of the common belief that "before the system of grades, everyone is equal," although we can see from this study that higher parental socioeconomic status is certainly associated with better academic functioning. However, in recent years, some prestigious universities introduced an "early admission program" that bases their admissions not only on academic achievement but also on performance in some extracurricular activities, such as drawing and playing an instrument. As cultural capital research has consistently demonstrated, students from families with high socioeconomic status are more likely participate in these highbrow cultural activities. Therefore, the early admission policy could further decrease the chances for students with low socioeconomic family background to enroll in prestigious universities.

The Financial Aid System

Although the Chinese government recognized the enormous financial challenges faced by low-income students in achieving access to higher education and thus established a financial aid system in the late 1990s, the availability of financial aid is not well advertised. This study found that very few low-income students and parents were aware of the existence of need-based grants and student loans and had no idea how to apply for them. Moreover, besides bad publicity, there are quite a few problems with the current financial aid system.

The most substantial problem in the financial aid system in China is the austerity of funding. The grants that needy students can receive are inadequate and far from covering the tuition and fees, not to mention covering living expenses. The average grant needy students could be awarded was around RMB 400 a year in 2002, while the average tuition charged in all levels of the university was RMB 5,000 for an academic year (Liu, 2002). Li and Min's study (2002) examines the different channels of income for students and their families to pay tuition and fees in Beijing. Their research indicates that need-based grants account for a very small proportion of the total income, which is only about 8 percent (p. 10). Therefore, the Chinese government should be concerned with the extremely low capacity of existing sources of need-based aid to provide access to and choice in higher education.

In today's fiscal and educational policy circumstances in China, loans are needed to make up the gap between the gross tuition and the grants available to students. Nevertheless, there are a lot of difficulties involved in formulating a comprehensive policy for student loans. A fundamental problem with lending to students is the lack of general availability of student loans in China. According to Johnstone (2002), the general availability refers to student loans "that are available to all eligible students." (p. 3). As indicated in the chapter on Chinese higher education reforms, only 32 percent of qualified students received student loans in 2001, and they received about 37 percent of what they applied for (Jiang, 2001, p. 2). Another substantial problem with the student loan program is the high default rate, which is "almost to be expected from student loans absent a culture that accepts the appropriateness of borrowing for higher education and absent systematic and vigorous efforts to secure repayment" (Johnstone, 2002). First of all, China has not established a comprehensive system to evaluate and track its citizens' creditworthiness (Beemer, 2003). Because of the high mobility of college graduates, it is very difficulty and costly to track down students for repayment. Second, the extremely short repayment period is another reason why the default rate is so high. It is not reasonable to expect students repay the loans within four years after graduation. Third, the high rates of unemployment and low-paying jobs among college graduates in China make loan repayment even more difficult.

In light of the fundamental problems and limitations discussed above, it is clear that there is a long way to go toward developing a comprehensive and justified financial aid system in China to overcome financial barriers for low-income students to receive a college education. As suggested by a number of American researchers, an adequate financial package is a necessity to make higher education affordable to all (Cronin & Simmons, 1987; Fecso, 1993; Hauptman & Koff, 1991; Lee, 1999). The package should include need-based grant assistance for the most promising students from low-income families, student loan programs that are available to all eligible students, and a work-study program. The grants and loans should be sufficient in amount to make possible the enrollment of financially disadvantaged but academically qualified students. In the following paragraphs I suggest a few strategies that can be employed to improve the current financial aid system in China by referring to some relative policies in American higher education.

First, the Chinese government should consider limiting merit-based scholarships and increase need-based grants. Research on American higher education (Gladieux, 2002; Heller, 2002; Lee, 2002; McPherson & Schapiro, 1998) reveals that grant dollars are more effectively targeted to low-income students and encourage enrollment. The Chinese government may survey the whole higher education scene and aim to concern itself with students who are most likely not to go to college without its help. The government should minimize politically popular merit-based scholarships. According to research conducted in American higher education (Cabrera & La Nasa, 2001; Coleman, 1988; Perna, 2000), there is a powerful correlation between good academic performance and high family socioeconomic status. That is to say, students from families of lower socioeconomic status are less likely than others to earn high achievements that are good enough to qualify for an award. Therefore, when aid is based on personal achievements, such as academic performance, the students who are most in need of financial assistance to make a college education even possible are the least likely to get a scholarship. One of the arguments for merit-based programs is that the presence of merit awards might induce students to perform well in both academic achievements and extracurricular activities, which will in turn bring in more societal benefits (McPherson & Schapiro, 1998). Nevertheless, I believe that the system of selective admissions in China already provides much incentive for good high school performance and a powerful mechanism to choose the most promising students. Within such a system, students who have made their way to universities and colleges are those who are most capable of learning. Most obviously, there is simply no reason from this point of view for the Chinese government to promote merit-based scholarships.

Second, the problems with the student loan program also need to be addressed. In this area, the experiences of American higher education might provide some good lessons. In the early years of the guaranteed student loan program in American higher education, it had exactly the same difficulties as China is experiencing (Fesco, 1993; Mumper, 1999). On the one hand, low-income students and their families were hesitant to borrow. On the other hand, lenders were reluctant to lend because of high administrative costs and uncertain returns. In order to encourage students to borrow, in the mid-1970s the federal government began to lower the interest rates of student loans and made them well below prevailing commercial rates. This strategy made the loans more appealing to students, but it made originating them less attractive to banks. In order to address this problem, the federal government compensated lenders with fees and subsidies for keeping the rates low. Moreover, student loans are largely protected from default risk by a federal guarantee and thus become a virtually risk-free source of revenue for banks. The federal government also helped set up an agency in each state to review all student loans and monitor both borrowers and lenders. These agencies are also responsible for collecting default student loans and paying the lenders any unpaid principal and interest. As indicated by Fesco (1993), "This complex arrangement has been remarkably successful at making low-interest capital available to the vast majority of students enrolled in postsecondary education" (p. 39).

In China, although banks are overwhelmingly state owned, as for-profit organizations they would not be willing to make any investments on student loans unless they could gain from it. Therefore, in order to make the loan amount sufficient, lenders should be paid a subsidy in addition to the interest charged as students repay their loans. Second, the Chinese government should shoulder the responsibility for borrowers who fail to repay their loans, not the students' parents as it is now prescribed in China. Third, the Chinese government may absorb some of the administrative costs, including originating the loans, determining the student's eligibility, and collecting the repayments. In today's China, the government agency the Student Loan Center is only responsible for reviewing application materials to ensure student eligibility. Banks play an essential role in providing capital sources, keeping track of repayments and making special efforts to collect repayments. Such a policy seriously discourages banks from making student loans, which is the reason why banks refused to allocate the RMB 400 million promised by the government to students in 2001 (Jiang, 2001).

To make loans more attractive and affordable to students, the Chinese government should also lengthen the repayment period. In the United States, under federal student loan programs such as the Stafford Loan and Perkins Loan, students have up to ten years after graduation to repay the loans (Heller, 2002; Lee, 1999). A longer repayment term than four years is more reasonable for the government and banks to expect whole repayment from students. In addition, the central government should pay the interests while the students are still in school. Finally, some researchers suggest expanding income-contingent loan forgiveness as an alternative form of financial assistance (Kane, 1999; Johnstone, 2001). In the United States, the 1992 reauthorization of the Higher Education Act created the income-contingent loan option (Kane, 1999). As Kane stated, "Rather than continue to base public subsidies solely on a means test that evaluates parents' and students' resources at college entry, a large share of the subsidy could be tied to the future income of students through forgiving some part of the loan if the former student earns a relatively low income" (Kane, 1999. p. 72). The U.S. government also encourages students to pursue some less marketable careers or work in a less attractive region by forgiving a portion of the student loans (Johnstone, 2001). The Chinese government may also consider these two policies as options to relieve students' pressure to repay loans.

Increasing Early Awareness of and Readiness for College Education

Undoubtedly, financial aid is important to narrow the class-based gaps in college participation. However, as this study has pointed out, merely making financial aid available to low-income students is not enough to ensure that they have equal access to college education. As indicated by cultural capital theory and confirmed by this research, cultural capital plays a critical role in determining college enrollment behavior. Therefore, the Chinese government must provide some academic and social support to students with low socioeconomic status to improve their academic preparation and college readiness. Two early information programs sponsored by the federal government in the United States provide a good example. The most widely known are TRIO programs, which include six federal outreach programs designed to provide students from disadvantaged backgrounds with academic and social support so that they can be college ready (U.S. Department of Education, 2008a). The more recent establishment of GEAR UP (Gaining Early Awareness and Readiness through Undergraduate Preparation) is another attempt by the federal government to deliver the message to students from disadvantaged social groups that a college education is within reach (U.S. Department of Education, 2008b). The common goals of those outreach programs are to promote "college attendance, college awareness, and college exposure" of economically and socially disadvantaged students (Swail & Perna, 2002). The early intervention programs often involve parents, improve students' academic skills, engage students in cultural activities, increase students' self-esteem, and provide information about college and financial aid (Swail & Perna, 2002). Some evaluative studies (The College Board, 2001; Ohio College Access Network, 2005) reveal that early awareness programs can effectively improve disadvantaged students' chances of enrolling in college. Therefore, while recognizing the importance of financial factors in the college access process, the Chinese government needs to effectively address the nonfinancial components that affect students' decisions to participate in higher education. Policy makers in China should begin to look at the possibility of developing and launching successful early awareness programs.

CONCLUSION

Higher education in China was open to a small proportion of the young adult-age group—although generally as a matter of right to all who have passed the rigorous requirements of the academic secondary track—until the 1990s. Given such a long tradition of free higher education, charging tuition is certainly a crucial step taken by the Chinese government in the reform of the higher educational system. In the past decade, the average tuition charged in Chinese institutions of higher learning has dramatically increased. Escalating college costs are putting direct pressure on students and their families as career paths are chosen and as factors related to enrollment and retention are considered. In the absence of countervailing measures, it is possible that some low-income students could be forced to terminate their higher education; others could be discouraged from applying for university admission. The whole Chinese society will be affected by a loss of access, choice, and equity. Therefore, the Chinese government needs to search for new and less painful ways for families to pay for a college education. How to broaden opportunities, increase fairness, and raise the quality of higher education should be the primary concern of policy makers in China and requires more exploration in future research.

Appendix A

List of Universities in Project 985

1. Tsinghua University
2. Peking University
3. University of Science and Technology in China
4. Nanjing University
5. Fudan University
6. Shanghai Jiao Tong University
7. Xi'an Jiaotong University
8. Zhejiang University
9. Harbin Institute of Technology
10. Nankai University
11. Tianjin University
12. Southeast University
13. Huazhong University of Science and Technology
14. Wuhan University
15. Xiamen University
16. Shandong University
17. Hunan University
18. Ocean University of China
19. Central South University
20. Jilin University
21. Beijing Institute of Technology
22. Dalian University of Technology
23. Beihang University
24. Chongqing University
25. University of Electronic Science and Technology
26. Sichuan University

27. South China University of Technology
28. Sun Yat-Sen University
29. Lanzhou University
30. Northeastern University
31. Northwestern Polytechnical University
32. Tongji University
33. Beijing Normal University
34. Renmin University of China
35. East China Normal University
36. China Agricultural University
37. National University of Defense Technology
38. Central University for Nationalities
39. Northwest Sci-Tech University of Agriculture and Forestry

Appendix B
Background Characteristics of the 14 Cases Excluded

Case	Family Background	School Type	Gender	Class Ranking	Parental Education (Father, Mother)
Sun Fengyun	Middle-Class	Key School	Male	5	MS, MS
Lei Meng	Middle-Class	Key School	Female	12	BA, MS
Yu Min	Middle-Class	Key School	Female	20	BA, MS
Chen Songxin	Middle-Class	Key School	Male	26	BA, BS
Li Jinwen	Working-Class	Key School	Male	17	HS, HS
Zheng Yuhui	Working-Class	Key School	Male	21	HS, Associate Degree
Shi Yan	Working-Class	Key School	Female	24	Middle School, HS
Guo Qiaochun	Working-Class	Ordinary School	Female	10	HS, Illiterate
Wang Yin	Working-Class	Ordinary School	Female	14	Middle School, Middle School
Fang Ziyi	Working-Class	Ordinary School	Male	29	HS, HS
Pan Gang	Working-Class	Ordinary School	Male	35	HS, HS
Zhu Qiang	Working-Class	Ordinary School	Male	47	HS, Middle School
Xia Guinan	Farming Family	Key School	Female	30	Elementary School, Illiterate
Zhuo Yue	Farming Family	Ordinary School	Female	45	Illiterate, Illiterate

Sun Fengyun is from a middle-class family. His father holds a baccalaureate degree in geography and a master's degree in politics. He is currently working as a manager of the sales department at a private company. Fengyun's mother has a baccalaureate degree in Chinese literature and a master's degree in literature critiques. She now works as an editor for one of the local newspapers. Fengyun is an excellent student in the science class at Fuzhong high school. He targets his college choices only at a few top science and engineering universities in the nation.

Lei Meng's parents are both college educated. Her father has a baccalaureate degree in mathematics and is a math teacher at an ordinary middle school. Her mother has a baccalaureate degree and a master's degree in history and is now an associate library director at Wuhu Municipal Public Library. Meng is an academically superior student. She plays piano and has a strong interest in art history. Her top college choices are the two prestigious universities with comprehensive undergraduate programs: Beijing University and Fudan University.

Yu Min's father has a baccalaureate degree in mechanical engineering and is now running a small store that has four employees. The store mainly sells hand tools, hardware, power tool accessories, and small electronics. Min's mother has a baccalaureate degree in law and a master's degree specializing in business and financial law. She is now an associate judge at Xinwu District's Court in Wuhu. Their annual family income is about 350,000 Chinese yuan, which they claim is mainly from her father's small business. Min is an average student at Fuzhong. Her college goal is to enroll in a national key university in some major metropolitan areas.

Chen Songxin's parents are both college educated. His father has a baccalaureate degree in electrical engineering and now works as an engineer at Wuhu Motor Company. His mother has a baccalaureate degree in English and is an English teacher at Fuzhong middle school. Songxin's academic achievement is a little below the average in the science class at Fuzhong. Nevertheless, he still wishes to go to a national key university. He has a strong interest in aerospace engineering, and the top two universities on his college choice set are Beijing University of Aeronautics and Astronautics and Northwestern Polytechnical University.

Li Jinwen's parents are both high school graduates. His father graduated from a specialized secondary school that is associated with the Wuhu Railway Bureau. He is now working at Wuhu Train Station as a railroad switch operator. His mother also graduated from a specialized secondary school, majoring in early childhood education. She is now a kindergarten teacher.

Jinwen is academically well prepared and he targets his college goal on two national key universities in the neighboring province: Nanjing University and Zhejiang University.

Zheng Yuhui's father has a high school diploma. He was a worker at Wuhu concrete factory but got laid off in 1997. He had a few part-time and short-term jobs afterward, and he is now a bus driver. Yuhui's mother has an associate degree in Chinese traditional medicine and works as a clerk at a large bookstore owned by Anhui Normal University. Yuhui's academic performance is about the average in class. His dream college is Shanghai Transportation University.

Shi Yan is from a working-class family. Her father is a middle school graduate, and her mother holds a high school diploma. Both of her parents were laid off from a Wuhu textile factory in the mid-1990s. Her father now works as a security guard at one of the local hotels. Her mother was rehired by the textile factory two years later and is now a fabric worker. Yan was one of the few lucky ones who won the lottery to Fuzhong middle school. Her academic performance is about the average at Fuzhong high school. She only considers colleges and universities in Wuhu or neighboring cities.

Guo Qiaochun's home is only five minutes from Nancheng high school. It's a nearly burned-out area. Her mother is illiterate and unemployed. She sells some homemade preserved vegetables in the farmer's market in the neighborhood. Her father has a high school diploma and is a salesperson at a local clothing store. Her family income is about 18,000 yuan. Qiaochun is a cheerful and diligent student and has a good academic record. She wishes to go to a four-year university. However, being aware of the financial difficulties her family faces, she does not plan to go out of town for her college education.

Wang Yin's parents are both middle school graduates. Her father works as a janitor at a luxury apartment complex. Her mother is an assistant at a local tailor's store. Yin is a joyful girl and has a positive attitude about life in general. Her academic performance at Nancheng high school is fine. Knowing that students at Nancheng high school are not very competitive, Yin thinks that a community college is a more feasible choice for her.

Fang Ziyi's parents are both high school graduates. His father was a worker at a Wuhu paper factory. He got laid off in 1998 and now he has a night-shift security job at a warehouse. His mother works as a sorter at a local soap factory who sorts through different kinds of soaps for packaging. Ziyi's academic performance is about the average in his class at Nancheng high school. He values higher education, but he is not sure he could make it to college. He thinks the best he can achieve might be a community college.

Pan Gang's father graduated from a vocational school and specialized in mechanics. He is a production line maintenance mechanic at the local textile factory. His mother obtained a high school diploma. She used to work for the same textile factory and was laid off during the mid-1990s when state-owned industries were massively laying off their employees. She is currently unemployed. Their annual family income is about 35,000 yuan. Gang does not think a college education is worth pursuing. He plans to go to an advanced vocational school after high school and become a mechanic like his father, who has a job with decent pay and good job security.

Zhu Qiang's father is a high school graduate, who served in the army for two years. He is now doing some labor work for a construction company. His mother is a middle school graduate and is now a waitress at a small restaurant. Qiang has been struggling in school, and shows no interest in continuing his education beyond high school. He takes a wait-and-see attitude, and does not have a clear plan for the future.

Xia Guinan is from a farming family. Her father is a middle school graduate, and her mother is illiterate. Her parents do general labor work for the farm, such as hedging, ditching, and drainage. Her father also works for the head of the village as a part-time secretary. Guinan is an outstanding student and is particularly good in mathematics and physics. She was recruited by the special recruiting team from Fuzhong high school. She targets her college goal at a couple of key national universities in the area.

Zhuo Yue is from a farming family. Neither of her parents received any formal school education. Her mother's brother owns a small restaurant in the suburbs of Wuhu and has hired some relatives from the countryside to work for him. Both of Yue's parents are now working at the restaurant. Yue thinks that she is not academically ready for a college education. She shares that she will probably work for her uncle's restaurant after graduating from high school. She might be interested in pursuing higher education later on in her life. She is not explicit about her plan but does not deny the possibility either.

Bibliography

Alexander, K., et al. (1978). *Status Composition and Educational Goals: An Attempt at Clarification.* Washington, DC: National Institute of Education.

Apple, M. W. (1982). "Reproduction and Contradiction in Education: An Introduction." In *Cultural and Economic Reproduction in Education: Essays on Class, Ideology, and the State,* edited by Apple, M. W. London: Routledge and Kegan Paul.

———. (1990). "Ideology and Cultural and Economic Reproduction." In *Ideology and Curriculum,* 2nd ed, edited by Apple, M. W., 26–42. New York: Routledge.

Aschaffenburg, K., and Maas, I. (1997). "Cultural and Educational Careers: The Dynamics of Social Reproduction." *American Sociological Review* 62, no. 4: 573–587.

Asian Development Bank (2010). *Key Indicators for Asia and the Pacific 2010.* India: Asian Development Bank.

Beemer, L. (2003). *Facework in 19th-Century Chinese-Authored Business Letters.* Paper presetned at the 2003 Association for Business Communication Annual Convention, California State University, Los Angeles.

Behrman, J. R., Pollak, R., and Taubman, P. (1989). "Family Resources, Family Size, and Access to Financing of College Education." *Journal of Political Economy* 97, no. 2: 398–419.

Bempechat, J. (1998). *Against the Odds: How "At-Risk" Children Exceed Expectations.* San Francisco: Jossey-Bass.

Berg, I. (1970). *Education and Jobs: The Great Training Robbery.* New York: Praeger.

Bernstein, B. (1982). "Codes, Modalities, and the Process of Cultural Reproduction: A Model." In *Cultural and Economic Reproduction in Education: Essays on Class, Ideology, and the State,* edited by Apple, M. W. London: Routledge and Kegan Paul.

———. (1997). "Class and Pedagogies: Visible and Invisible." In *Education: Culture, Economy, and Society,* edited by Halsey et al. Oxford: Oxford University Press.

Bian, Y., Breiger, R., Davis, D., and Galaskiewicz, J. (2005). "Occupation, Class, and Social Networks in Urban China." *Social Forces* 83, no. 4: 1443–1468.

Bian, Y., and Logan, J. R. (1996). "Market Transition and the Persistence of Power: The Changing Stratification System in Urban China." *American Sociological Review* 61: 739–758.

Blau, P. M., and Duncan, O. D. (2000). "The Process of Stratification." In *The Structure of Schooling: Readings in the Sociology of Education*, edited by Arum, R., and Beattie, I. R. London: Mayfield.

Bourdieu, P. (1971). "Intellectual Field and Creative Project." *Knowledge and Control: New Directions for the Sociology of Education*, edited by Young, M. F. D.. London: Collier-Macmillan.

———. (1977a). "Cultural Reproduction and Social Reproduction." In *Power and Ideology in Education*, edited by Karabel, J. and Halsey, A. H., 487–511. New York: Oxford University Press.

———. (1977b). *Outline of a Theory of Practice*. Cambridge: Cambridge University Press.

———. (1977c). "Symbolic Power." In *Identity and Structure: Issues in the Sociology of Education*, edited by Gleason, D., 112–119. Dimiffield, England: Nefferton.

———. (1984). *Distinction: A Social Critique of Judgment of Taste*. Cambridge: Cambridge University Press.

———. (1990). *In Other Words: Essays Towards a Reflexive Sociology*. Stanford: Stanford University Press.

———. (1997). "The Forms of Capital." In *Education: Culture, Economy, and Society*, edited by Halsey et al. Oxford: Oxford University Press.

Bourdieu, P., and Passeron, J. (1977). *Reproduction in Education, Society, and Culture*. London: Sage Publications.

Bowen, H. (1996). *Investment in Learning: The Individual and Social Value of American Higher Education*. New Brunswick, NJ: Transaction Publishers.

Bowles, S., and Gintis, H. I. (1976). *Schooling in Capitalist America*. New York: Basic Books.

Braverman, H. (1998). *Labor and Monopoly Capital: The Degradation of Work in the Twentieth Century*. New York: Monthly Review Press.

Breneman, D. W., and Merisotis, J. P. (2002). "Beyond Money: Support Strategies for Disadvantaged Students." In *Condition of Access: Higher Education for Lower Income Students*, edited by Heller, D. E. Westport: Praeger Publishers.

Burawoy, M. (1985). *The Politics of Production*. London: Verso.

Cabrera, A. F., and La Nasa, S. M. (2001). "On the Path to College: Three Critical Tasks Facing America's Disadvantaged." *Research in Higher Education* 42: 119–149.

Central Education Research Institute. (2001). "An Investigation into Higher Education Institutions' Tuition and Financial Aid to Needy Students." *Chinese Education and Society* 34, no. 4 (July/August 2001): 29–53.

Chapman, D. W. (1981). "A Model of Student College." *Journal of Higher Education* 52, no. 5: 490–505.

Chen, B. K., Zhang, P. F., and Yang, R. D. (2010). *Government Educational Expenditure: Human Capital Investment, and Income Inequality* (in Chinese). www.chinaes.org.cn/Article/UploadFiles/201003/2010032121195854.doc (accessed June 2010).

Cheung, H., and Ng, L. (2003). "Chinese Reading Development in Some Major Chinese Societies: An Introduction." In *Reading Development in Chinese Children*, edited by McBride-Chang, C., 3–17. Westport, CT: Praeger.

China Education News. (2001). *The Financial Aid System in Higher Education* (in Chinese). http://www.edu.cn/20010823/207517.shtml (January 2006).

——. (2002). *National Outstanding Needy Student Scholarship* (in Chinese). http://www.edu.cn/20020210/3020352.shtml (January, 2006).

China Education and Human Resource Task Force. (2003). Task Force on Issues of Education and Human Resources in China: Stride from a Country of Tremendous Population to One of Profound Human Resources (in Chinese). Beijing: Higher Education Press, 2003

Chinese Ministry of Education. (1985). *The Statistics of Educational Achievements of China (1949–1989)*. Beijing: Renming Education Press.

——. (2000). *Yearly Book of Chinese Education: 1990–2000*. Beijing: People's Education Press.

——. (2001). Questions and Answers about the Student Loan Program (in Chinese).
http://www.edu.cn/20010101/3201.shtml (January 2006).

——. (2002). *China Education Finance Statistical Yearbook*. Beijing: China Statistics Press.

Chinese National Department of Culture. (2005). Report on Cultural Activities of Chinese Farmers. http://www.fosu.edu.cn/xiaobao/news_view.asp?newsid=401 (retrieved on May 2011)

Chinese National Statistics Bureau (2000). *China National Statistics Yearbook 2000*. Beijing: China Statistics Press.

Cohn, E., and Geske, T. G. (1990). *The Economics of Education*. 3rd ed. New York: Pergamon Press.

Coleman, J. C. (1990, 1994). *Foundations of Social Theory*. Cambridge, MA: Harvard University Press.

Coleman, J. S. (1988). "Social Capital in the Creation of Human Capital." *American Journal of Sociology* 94: S95–S120.

The College Board. (2001). *Outreach Program Handbook*. Washington, DC: Educational Policy Institute.

"College-Bound Black Students: Often Poor but Still You Must Show Us Your Money." (2001). *The Journal of Blacks in Higher Education, 32*: 8–11.

Collins, R. (1979). *The Credential Society*. New York: Academic Press.

Conklin, M. E., and Dailey, A. R. (1981). "Does Consistency of Parental Educational Encouragement Matter for Secondary Students?" *Sociology of Education 5*, no. 4: 254–262.

Creswell, J. W. (1997). *Qualitative Inquiry and Research Design*. London: Sage Publications.

Cronin, J. M. and Simmons, S. Q. (1987). *Student Loans: Risks and Realities*. Dover, MA: Auburn House Publishing.

Crook, C. (1997). *Cultural Practices and Socioeconomic Attainment: The Australian Experience*. Westport, CT: Greenwood Press.

Crosnoe, R. (2004). "Social Capital and the Interplay of Families and Schools." *Journal of Marriage and Family* 66: 267–280.

de Graaf, P. M. (1986). "The Impact of Financial and Cultural Resources on Educational Attainment in the Netherlands." *Sociology of Education* 59, no. 4: 237–246.

———. (1988). "Parents' Financial and Cultural Resources, Grades, and Transition to Secondary School in the Federal Republic of Germany." *European Sociology Review* 4, no. 3: 209–221.

———, et al. (2000). "Parental Cultural Capital and Educational Attainment in the Netherlands: A Refinement of the Cultural Capital Perspective." *Sociology of Education, 73*: 92–111.

DeMarrais, K. B., and LeCompte, M. D. (1998). *The Way Schools Work: A Sociological Analysis of Education.* 3d. Boston, Ma: Addison Wesley Longman, Inc.

Denzin, N. K., and Lincoln, Y. S. (1994). *Handbook of Qualitative Research.* Thousand Oaks, CA: Sage Publications.

DiMaggio, P. (1979). "On Pierre Bourdieu." *American Journal of Sociology 84,* no. 6: 1460–1474.

———. (1982). "Cultural Capital and School Success: The Impact of Status Culture Participation on the Grades of U.S. High School Students." *American Sociological Review* 47: 189–201.

DiMaggio, P., and Mohr, J. (1985). "Cultural Capital, Educational Attainment, and Marital Selection." *American Journal of Sociology* 90: 1231–1261.

Du, R. (1992). *Chinese Higher Education.* New York: St. Martin's Press.

Dumais, S. A. (2002). "Cultural Capital, Gender, and School Success: The Role of Habitus." *Sociology of Education* 75, no. 1: 44–68.

Ekstrom, R. B. (1985). *A Descriptive Study of Public High School Guidance: Report to the Commission for the Study of Precollegiate Guidance and Counseling.* Princeton, NJ: Educational Testing Services.

Elsworth, G., et al. (1982). *From High School to Tertiary Study: Transition to College and University in Victoria.* Hawthorn, Victoria: Australian Council on Education.

Fagerlind, I., and Saha, L. J. (1989). *Education and National Development: A Comparative Perspective.* Oxford: Pergamon Press.

Fesco, R. S., ed. (1993). *Quality in Student Financial Aid Programs: A New Approach.* Washington, DC: National Academy Press,

Fisch, R., Smith, M., and Phinney, M. Y. (1997). "Project Read—The Importance of Early Learning; RX: Read to Your Child." *American Family Physician 56,* no. 9: 2195–2198.

Fitzgerald, B. K. and Delaney, J. A. (2002). "Educational Opportunity in American." In *Condition of Access: Higher Education for Lower Income Students,* edited by Heller, D. E. Westport, CT: Praeger Publishers.

Freire, P. (2000). *The Pedagogy of the Oppressed.* New York: Continuum.

Gallagher, B. G. (1950). "The Need for Federal Aid to Students." *Journal of Higher Education 21,* no. 7: 344–347.

Galt, H. S. (1992). *The Development of Chinese Educational Theory.* Shanghai: Commercial Press.

Gandara, P. (1995). *Over the Ivy Walls: The Educational Mobility of Low-Income.* Albany: State University of New York Press.

Gerth, H. H., and Mills, C. W. (1958). *From Max Weber: Essays in Sociology.* New York: Oxford University Press.

Gingrich, P. (1999). *Multiple Sources of Power—Class, Status, and Party.* http://uregina
.ca/~gingrich/o5f99.htm (December, 2005)

Gladieux, L. E. (2002). "Federal Student Aid in Historical Perspective." In *Condition
of Access: Higher Education for Lower Income Students,* edited by Heller, D. E. Westport, CT: Praeger Publishers.

Goetz, J. P., and LeCompte, M. D. (1984). *Ethnography and Qualitative Design in
Educational Research.* New York: Academic Press.

Graaf, N., Graaf, P., and Kraaykamp, G. (2000). "Parental Cultural Capital and
Educational Attainment in the Netherlands: A Refinement of the Cultural Capital
Perspective." *Sociology of Education, 73:* 92–11.

Grabb, E. G. (1990). *Theories of Social Inequality: Classical and Contemporary Perspectives.* 2nd ed. Canada: Holt, Rinehart, and Winston of Canada.

Guba, E. G., and Lincoln, Y. S. (1989). *Fourth Generation Evaluation.* Newbury Park,
CA: Sage Publications.

Gui, J. (2002). *The Students Getting Financial Aid in Beijing in 2001* (in Chinese).
http://www.edu.cn/20021022/3070515.shtml (January 2006).

Hagedorn, L. S., and Fogel, S. (2002). "Making School to College Program Work:
Academics, Goals, and Aspirations." In *Increasing Access to College: Extending Pos-
sibilities for All Students,* edited by Tierney, W. G., and Hagedorn, L. S. Albany, NY:
State University of New York Press.

Han, X. P. (2002). "Soaring Fees at Institutions of Higher Learning." *Chinese Education and Society 35,* no. 1: 21–27.

Hannum, E. (1999). "Political Change and the Urban-Rural Gap in Basic Education
in China, 1949–1990." *Comparative Education Review 43,* no. 2: 193–211.

Harris, S. E., ed. (1964). *Economic Aspects of Higher Education.* Paris: The Organisa-
tion for Economic Cooperation and Development.

Hauser, R. M. (1993). "The Decline in College Entry among African Americans:
Findings in Search of Explanations." In *Prejudice, Politics, and the American Di-
lemma,* edited by Sniderman, P. M., Tetlock, P. E., and Carmines, E. G., 271–306.
Palo Alto, CA: Stanford University Press.

Hauptman, A.M., and Koff, R.H. (1991). *New Ways of Paying for College.* New York:
Macmillan Publishing Company.

Hayhoe, R. (1984). "The Evolution of Modern Chinese Educational Institutions." In
Contemporary Chinese Education, edited by Ruth Hayhoe, 26–46. London: Croom
Helm.

———. (1989). *Chinese Universities and the Open Door.* Armonk, NY: M. E. Sharpe.

———. (1996). *China's Universities, 1895–1995: A Century of Cultural Conflict.* New
York: Garland Publishing.

Heller, D. E. (2002). "State Aid and Student Access: The Changing Picture." In *Condition of Access: Higher Education for Lower Income Students,* edited by Heller, D. E.
Westport, CT: Praeger Publishers.

Horvat, E. M., Weininger, E., and Lareau, A. (2003). "From Social Ties to Social Capital: Class Differences in the Relations between Schools and Parent Networks."
American Educational Research Journal 40, no. 2: 319–351.

Hossler, D., Braxton, J., and Coopersmith, G. (1989). "Understanding Student College Choice." In *Higher Education: Handbook of Theory and Research, Vol. 5.,* edited
by Smart, J., 231–288. New York: Agathon Press.

Hossler, D., and Gallagher, K. (1987). "Studying Student College Choice. A Three-Phase Model and the Implications for Policy Makers." *College and University, 2:* 207–221.

Hossler, D., Schmidt, J., and Vesper, N. (1999). *Going to College: How Social, Economic, and Educational Factors Influence the Decisions Students Make.* Baltimore, MD: Johns Hopkins University Press.

Hossler, D., and Stage, F. K. (1992). "Family and High School Experience Influences on the Postsecondary Educational Plans of Ninth-Grade Students." *American Educational Research Journal 29,* no. 2: 425–451.

Hurn, C. J. (1985). *The Limits of Possibilities of Schooling.* 2nd ed. Boston, MA: Allyn and Bacon.

International Comparative Higher Education Finance and Accessibility Project. (2006). *A Brief Description of Chinese Higher Education System.*

"Inside the Knowledge Factory." (1997). *The Economist,* October 4.

International Comparative Higher Education Finance and Accessibility Project. (2006) *A Brief Description of Chinese Higher Education System.* http://www.gse.buffalo.edu/org/inthigheredfinance/region_asiaCN.html (accessed January 2006).

Ishida, H. (1993). *Social Mobility in Contemporary Japan.* Stanford: Stanford University Press.

Jackson, G. A. (1982). "Public Efficiency and Private Choice in Higher Education." *Educational Evaluation and Policy Analysis 4,* no. 2: 237–247.

Jackson, J. (1978). "In Pursuit of Equity, Ethics, and Excellence: The Challenge to Close the Gap." *Phi Delta Kappan, 60:* 191–193.

Jencks, C., et al. (2000). "Inequality in Educational Attainment." In *The Structure of Schooling: Readings in the Sociology of Education,* edited by Arum, R. and Beattie, I. R., 168–181. Columbus, OH: McGraw-Hill.

Jenson, E. L. (1984). "Student Financial Aid and Degree Attainment." *Research in Higher Education, 20*(1): 117–127.

Jian, J. (1998). "Moving the Reform of the Higher Education Administrative System into Great Depth Enthusiastically and Steadily." *Chinese Education and Society, 31*(6): 5–27.

Jiang, X. Q. (2001). "In China, Student Loans May Be Expanding Societal Gaps They Were Supposed to Close." *Chronicle of Higher Education, 48*(15): 37–39.

Johnstone, D. B. (2000). *Student Loans in International Comparative Perspective: Promises and Failures, Myths and Partial Truths.* Buffalo, NY: International Comparative Higher Education Finance and Accessibility Project.

———. (2001). *Student Loans in International Perspective: Promises and Failures, Myths and Partial Truths.* http://www.gse.buffalo.edu/org/inthigheredfinance/publicationsLoans1.html (January 2006).

Johnstone, D. B. (2002). *Chinese Higher Education in the Context of the Worldwide University Change Agenda.* http://www.gse.buffalo.edu/org/inthigheredfinance/publications_chinapaper.htm (January, 2006).

Johnstone, D. B., and Shroff-Mehta, P. (2000). "Higher Education Finance and Accessibility: An International Comparative Examination of Tuition and Finance Assistance Policies." In *Higher Education Reform,* edited by Heather, E. London: Society for Research into Higher Education.

Jonsson, J. O. (1987). "Class Origin, Cultural Origin, and Educational Attainment: The Case of Sweden." *European Sociological Review, 3*(3): 229–242.

Jun, A., and Colyar, J. (2002). "Parental Guidance Suggested: Family Involvement in College Preparation Programs." In *Increasing Access to College: Extending Possibilities for All Students*, edited by Tierney, W. G., and Hagedorn, L. S. Albany: State University of New York Press.

Kalmijn, M., and Kraaykamp, G. (1996). "Race, Cultural Capital, and Schooling: An Analysis of Trends in the United States." *Sociology of Education*, 69(1): 22–34.

Kane, T. J. (1999a). *The Price of Admission: Rethinking How Americans Pay for College*. Washington, DC: Brookings Institution Press.

———. (1999b). "Reforming Public Subsidies for Higher Education." In *Financing College Tuition*, edited by Kosters, M. H. Washington, DC: The AEI Press.

Katsillis, J., and Rubinson, R. (1990). "Cultural Capital, Student Achievement, and Educational Reproduction: The Case of Greece." *American Sociological Review*, 55(2): 270–279.

Kerbo, H. R. (1991). *Social Stratification and Inequality: Class Conflict in Historical and Comparative Perspective*. 2nd ed. Columbus, OH: McGraw-Hill.

Kuo, D. H., and Hauser, R. M. (1995). "Trends in Family Effects on the Education of Black and White Brothers." *Sociology of Education*, 68: 136–160.

Lamb, Stephen. (1989). "Cultural Consumption and the Educational Plans of Australian Secondary School Students." *Sociology of Education*, 62(2): 95–108.

Lamont, M., and Lareau, A. (1988). "Cultural Capital: Allusions, Gaps and Glissandos in Recent Theoretical Developments." *Sociological Theory*, 6(2): 153–168.

Lareau, A. (1987). "Social Class Differences in Family-School Relationships: The Importance of Cultural Capital." *Sociology of Education*, 60(2): 73–85.

Lee, C. K., and Selden, M. (2007). "China's Durable Inequality: Legacies of Revolution and Pitfalls of Reform." *Japan Focus*, January 24.

Lee, J. B. (1999). "How Do Students and Families Pay for College?" In *Financing College Education: How It Works, How It's Changing*, edited by King, J. E. Phoenix, AZ: Oryx Press.

———. (2002). "An Issue of Equity." In *Increasing Access to College: Extending Possibilities for All Students*, edited by Tierney, W. G., and Hagedorn, L. S. Albany: State University of New York Press.

Lee, T. H. (2000). *Education in Traditional China: A History*. Leiden: E. J. Brill.

Li, S. P. (2004). *Chinese Calligraphy*. http://www.csulb.edu/~sanpaoli/ (December 2007).

Li, W. L., and Min, W. F. (2000). *Tuition, Private Demand, and Higher Education in China*._http://www.teacherscollege.edu/centers/coce/pdf_files/v4.pdf (January 2006).

———. (2002). *Study on University Students' Private Education Expenditure and Willingness to Pay* (in Chinese). http://www.teacherscollege.edu/centers/coce/pdf_files/c4.pdf (December 2006).

Lin, J. (1991). *The Red Guards' Path to Violence: Political, Educational, and Psychological Factors*. New York: Praeger.

———. (2006). "Class Stratification and Education in China: The rise of the new middle class and Their Impact on Education." In *Education and Social Change in China: Inequality in a Market Economy*, edited by Postiglione, G., 179–198. New York: M. E. Sharp.

Lin, J., and Sun, X.Y. (2010). "Higher Education Expansion and China's Middle Class." In *China's Emerging Middle Class: Beyond Economic Transformation*, edited by Li, C., 217–242. Washington DC: Brookings Institution Press.

Lin, N. (1999). "Social Networks and Status Attainment." *Annual Review of Sociology*, 25: 467–487.

Litten, L. H. (1982). "Different Strokes in the Applicant Pool: Some Refinements in a Model of Student College Choice." *Journal of Higher Education*, 53(4): 383–402.

Liu, J., and Liu, D. (2002). *Green Path Open for Low-Income Students in Shanghai* (in Chinese). http://www.edu.cn/20020902/3066147.shtml (retrieved on January 2006).

Liu, W. Y. (2002). *How Do Financially Disadvantage Students Pay for College Education?* (in Chinese). http://www.edu.cn/20021011/3069778.shtml (retrieved on January 2006).

Liu, W. Y., and Lan, Y. (2002). *The Central Government Set Up National Scholarship for Outstanding Low-Income Students* (in Chinese). http://www.edu.cn/20020522/3026845.shtml (retrieved on January 2006).

Marks, G. N. and McMillan, J. (2003). "Declining Inequality? The Changing Impact of Socioeconomic Background and Ability on Education in Australia." *British Journal of Sociology*, 54(4): 453–471.

Marshall, C., and Rossman, G. B. (1999). *Designing Qualitative Research*. 3rd ed. Thousand Oaks, CA: Sage Publications.

Matthay, E. R. (1989). "A Critical Study of the College Selection Process." *School Counselo*, 36: 359–370.

Maxwell, J. A. (1996). *Qualitative Research Design: An Interactive Approach*. Thousand Oaks, CA: Sage Publications.

McDonough, P. M. (1988). *Classmates? How Students Prepare for Different College Futures*. Paper presented at the annual meeting of the American Educational Research Association, New Orleans.

———. (1997). *Choosing Colleges: How Social Class and Schools Structure Opportunity*. Albany: State University of New York Press.

McDonough, P. M., Korn, J., and Yamasaki, E. (1997). "Access, Equity, and the Privatization of College Counseling." *Review of Higher Education*, 20(3): 297–317.

McMurtie, B. (1999). "Banks Will Provide New Loans for Chinese Students." *Chronicle of Higher Education*, 46(2): 89.

McPherson, M. S., and Schapiro, M. O. (1998). *The Student Aid Game: Meeting Need and Rewarding Talent in American Higher Education*. Princeton, NJ: Princeton University Press.

———. (2002). "Changing Patterns of Institutional Aid: Impact on Access and Education Policy." In *Increasing Access to College: Extending Possibilities for All Students*, edited by Tierney, W. G., and Hagedorn, L. S. Albany: State University of New York Press.

Merriam, S. B. (1998). *Qualitative Research and Case Study Applications in Education*. 2nd ed. San Francisco, CA: Jossey-Bass.

Mertens, D. M. (1997). *Research Methods in Education and Psychology: Integrating Diversity with Quantitative and Qualitative Approaches*. Thousand Oaks, CA: Sage Publications.

Mumper, M. (1999). "The Student Aid Industry." In *Financing College Education: How It Works, How It's Changing*, edited by King, J. E. Phoenix, AZ: Oryx Press.

Nee, V. (1989). "A Theory of Market Transition: From Redistribution to Markets in State Socialism." *American Sociological Review*, 54: 663–681.

Niu, X. D. (1992). *Policy Education and Inequalities.* Lanham, MD: University Press of America.

Nora, A. (1993). "Two-Year Colleges and Minority Students' Educational Aspirations: Help or Hindrance?" *Higher Education: Handbook of Theory and Research,* Vol. 9. Edited by Smart, J. New York: Agathon Press.

Nora, A., and Cabrera, A. F. (1992). *Measuring Program Outcomes: What Impacts are Important to Assess and What Impacts are Possible to Measure for the Talent Search Program.* U.S. Department of Education: Office of Policy and Planning.

Ohio College Access Network. (2005). *Advisory Services Guidebook for Pre-College Outreach Programs.* Arlington, VA: Educational Policy Institute.

Parkin, F. (1971). "The Dimensions of Class Inequality." In *Class Inequality and Political Order,* edited by Parkin, F. New York: Praeger Publishers.

———. (1994). "The 'Boundary Problem' in Sociology." In *Social Stratification,* edited by Grusky, D, 162–177. Boulder: Westview.

Parsons, T. (1959). "The School Class as a Social System: Some of Its Functions in American Society." *Harvard Educational Review, 29:* 297–318.

Patton, M. Q. (1990). "Designing Qualitative Studies: Critical Trade-Offs." In *Qualitative Evaluation and Research Methods,* edited by Patton, M. Q., 162–186. Newbury Park, CA: Sage Publications.

Peng, B. (2004). "A Report on 17 Middle School Graduation Rates." *China Youth Daily,* June 14.

Peng, S. S. (1977). "Trends in the Entry to Higher Education: 1961–1972." *Educational Researcher, 6*(1): 15–19.

Peng, S. S., Bailey, P., and Ekland, B. (1977). "Access to Higher Education: Results from the National Longitudinal Study of the High School Class of 1972." *Educational Researcher, 6*(11): 3–7.

Perna, L. W. (2000). "Differences in the Decision to Enroll in College among African Americans, Hispanics, and Whites." *Journal of Higher Education, 71:* 117–141.

———. (2002). "The Key to College Access: Rigorous Academic Preparation." *Nine Propositions Relating to the Effectiveness of College Preparation Programs,* edited by Tierney, W. G. Albany: State University of New York.

Phillips, B. M., and Lonigan, C. J. (2007). "Social Correlates of Emergent Literacy." In *The Science of Reading: A Handbook,* edited by Hulme, C., and Snowling, M., 173–187. Malden, MA: Blackwell.

Premfors, R. (1984). "Numbers and Beyond: Access Policy in an International Perspective." *Journal of Higher Education, 55*(1).

Ridgway, T. (2003). "Literacy and Foreign Language Reading." *Reading in a Foreign Language, 15*(2).

Riskin, C., Zhao, R., and Li, S. (2001). *China's Retreat from Equality.* Armonk, NY: M. E. Sharpe.

Roscigno, V. J., and Ainsworth-Darnell, J. W. (1999). "Race, Cultural Capital, and Educational Resources: Persistent Inequalities and Achievement Returns." *Sociology of Education, 72*(3): 158–178.

Schofield, J. W. (1990). "Increasing the Generalization of Qualitative Research." In *Qualitative Inquiry in Education: The Continuing Debate,* edited by Eisner, E. W., and Peshkin, A., 201–232. New York: Teachers College Press.

Seeberg, V., and Zhang, W. (2001). "Guest Editor's Introduction." *Chinese Education and Society, 34*(4) (July/August): 3–17.

Sewell, W., Hauser, R., and Wolf, W. (1980). "Sex, Schooling, and Occupational Status." *American Journal of Sociology*, 86(3): 551–583.

Shanghai Academy of Education and Technology. (2002). *Enrollment Expansion to Higher Education.* http://www.edu.cn/20021106/3071663.shtml (December 2003).

Shi, J. (2007). *College Entrance Examination Online Reporting Needs to Grasp the Principle of Voluntary Reporting.* http://www.jnyulu.com/News/Article.do?articleID=177 (retrieved on May 17, 2011).

Shulman, L. S. (1988). "Disciplines of Inquiry in Education: An Overview." In *Complementary Methods for Research in Education*, edited by Jaeger, R. M., 3–17. Washington, DC: American Educational Research Association.

So, A. Y. (2003). "The Changing Pattern of Classes and Class Conflict in China." *Journal of Contemporary Asia*, 33(3) (August): 363–376.

Soper, E. L. (1971). *A Study of Factors Influencing the Postsecondary Educational Plans of Utah High School Students.* Washington, DC: National Center for Educational Statistics.

Spring, J. H. (1998). *Conflict of Interests: The Politics of American Education.* Columbus, OH: McGraw-Hill.

Stafford, K. L., Lundstedt, S., and Lynn, A. D. (1984). "Social and Economic Factors Affecting Participation in Higher Education." *Journal of Higher Education*, 55(5) 590–608.

Stake, R. E. (1995). *The Art of Case Study Research.* Thousand Oaks, CA: Sage Publications.

Steelman, L. C., and Powell, B. (1989). "Acquiring Capital for College: The Constraints of Family Configuration." *American Sociological Review*, 54(5): 844–855.

———. (1991). "Sponsoring the Next Generation: Parental Willingness to Pay for Higher Education." *American Journal of Sociology*, 96(6): 1505–1529.

Sullivan, A. (2001). "Cultural Capital and Educational Attainment." *British Journal of Sociology*, 35(4): 893–912.

Swail, W. S., and Perna, L. W. (2002). "Pre-College Outreach Programs: A National Perspective." In *Increasing Access to College: Extending Possibilities for All Students*, edited by Tierney, W. G., and Hagedorn, L. S. Albany: State University of New York Press.

Szelenyi, I. (1978). "Social Inequalities in State Socialist Redistributive Economies." *International Journal of Comparative Sociology*, 19: 63–87.

Tan, L. H., Spinks, J. A., Eden, G., Perfett, C. A., and Siok, W. T. (2005). *Reading Depends on Writing, in Chinese.* Proceedings of the National Academy of Science, USA, 102, 8781–8785.

Tang, J. (2006). Interview at Fuzhong High School, April 20.

Tang, J. L. (1998). "1997: Track Merging Across the Board." *Chinese Education and Society*, 31(6) (November/December): 34–38.

———. (1998b). "A Strategy for Reforming the Higher Education Administrative System." *Chinese Education and Society*, 31(6).

Task Force on Higher Education. (2000). *Higher Education in Developing Countries: Peril and Promise.* Washing, DC: World Bank.

Taylor, G. D. (1994). "Sociological Interpretations of Schooling: The Functional Perspective." In *Sociology of Education in Canada: Critical Perspectives on Theory,*

Research and Practice, edited by Erwin, L., and Maclennan, D. Toronto: Copp Clark Longman.

Terenzini, P. T., Cabrera, A. F., and Bernal, E. M. (2001). "Swimming against the Tide: The Poor in American Higher Education." *The College Board Research Repot,* no. 2001-1. New York: College Board.

Thomas, G. E., Alexander, K. and Eckland, B. (1979). "Access to Higher Education: The Importance of Race, Sex, Social Class, and Academic Credentials." *The School Review* 87, no. 2: 133-156.

Tierney, W. G., and Hagedorn, L. S. (2002). "Introduction: Cultural Capital and the Struggle for Educational Equity." In *Increasing Access to College: Extending Possibilities for All Students,* edited by Tierney, W. G., and Hagedorn, L. S. Albany: State University of New York Press.

Tillery, D. (1973). *Distribution and Differentiation of Youth: A Study of Transition from School to College.* Cambridge, MA: Ballinger.

Tokuhama-Espinosa, T. (2001). *Raising Multilingual Children: Foreign Language Acquisition and Children.* Westport, CT: Bergin and Garvey.

"Tuition Costs at Highly Selective Colleges: Where's the Level Playing Field?" (1994). *The Journal of Blacks in Higher Education,* 5: 22-24.

Tuttle, R. (1981). *A Path Analytical Model of the College Going Decision.* Boone, NC: Appalachian State University.

U.S. Department of Education. (2008a). *Federal TRIO Programs.* http://www.ed.gov/about/offices/list/ope/trio/index.html (accessed March 2008).

U.S. Department of Education. (2008b). *Gaining Early Awareness and Readiness for Undergraduate Programs.* http://www.ed.gov/programs/gearup/index.html (accessed March 2008).

Wagner, D. (2010). "China's Ubiquitous Middle Class." http://www.huffingtonpost.com/daniel-wagner/chinas-ubiquitous-middle-_b_799599.html (accessed December 2010).

Wang, M., Perfetti, C.A., and Liu, Y. (2003). "Alphabetic Readers Quickly Acquire Orthographic Structure in Learning to Read Chinese." *Scientific Studies of Reading,* 7(2): 183-207.

Wang, X. (2001). "A Policy Analysis of the Financing of Higher Education in China: Two Decades Reviewed." *Journal of Higher Education Policy and Management,* 23(2): 205-217.

Wei, X. (1999). *Contributions of Scale Expansion of Higher Education to the Economic Growth* (in Chinese). http://www.hedu.pku.edu.cn/kuozhao/kzhkt.html (accessed January 2006).

Wexler, P. (1982). "Structure, Text, and Subject: A Critical Sociology of School Knowledge." *Cultural and Economic Reproduction: Essays on Class, Ideology and the State,* edited by Apple, M. W. London: Routledge and Kegan Paul.

Wong, R. (1998). "Multidimensional Influences of Family Environment in Education: The Case of Socialist Czechoslovakia." *Sociology of Education,* 71(1): 1-22.

Worden, R. L., Savada, A. M., and Dolan, R. E. (1987). *China: A Country Study,* 4th ed. Washington, DC: Library of Congress.

World Bank. (1986). *China: Management and Finance of Higher Education.* Report No. 5912-CHA. Washington, DC: Projects Department, East Asia and Pacific Regional Office.

———. (1999). *Project Appraisal Document On A Proposed Loan of US$ 20.0 Million and a Proposed Credit of SRD 36.8 Million (US$ 50 Million) to the People's Republic of China.* Report No. 19146–CHA. Washington, DC: Human Development Sector Unit, East Asia and Pacific Regional Office.

———. (2001). *Sources of China's Economic Growth: 1952–99—Incorporating Human Capital Accumulation.* Report No. WPS 2650. Washington, DC: Economic Policy and Poverty Reduction Division.

Wu, G. (2002). "Relationship Between Education and Society in the Period of Transformation." *China Education: Studies and Reviews*, Volume 2. Edited by Ding, G. Beijing: Education and Science Publishing House.

Wu, X., and Treiman, D. J. (2002). *The Household Registration System and Social Stratification in China: 1955–1996.* Los Angeles: California Center for Population Research

Wuhu Bureau of Education. (2006). http://www.whedu.net/cms/data/html/doc/2007-01/03/37922/index.html (accessed November 2007)

Wuhu Statistics Bureau. (2001). *Wuhu Statistical Yearbook 2001.*

———. (2002). *Wuhu Statistical Yearbook 2002.*

———. (2003). *Wuhu Statistical Yearbook 2003.*

———. (2004). *Wuhu Statistical Yearbook 2004.*

———. (2005). *Wuhu Statistical Yearbook 2005.*

Xiao, H. (2000). "Structure of Child-Rearing Values in Urban China." *Sociological Perspectives, 43*(3): 457–471.

Yin, R. K. (2002). *Case Study Research: Design and Methods.* 3rd ed. Thousand Oaks, CA: Sage Publications.

Zha, Q. (2007). *China's Move to Mass Higher Education: The Policy Process.* Paper Presented at the 32nd Annual Conference of American Society of Higher Education, Kentucky.

Zhang, H. J. (2001). "Strengthening the Financial Aid System to Help Poor Students at Higher Education Institutions." *Chinese Education and Society, 34*(4) (July/August): 54–62.

Zhao, F. (1998). "A Remarkable Move of Restructuring: Chinese Higher Education." *The Education Policy Analysis Archives, 6*(5). http://epaa.asu.edu/epaa/v6n5.html (accessed March 2009).

Zhou, X. (2000). "Economic Transformation and Income Inequality in Urban China: Evidence from Panel Data." *American Journal of Sociology, 105*:1135–1174.

Zhou, X., Moen, P., and Tuma, N. B. (1998). "Educational Stratification in Urban China, 1949-94." *Sociology of Education* 71:199–222.

Zhou, X.; Tuma, N. B., and Moen, P. (1996). "Stratification Dynamics under State Socialism: The Case of Urban China, 1949-1993." *Social Forces*, 74: 759–796.

Zhu, K. X. (1995). "Actively and Intensively Promoting Reforms in Higher Education Administrative System." *China Education Daily* (November).

Index

academic preparation, 26, 34, 180–181; academic performance, academic achievement, 16, 18, 27, 33, 155–158

Blau, P. M., and Duncan, O. D., 23–24
Bourdieu, Pierre, 7–12

case study, 60–61, 65–67
China, economic reform in, 37–39; higher education in, 42–45, 55–56
Chinese calligraphy, 84–86, 93, 97–98, 146–148
Coleman, James, 16, 18
college access, 23–27, 32, 56, 175–177
college admission policies, 43
college application, 80–81
college choice, 57
college choice process, 290
college costs, 184–185
college participation rates, 1, 24–25, 46, 56, 157
college planning, 35–36, 158–160, 183, 185, 187
college visit, 164–168
cultural capital, 7–19, 32–34, 143–145, 148–149
cultural capital effect, background effect, 14

cultural classes, 28n2
cultural consumption, cultural formation, 15, 73
cultural exclusion, 9–10

de Graaf, Paul, 20–21
DiMaggio, Paul, 19–20
dual-elite model, 40
Dumais, Susan, 22

early admissions, 89, 94, 107–109, 119, 181
early childhood education, importance of, 33, 143–144; early family education, 148–152
early intervention programs, 193
education reform, 42
educational resources, 15
educational system and social inequality, 12–14

family income, 18–19, 23–25, 35
field, concept in Bourdieu's social reproduction model, 11–12
financial aid policy, 26–27, 51–55, 18–192
financially needy students, 51–52
financing higher education, 48–50

Fitzgerald, B. K., and Delaney, J. A., 1, 19, 23–24
forms of cultural capital, 9

habitus, 10–12, 22, 182
high schools, 25–26, 78–80; role of teachers in, effect of peer culture in, 187
higher education expansion, 18, 45–48
higher education reform, 44–48
Hossler, D., Braxton, J., and Coopersmith, G., 30
Hossler, D., and Gallagher, K., 32–33

inequalities in Chinese higher education, 55–57
institutional amalgamation policy, 44–46
investment in higher education, 46–47

key schools, 62, 76–77, 160, 177n1

Lamont, M., and Lareau, A., 10, 13, 15
Lareau, Annette, 22–23

market economy, 38–39
middle class, 40–41, 69n2

National College Entrance Examination (NCEE), 80

parental education, 15, 23–25, 158–160
parental involvement, 17, 22, 25, 33–35, 183–184; parental expectation,16, 158–160, 177, 183; parental preferences, 33–34, 182
parental network, 18
parents' willingness to pay, 19, 33–35, 171–175
"Pay-to-Learn" policy, cost-sharing policy, 48–50
Perna, Laura, 10, 18, 23–26, 33–34

poem recitation, 84, 90–91, 97, 143
probability sampling and purposeful sampling, 62
Project 211, 56
Project 985, 57, 195–196

qualitative research, 59–60

redistributive economy, 38

scholarships and grants, 52–53
self-expectation, 11, 26. See also habitus
social capital, 12, 16, 18, 27n1
social economic status, 23
social exclusion, 9–10
social inequality, 2, 7–8, and educational system, 12–14
social network, 16–17. See also parental network
social stratification, 40–42
Soviet Model, 42
Stake, Robert, 60–61, 65
student college choice, 29–32; economics models of, 29–30; status-attainment models of, 30; three phases of, 31
student loans, 53–55
Sullivan, Alice, 21

Task Force on Higher Education and Society, 2
three-tiered examination system, 5n1
tuition and fees, 49

urban-rural cleavage, 73–74

value of college education, 2, 52
voucher system, 78

Wong, Sin-Kwok , 21
World Bank, 1, 46

Yin, Robert, 61, 65, 67

About the Author

Lan Gao is working at Harvard University as a senior project analyst. Dr. Gao is interested in international issues related to higher education opportunity and access, with a special focus on underserved populations, including access and success for low-income students, college readiness and preparation, and financial aid. Dr. Gao received her B.A. in Chinese literature and education from Beijing Language and Culture University in China and her Ph.D. in higher education administration and international education from the University of Maryland, College Park.

Lightning Source UK Ltd.
Milton Keynes UK
UKOW050131110412

190416UK00004B/2/P